Common Good, Uncommon Questions

Common Good, Uncommon Questions

A Primer in Moral Theology

Timothy Backous, O.S.B.
William C. Graham
Editors

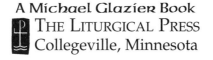

A Michael Glazier Book
THE LITURGICAL PRESS
Collegeville, Minnesota

Cover design by Mary Jo Pauly

A Michael Glazier Book published by The Liturgical Press

1   2   3   4   5   6   7   8

Library of Congress Cataloging-in-Publication Data

Common good, uncommon questions : a primer in moral theology / edited
  by Timothy Backous and William C. Graham.
        p.   cm.
      "Michael Glazier book."
      Collection of previously published essays, stories, etc. from
  various sources.
      Includes bibliographical references and index.
      ISBN 0-8146-5920-9
      1. Christian ethics—Catholic authors.   I. Backous, Timothy,
  1953– .   II. Graham, William C., 1950– .
  BJ1249.C46   1997
  241'.042–dc21   96-40323
                                                                CIP

Dedicated to the memory of Alfred Deutsch, O.S.B.

What has been is what will be,
and what has been done is what will be done;
and there is nothing new under the sun.

−Ecclesiastes 1:9

And the One who sat upon the throne said,
"Behold, I make all things new."

−Revelation 21:5

It is the eternal cry of the clay to the potter,
"Why hast Thou made me thus?"
He will translate it,
and after many days he will translate the answer,
which is no answer in logic,
but in excess of light.[1]

−Helen Waddell

Life is a struggle,
but not a warfare.

−John Burroughs (1837–1921)

The greatest discovery of my generation
is that a human being can alter his life
by altering his attitudes of mind.

−William James (1842–1910)

If you don't like what you're doing,
you can always pick up your needle
and move to another grove.

−Timothy Leary (1920–1996)

We are here on earth
to do good to others.
What the others are here for, I don't know.

−W. H. Auden (1907–1973)

---

[1] *Poetry in the Dark Ages,* The Eighth W. P. Ker Memorial Lecture delivered in the University of Glasgow, October 28, 1947 (Glasgow: Jackson, Son & Co., 1948) 30.

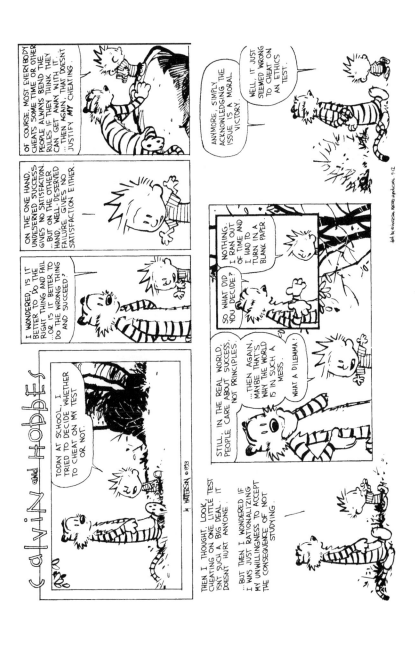

Contents

Acknowledgments

For the reprinting of material in this volume that is not in public domain or within the fair-use practice, the editors and the publisher of *Common Good, Uncommon Questions: A Primer in Moral Theology* are grateful to the copyright holders of the titles cited below for the permissions received.

The Scripture quotations are from the New Revised Standard Version Bible, Catholic edition, © 1989 by the Division of Christian Education of the National Council of Churches of Christ in the USA. Used by persmission. All rights reserved.

Excerpts from *Vatican Council II: The Conciliar and Post Conciliar Documents, New Revised Edition* edited by Austin Flannery, O.P., copyright © 1992, Costello Publishing Company, Inc., Northport, NY are used by permission of the publisher, all rights reserved. No part of these excerpts may be reproduced, stored in a retrieval system, or transmitted in any form or by any means—electronic, mechanical, photo-copying, recording or otherwise, without express permission of Costello Publishing Company.

CALVIN AND HOBBES © Watterson. Dist. by UNIVERSAL PRESS SYNDICATE. Reprinted with permission. All rights reserved.

ZIGGY © ZIGGY AND FRIENDS, INC. Dist. by UNIVERSAL PRESS SYNDICATE. Reprinted with permission. All rights reserved.

RUBES by Leigh Rubin. By permission of Leigh Rubin and Creators Syndicate, Inc.

SIN HAPPENS by permission of Harley L. Schwadron.

B.C. by permission of Johnny Hart and Creators Syndicate, Inc.

Paragraphs 2288–2291, 2293–2294, 2357, 2415, and 2448 from the English translation of the *Catechism of the Catholic Church* for the United States of America, copyright © 1994, United States Catholic Conference, Inc.–Libreria Editrice Vaticana.

"An Echo in the Soul: Grace and Human Response" by Dominic Colonna.

Excerpts from "A Man for All Seasons" by Robert Bolt. Copyright © 1960, 1962 by Robert Bolt. Reprinted by permission of Random House, Inc., New York City, and Heinemann Educational Publishers, A Division of Reed Educational & Professional Publishing Limited, Oxford, United Kingdom.

"Civility" by Lawrence S. Cunningham, *Notre Dame Magazine* (Spring 1994) 75–77.

"Developing a Christian Social Conscience" by Max Oliva, S.J., *Review for Religious* 42:4 (July–August 1983) 585–90.

"I Am Going to Leave This World a Happy Man" by Mark Hollenhorst, *More Urgent Than Usual: The Final Homilies of Mark Hollenhorst,* © 1995 by The Order of St. Benedict, Inc., The Liturgical Press, Collegeville, Minnesota.

"How Long Must We Preserve Life? Catholic Ethics at the End of Life" by Thomas A. Shannon, *Commonweal* (December 3, 1993) 12–15.

"Killing the Patient" by Richard McCormick, *The Tablet,* London, England, John Wilkins, Editor.

"Even I Can't Back Death Penalty: Forgiveness, Not Vengeance, Is Best Reply to a Murderer" by Antoinette G. Bosco.

"Does College Kill Faith?" by Lawrence S. Cunningham, *Notre Dame Magazine* (Spring 1994) 14–15.

"A Way Through, Not a Way Out" by Don Talafous, O.S.B., from *The Risk in Believing,* © 1982 by The Order of St. Benedict, Inc., The Liturgical Press, Collegeville, Minnesota.

"What Keeps Women 'in Their Place'?" by Anthony Layng, reprinted from *USA TODAY MAGAZINE* (May 1989) © 1989 by the Society for the Advancement of Education.

"What's Right with the Catholic Church?" by Joan Chittister, O.S.B., *WomanStrength: Modern Church, Modern Women* © 1990 by Sheed & Ward, Kansas City, Missouri.

"Lazarus In Our City?" by Anne Buckley, Editor-in-Chief, *Catholic New York,* newspaper of the Archdiocese of New York, in which this column appeared, October 8, 1992.

"For Pete's Sake: Our Homeless Parishioner" by Pastor Urbanus, *America* (April 10, 1993)12–13. Reprinted with the permission of America Press, Inc., 106 West 56th Street, New York, NY 10019 in the absence of Pastor Urbanus. © 1993. All rights reserved.

"Advocacy for the Homeless" by Kim Hopper, *Charities USA* (April 1986) 17–22.

"The Catholic Church and Homelessness" by Timothy A. Mitchell, *Social Justice Review* (July/August 1992) 99–100.

"Oh, Give Me a Home" by Douglas D. Watson, *Social Justice Review* (July/August 1992) 101–103.

"Helping the Homeless: How Individuals Can Make a Difference" by Gary M. Stern, *Social Justice Review* (July/August 1992) 103–106.

"Hair of a Different Color" by Molly Stein, *The Senior Reporter* (August 1994) 27.

"Homosexuality" by Richard C. Friedman, M.D., and Jennifer I. Downey, M.D., *The New England Journal of Medicine* 331:14 (October 6, 1994) 923–930.

"Science, Homosexuality, and the Church" by Sr. Renée Mirkes, *Ethics & Medics* 17:6 (June 1992) 1–3. *Ethics & Medics* is a newsletter published by the Pope John Center, 186 Forbes Road, Braintree, MA 02184. Phone: 617-848-6965.

"Christianity and The Rise of the Nuclear Family by Robert W. Shaffern. Reprinted with the permission of Robert W. Shaffern and America Press, Inc., 106 West 56th Street, New York, NY 10019. Originally published in *America* 170:16 (May 7, 1994) 13–15.

RB 1980: The Rule of St. Benedict, Timothy Fry, O.S.B., Editor, © 1981 The Order of St. Benedict, Inc., The Liturgical Press, Collegeville, Minnesota.

"The Lofty Side of Marriage" by Molly K. Stein and William C. Graham, *The Catholic Wedding Book,* © 1988 by Paulist Press.

"The Retreat" by Bobbie Ann Mason from *Shiloh and Other Stories,* copyright © 1982 by Bobbie Ann Mason. Reprinted by permission of Harper-CollinsPublishers, Inc.

"When People's Concerns Meet Jesus Christ, Church Lives" by John Carmody. This article originally appeared in the October 1, 1993 *National Catholic Reporter,* Kansas City, Missouri.

"Ethnic Snub at Child's Party Hurts 50 Years Later" by Robert F. Drinan, S.J., *National Catholic Reporter* (October 21, 1994). Reprinted with permission of the *National Catholic Reporter* and Father Drinan.

"Old Values Needed to Curb Violence" by Bishop John H. Ricard, S.S.J., *Daily News* (December 11, 1994).

"Sheen Sham." Reprinted from the pages of the *TV Guide®* Magazine Grapevine (September 4–10, 1993) copyright © 1994 by News America Publications, Inc.

"Why Good Works Are So Good for You" by Laura M. Grimes, *U.S. Catholic* (November 1993).

"When Fear Moves In" by Molly K. Stein, *The Catholic Outlook* (March 1994) 18.

Excerpts from *Humanae vitae* by Pope Paul VI. Reprinted with permission of Libreria Editrice Vaticana, 00120 Città del Vaticano.

"Sex, Natural Law, and Bread Crumbs" by Robert P. Heaney, M.D., John A. Creighton University Professor and Professor of Medicine, Creighton University.

"This We Can Do" by Brian Wren, copyright © 1975 by Hope Publishing Co, Carol Stream, IL 60188. All rights reserved. Used by permission.

Excerpts from *Centessimus annus* by Pope John Paul II. Reprinted with permission of Libreria Editrice Vaticana, 00120 Città del Vaticano.

"The Horrors of the Century" by Brian Wren, copyright © 1975 by Hope Publishing Co, Carol Stream, IL 60188. All rights reserved. Used by permission.

"Is this consequentialism?" *Commonweal* (October 21, 1994). Copyright © 1994 by the Commonweal Foundation. Reprinted with permission of the Commonweal Foundation.

Introduction to *Christianity and the Social Crisis* by Walter Rauschenbusch © 1991 by Westminster/John Knox Press.

"Chastisty as Shared Strength: An Open Letter to Students" by Mary Patricia Barth Fourqurean and David N. Fourqurean. Reprinted with the permission of the authors and America Press, Inc., 106 West 56th Street, New York, NY 10009. Originally published in *America* (November 6, 1993) 10–13.

"Declaration on Certain Questions Concerning Sexual Ethics" by Pope John Paul II. Reprinted with permission of Libreria Editrice Vaticana, 00120 Città del Vaticano.

"Can We Get Real About Sex?" by Lisa Sowle Cahill, *Commonweal* (September 14, 1990) 497–503. Copyright © 1990 by the Commonweal Foundation. Reprinted with permission of the Commonweal Foundation.

"Reverence for the Earth as a Religious Concern?" by Rose Zuzworsky.

"Giving Up the Gift" by Madeleine Gray, a pseudonym of a free-lance writer who lives in Wisconsin. This article originally appeared in *Commonweal* (February 25, 1994) 13–15.

"Inconvenient Human" by Meg Abbey, *America* (March 12, 1994).

"Something More About Alcohol" by Roman Paur, O.S.B., *Saint John's* (May 1992) Collegeville, Minnesota.

"Dorothy Day: A Radical Simplicity" by Jim Forest. Reprinted with permission from *Sojourners*, 2401 15th Street N.W., Washington, DC 20009.

"Jerusalem, My Happy Home," arranged by Richard Proulx, © 1975 by GIA Publications, Inc., Chicago.

The editors of *Common Good, Uncommon Questions* are grateful to all who, in any way and many ways, have contributed to getting this work into print:

St. John's University in Collegeville, Minnesota, and Caldwell College in Caldwell, New Jersey, provided space and resources;

Five young scholars assisted us in the preparation of the final manuscript: from St. John's, Jason McLellan, Aaron Carpenter, and Brian Sharpe, undergraduates, and George Maurer, a student in the graduate program; and Jef Hrusko of Caldwell. All were eager, proficient, and competent; and,

Finally and especially, our students at Caldwell College who road-tested the first drafts and who, with our students at Fordham University and the College of St. Benedict/St. John's University, by perceptive questions and comments, helped shape this discussion.

To all who assisted us, we are happy to offer thanks. However, any shortcomings in this text are our responsibility alone.

Introduction

Genesis teaches us that God has created the earth good and given it as gift to humankind. It is on the earth that we encounter God, for here has God chosen to dwell among us. Both popular and high culture continue to present opportunities to see God at work even now, entering into life in this very day and age. Like Pope Paul VI, who understood that the sacred was the secular seen in the light of God's plan, modern men and women are invited to see the divine plan in the developing earth.

Working together, honoring the present Christ in each man and woman, girl and boy, we advance the coming reign of God, enjoying in our efforts in the earthly city a foretaste and promise of the paschal feast of heaven.

The common good is enhanced by questions both common and uncommon. Our hope is that these Scripture pericopes, coupled with Church teachings, will provoke readers to look for signs of promise in the articles, stories, hymns, and poems that follow. Examples of righteousness and models of temptation both are intended to begin the discussion which will not conclude until Christ returns in glory.

The genesis of this book is in our classroom work with students at Caldwell College, Fordham University, and the College of St. Benedict/ St. John's University. We were prompted to gather these assorted works in response to our students' desire to delve into significant issues while learning and taking seriously what the Church has to say about life in the modern world. Our hope is that by bringing these authors together between two covers, we will facilitate both reading and conversing in classrooms and for study groups.

By no means have we collected all definitive church teachings on any given topic. Nor are the Scripture pericopes intended as proof texts. Points of view expressed by individual authors are not necessarily our own, nor do they necessarily represent official Church teaching. Our point is to show that modern issues do have a history, and that discussion and discernment are duties for all Christians. Readers will do well to remember the assertion of John Henry Cardinal Newman that conscience is the first Vicar of Christ.

This book is a work in progress; it has been designed as such. The very nature of this text suggests that the discussion which has begun is far from complete.

Timothy Backous, O.S.B.
William C. Graham
St. John's University
Collegeville, Minnesota
July 11, 1997
Feast of St. Benedict

1
Grace and Human Response

An Echo in the Soul: Grace and Human Response
Dominic Colonna

Preliminary Questions

What does it mean to say that human beings are free and responsible for their actions? How does the Christian doctrine of grace affect an understanding of human freedom and responsibility?

Introduction

Christianity presumes that humanity is in an imperfect or sinful state of existence. In order to realize our full potential, in order to become the beings we are capable of becoming, in order to "go to heaven" (to use traditional language), we need help from God. We were not created in this imperfect way. God is not responsible for our sinfulness. God's creation is good. We are in some way responsible for our own imperfection. Despite our sinfulness, some basic goodness remains. This goodness is, in a sense, the seed from which a better existence might grow. Christian theologians teach that, on one level, we are free and responsible beings who are able to overcome our sinfulness. On a more fundamental level, we are dependent upon God for any ability to overcome sin. Many contemporary Roman Catholic theologians reconcile these two seemingly contradictory understandings in the fundamental-option theory.

The fundamental-option theory was originally formulated in the decades before the Second Vatican Council (1962–1965) through the decade or so after the Council. It represents a reformulation of the doctrine of grace in which the teachings of a neglected Christian tradition were retrieved and reformulated, drawing on aspects of modern understandings of freedom and responsibility. "Grace" describes the reality of God's transformative presence and our response to that presence. In the retrieved tradition, God is present to us immediately and personally. God's immediacy or closeness saves us from our sinful state of existence, restores our natural abilities and raises us up to a supernatural state of existence wherein we can strive for an even greater closeness to God.

Option

Basically, a *fundamental option* represents the necessary role human beings play in the reality called grace. Emphasis is placed on the personal character of the individual's encounter with God. Grace is likened to a communication between the divine and human persons. Our relationship with God is dialogical. God initiates the conversation, perpetually offering salvation and sanctification to all of humanity. We freely and responsibly opt to either accept or reject that offer. We respond to God's love by loving God. The mutual love makes the conversation effective. A real communication between persons occurs resulting ultimately in either salvation or damnation.

This description of the dialogical relationship between persons respects the freedom and responsibility of the human person. At the same time, it acknowledges the gratuity of the offer when it recognizes that God's offer ontologically precedes human acceptance of that offer. The grace-ful character of God's part of the dialogue consists in God's making possible the conversation, first, by initiating it and, second, by making human persons able to respond. Fundamental-option theorists embrace the idea that we share in the responsibility of our own salvation. The theory also accounts for the Christian notion that we are responsible for our own sinfulness or separation from God. Mutual participation is essential in order for a meaningful, effective communication to occur between the divine and human persons.

Fundamental

A fundamental option is a moral act. Opting for God, or opting to love God and live accordingly, constitutes a good moral act. It represents a free and responsible basic decision to do good and avoid evil. Opting against God constitutes a bad moral act. The Jesuit moral theologian Josef Fuchs (1912–) explains the relationship between one's fundamental option and the particular acts by which we concretely do good and avoid evil. Particular acts are moral acts "in the real and full sense" insofar as they "correspond to the depths of self-commitment in basic freedom," that is, insofar as they correspond to one's fundamental option and to the pattern of all of one's actions.[1] The term "fundamental" indicates that one's fundamental option is a significant determining cause of all of one's particular moral actions. In a fundamental option, we choose to live in one way rather than another. We commit ourselves to the performance of particular actions which constitute our acceptance or rejection of God's grace. One's free and responsible particular actions constitute and generally reflect one's basic commitment to God.

A fundamental option is fundamental insofar as it is said to be the ground for particular actions. Theologians suggest that we are not likely to change our basic commitment or orientation often. While it is possible to say that one might occasionally perform particular acts which are inconsistent with one's basic orientation, it is awkward to speak of one making multiple or contradictory fundamental options. A fundamental option represents a commitment to a particular personal relationship with God. To understand the personal commitment involved in a fundamental option it might be helpful to say that one's fundamental option describes who a person is as much as it describes what a person does. To say that we are capable of frequently changing who we essentially are does not fit with experience. Experience suggests that when we change, we change slowly. Multiple, radical changes in a lifetime seem unlikely. Fundamental-option theorists acknowledge the possibility that one might change one's basic orientation or one's identity in the course of a lifetime. ("Conversion" and "mortal sin" are traditional terms used to describe such radical changes, according to fundamental-option theorists.) They suggest, however, that the personal commitment involved in the fundamental option is such that it occurs infrequently.

Particular Acts

The fundamental option and particular moral acts mutually condition one another. Just as one's fundamental option determines the particular acts one performs in life, particular moral acts determine one's fundamental option. On the one hand, one's fundamental option

---

[1] "Basic Freedom" in *Human Values and Christian Morality* (Dublin: Gill and Macmillan Ltd., 1970) 102.

grounds particular acts. It does not strictly determine them but our particular acts tend to conform to our fundamental act, our commitment to a particular way of life. On the other hand, the accumulation of one's particular moral acts constitutes one's fundamental option. We love God, we make our fundamental option complete by living out, expressing, or manifesting our basic decision by means of particular acts. What one does affects who one is. Particular actions determine who one is.

According to Josef Fuchs, one is primarily engaged in realizing oneself as a person or making a fundamental option when one performs particular acts. People engage their fundamental option in some particular acts, however, more than in others. Fuchs argues that there are times when we perform particular acts and barely engage our fundamental option. Fuchs argues further that there are times when we act in a way inconsistent with our fundamental option. In such instances, an essentially good person might perform an act which would hinder self-realization or would be sinful, to use traditional language. Such acts, however, are not likely to constitute a fundamental rejection of God (mortal sin).

One's particular moral acts could, however, effect a reversal of one's fundamental option, according to the theorists. It is possible that one or a few acts might radically alter or represent a reversal of one's fundamental attitude toward God. We are not likely to alter significantly, however, our basic relationship with God by means of one or a few particular acts. This is true especially if such acts are not consistent with our innermost, basic attitude toward God. According to the theory, it is more likely that individual particular events, such as religious conversions and mortal sins, are more often than not the climax of a pattern or habit of disposing oneself toward or against God. In other words, although it is possible, it is not likely that one whose actions generally demonstrate a pattern indicating a love for God will commit a single, particular act which represents a rejection of God.

Consciousness

Theorists claim that the fundamental character of the fundamental option allows one a unique consciousness of that option. We cannot be conscious of our fundamental option as we are conscious of other realities. A fundamental option is a transcendental phenomenon. It provides the context for which we are conscious of other realities. It provides the background which gives meaning to or makes relevant particular moral acts. It is that moral act which, using a popular analogy, provides the "horizon" against which particular acts can be seen. Like a horizon, the fundamental option is a reality which can be approached only asymptotically. At times, it appears that we can be conscious of the horizon apart from the realities before it. Such an immediate consciousness, however, is an illusion. What happens at such times is we separate the most distant foreground reality one can see—the sky beyond the mountains beyond the far side of the valley beyond the river beyond the near side of the valley beyond the trees. If we were to move toward the horizon, however, we would see that the horizon recedes. It is itself a foreground of some more distant horizon.

Theologians who use this theory suggest that one can be conscious of a fundamental option in a way different than the way one is conscious of particular moral acts. Again, likening the fundamental option to a horizon is helpful here. We are conscious of our fundamental option as an indeterminate, continuously changing reality which acts as the background for other realities. We are conscious of the horizon but in a way different than the way we are conscious of the realities before it. We cannot perceive the exact dimensions of the horizon. Without some sort of simultaneous consciousness of the horizon, however, we would not be able to be conscious of realities before the horizon. Similarly, we are conscious of our fundamental option when we perform particular moral acts. We are conscious of our fundamental option as that mysterious, changing reality which grounds all particular moral acts. This consciousness is heightened through our performance of particular moral acts. The more we understand about the realities before the horizon, the more we learn about their relationship with the horizon and the horizon itself.

Evaluation

Pope John Paul II shows an appreciation for the idea that one makes a fundamental option in response to God's call but he is critical of the emphasis which some theologians place on the distinction between one's fundamental option and one's particular, concrete acts. In his encyclical *The Splendor of Truth* (*Veritatis splendor,* 1993), for example, the pope explains that emphasizing the distinction between the two types of acts makes any one particular, concrete act play a smaller role in the determination of one's relationship with God. This is so because fundamental-option theorists teach that any particular act is truly moral only when it corresponds to one's fundamental option and to the pattern of all of one's actions. Furthermore, the pope teaches that the description of the distinction between one's *consciousness* of one's fundamental option and one's particular acts suggests that one is unable to determine which particular acts are mortally sinful. This is so because one is never conscious of one's fundamental option in a way which allows one to fully express it in concepts or words. One is left using, therefore, a mysterious criterion by which to determine whether and to what degree any particular act is sinful. The emphasis on the distinction between one's fundamental option and one's particular acts, the pope concludes, leads to a defective reformulation of the doctrine of sin. That reformulation suggests that, although possible, it is unlikely that one can radically alter one's relationship with God through the performance of a single, particular act.

The pope teaches that radically altering one's relationship with God through the performance of a single, particular act is a very real possibility. Referring to a traditional teaching about sin, the pope teaches that certain particular acts are "intrinsically" or inherently evil. We can identify such acts through the use of natural law and by referring to revelation. Examples of such acts include lying, suicide, abortion, sterilization, masturbation, premarital and extramarital intercourse, and divorce. Such acts are said to violate an objective moral order. Such acts are defined, however, by more than their conformity to the objective moral order. They are also defined by the particular circumstances in which the acts are performed. The pope suggests that some fundamental-option theorists have overemphasized the role that particular circumstances play. He suggests that in emphasizing the fact that the morality of any individual act is to be judged according to its correspondence with one's fundamental option and the pattern of one's actions, some theologians neglect the need to consider the fact that some acts are intrinsically evil. In other words, the pope suggests that, although particular circumstances affect the morality of one's actions, some particular acts are sinful largely because they are intrinsically evil. The pope teaches that because one is able to perform intrinsically evil acts, one is able to radically alter one's relationship with God.

Grace and Human Response: Reflection Questions

1. What is grace? Why is grace necessary for us to become the beings we are capable of becoming?

2. Is the description of freedom offered in the fundamental-option theory meaningful? Does it correspond to your understanding of what it means to be free and responsible?

3. How does one determine whether and to what degree a particular act is good or evil?

4. Is it *possible* that one can significantly alter one's relationship with God through a single, particular act? Is it *likely* that one can do so? For example, is it possible and/or likely that one can commit a mortal sin or experience a religious conversion as the result of a single act? Can one and/or is one likely to perform a particular act which is largely out of character with the pattern of one's actions?

Officer Johnson runs into
one of those "gray areas" of the law.

Calvin and Hobbes

by Bill Watterson

2
Conscience

Romans 2:12-16

[12]All who have sinned apart from the law will also perish apart from the law, and all who have sinned under the law will be judged by the law. [13]For it is not the hearers of the law who are righteous in God's sight, but the doers of the law who will be justified. [14]When Gentiles, who do not possess the law, do instinctively what the law requires, these, though not having the law, are a law to themselves. [15]They show that what the law requires is written on their hearts, to which their own conscience also bears witness; and their conflicting thoughts will accuse or perhaps excuse them [16]on the day when, according to my gospel, God, through Jesus Christ, will judge the secret thoughts of all.

Dignity of Moral Conscience

16. Deep within his conscience man discovers a law which he has not laid upon himself but which he must obey. Its voice, ever calling him to love and to do what is good and to avoid evil, tells him inwardly at the right moment: do this, shun that. For man has in his heart a law inscribed by God. His dignity lies in observing this law, and by it he will be judged.[9] His conscience is man's most secret core, and his sanctuary. There he is alone with God whose voice echoes in his depths.[10] By conscience, in a wonderful way, that law is made known which is fulfilled in the love of God and of one's neighbor.[11] Through loyalty to conscience Christians are joined to other men in the search for

[9]Cf. Rom. 2:15-16.
[10]Cf. Pius XII, *radio message* on rightly forming the Christian conscience in youth, 23 March 1942; *AAS* 44 (1952) 271.
[11]Cf. Mt. 22:37-40; Gal. 5:14.

truth and for the right solution to so many moral problems which arise both in the life of individuals and from social relations.

—*Gaudium et spes* 16

A Man for All Seasons   Robert Bolt

In an age when any wrong doing can be seemingly justified by claiming ignorance or placing blame on someone else's shoulders, the plight of St. Thomas More may seem mysterious or even silly. This is the story of a man who is willing to die in order to keep his conscience clear. All he needs to do is sign a document and the king will grant him freedom. But for Thomas, to live without integrity is not really living at all.

The following are excerpts from the play *A Man for All Seasons* by Robert Bolt. The first recounts a conversation between More and a would-be-protégé, Roper. More explains to Roper how even the devil ought to be given benefit of the law. In another scene, More explains to Norfolk, the Duke, the perils of not following one's conscience. Finally, a piece of More's conversation with his daughter Margaret follows. She tries desperately to convince him to sign whatever is necessary to save his life.

MARGARET: Father, that man's bad.

MORE: There is no law against that.

ROPER: There is! God's law!

MORE: Then God can arrest him.

ROPER: Sophistication upon sophistication!

MORE: No, sheer simplicity. The law, Roper, the law. I know what's legal not what's right. And I'll stick to what's legal.

ROPER: Then you set man's law above God's!

MORE: No, far below; but let me draw your attention to a fact—I'm *not* God. The currents and eddies of right and wrong, which you find such plain sailing, I can't navigate. I'm no voyager. But in the thickets of the law, oh, there I'm a forester. I doubt if there's a man alive who could follow me there, thank God . . .
    (He says this last to himself)

ALICE (*Exasperated, pointing after* RICH)   While you talk, he's gone!

MORE: And go he should, if he was the Devil himself, until he broke the law!

ROPER: So now you'd give the Devil benefit of law!

MORE: Yes. What would you do? Cut a great road through the law to get after the Devil?

ROPER: I'd cut down every law in England to do that!

MORE: *(Roused and excited)*   Oh? *(Advances on* ROPER*)* And when the last law was down, and the Devil turned round on you—where would you hide, Roper, the laws all being flat? *(He leaves him)* This country's planted thick with laws from coast to coast—man's laws, not God's—and if you cut them down—and you're just the man to do it—d'you really think you could stand upright in the winds that would blow then? *(Quietly)* Yes, I'd give the Devil benefit of law, for my own safety's sake.

NORFOLK: *(Hardly responds to the insult; his face is gloomy and disgusted)* Oh, confound all this . . . *(With real dignity)* I'm not a scholar, as Master Cromwell never tires of pointing out, and frankly I don't know whether the marriage was lawful or not. But damn it, Thomas, look at those names . . . You know those men! Can't you do what I did, and come with us, for fellowship?

MORE: *(Moved)*   And when we stand before God, and you are sent to Paradise for doing according to your conscience, and I am damned for not doing according to mine, will you come with me, for fellowship? You want me to swear to the Act of Succession?

MARGARET: "God more regards the thoughts of the heart than the words of the mouth." Or so you've always told me.

MORE: Yes.

MARGARET: Then say the words of the oath and in your heart think otherwise.

MORE: What is an oath then but words we say to God?

MARGARET: That's very neat.

MORE: Do you mean it isn't true?

MARGARET: No, it's true.

MORE: Then it's a poor argument to call it "neat," Meg. When a man takes an oath, Meg, he's holding his own self in his own hands. Like water. *(He cups his hands)* And if he opens his fingers *then*–he needn't hope to find himself again. Some men aren't capable of this, but I'd be loathe to think your father one of them.

Civility   *Lawrence S. Cunningham*

There is much talk about the loss of civility in our world. One of the symptoms is the popularity in the mass media of persons and groups who make fortunes by vilification, scorn, and utterances that go well beyond the rude. Is there not something disquieting that we should grant celebrity to foul-mouthed rap groups who preach denigration of women, attacks on police and praise for gangs? And what does it say about us that we should pay attention to (indeed, enrich) loathsome toads like Howard Stern, Geraldo Rivera and Rush Limbaugh?

That such folk have a right to speak is beyond argument. That they should be celebrated is a disgrace. That they may be symptomatic of a deeper ill–a pervasive loss of common discourse–is a real possibility.

It is night thoughts like these, after a bout of watching various louts on television, that have led me to think about the need to rehabilitate *courtesy* as a virtue and not merely as a refinement of manners. That thought came to me even more urgently while, of all things, I was browsing through the *Summa* of Saint Thomas Aquinas, looking for something else.

Saint Thomas asks whether *affability* is a virtue. He uses the Latin word *affabilitas* as a synonym for friendship *(amicitia)*, even though we tend to think of affability simply as the personality trait of an easygoing, open and gregarious person. Thomas has something more technical in mind: Affability is that habit by which a person relates to other people so as to give each person what he or she is due.

That phrase, "is due," links affability to the virtue of justice. The sins against this virtue–and affability is a virtue, according to the Angelic Doctor–are flattery and quarrelsomeness. Affability is, Aquinas observes, part of the virtue of justice.

Affabilitas is one Latin word that was often used for courtesy. The other is *curialitas*, which means after the manner of the court (as does the English word *courtesy* itself). Unfortunately, for us courtesy is often reduced to a set of regulations by which we attempt to demonstrate our common civility in the company of others: Don't wipe your nose with the dinner napkin; don't be rude to customers; learn to say "please" and "thank you." Someone who masters these rules to a fault is often described as showing "elaborate courtesy" (this is a favorite cliché of bad novelists who wish to describe racist patricians in the Deep South: "Beauregard smiled sardonically but with elaborate courtesy . . .").

It is true that the medievals also viewed courtesy as the mastery of those rules which would serve one at court—the courteous person was a *courtier*—but courtesy was also part of the religious language of the day, where it indicated a cultivated virtue that steered between the shoals of untruthfulness (flattery) and irascibility. The former case overstated the character of a person; the latter did not give people their due.

If there ever was a theologian of courtesy, it was Saint Francis of Assisi. In his later years, for example, he suffered from a terrible eye disease, and one remedy inflicted on him was to have white-hot irons touched to his temples for the putative purpose of lessening his ocular pain. Stories about Francis say that when the surgeon stepped forward with the iron, Francis said: "Brother fire, I pray thee be courteous with me."

Courtesy was a word found not infrequently on the lips of Francis. He was described even from his youth as most courteous; he wanted speech to be courteous; he counseled his friars to be as courteous to the poor as they had been to him.

For him, to be courteous meant, in the first place, to be alert to the other, because the other was equally a creature of God and therefore endowed with the same dependence on God's providence as everyone else. The genius of Francis was to see that this notion of affability or courtesy could be extended to all creation, giving elements, animals, plants and the cosmos itself the respect due them as coming from God.

The Franciscan use of courtesy in this religious sense would enter into Christian vocabulary, so that by the 14th century one reads the great mystic Julian of Norwich applying the term "courteous" to God and to Jesus Christ: "For Our Lord himself is supreme familiarity and he is as courteous as he is familiar, for he is supreme courtesy."

It is easy, though, to understand how courtesy could become a façade when detached from its deepest meaning. One could effect a suave sense of *noblesse oblige* which passes for civility or concern for others—such a pose became characteristic of exaggerated concern for courtliness in the post-medieval period. Castiglione's great renaissance book *The Courtier* was a reference manual of "civilized" or "courtly" behavior; it preached the virtue *sprezzatura*—an Italian word that has the sense of "effortless mastery." I think the closest translation of *sprezzatura* is the word "cool"—that quality so admired in talk show hosts, artists and other celebrities (celebrity: one who is famous for being famous). Unfortunately, that is the common sense of courtesy today.

Aquinas was after something deeper. We can get to his understanding of courtesy by looking at flattery and quarrelsomeness, those sins which offend against it. Flattery sins against truth, either for illicit gain or to avoid telling a painful truth or to confirm someone who is on an evil course. Dante, a close reader of Aquinas, puts flatterers in the eighth circle of hell and, to make the punishment fit the crime, depicts them as immersed in a pit of human excrement.

Quarrelsomeness, by contrast, sins against charity; Aquinas sees the litigious person as having a defective sense of the other; one who will not view the other to whom he owes love as a fellow creature of God. Aquinas argues that quarrelsomeness is even a greater sin than flattery because it does more to create sadness in the other person: It shows contempt for them and is lethal to the truth that should be expressed between people.

It does not take a lot of reflection to see how badly we need to rediscover the virtue of courtesy in Aquinas's sense of the term. Our mass media are filled with lugubrious accounts of persons who kill, maim and injure people over the most inane of matters. To shoot someone because the shooter feels he has been "dissed" (that is, shown disrespect) is the most extreme form of lack of courtesy. At less lethal levels, the deficiency that turns irate motorists into avengers, or the unhappy into those who will kill a person's reputation by oceans of public gossip, render ordinary life precarious and uncivilized. Such acts are all rooted in a lack of concern for the other.

It is often said that urban living is becoming more of a trial today not because of specific problems but through a whole spectrum of things that break down a sense of communal living. How does one psychically manage a life surrounded by a blight of graffiti, an accumulation of garbage, the wreckage of once proud neighborhoods, roaming gangs of rapists and robbers, neglected bands of the mentally ill and addicted huddled about our grates, vandalized public services and the indifference of public servants?

Each of these circumstances arises from an indifference to others—from that unwillingness to concern oneself with the other. This is a

blow both to the person and to the commonweal. When our most respected voices argue that the crisis of our age is a crisis in values, they
are really saying that we have undercultivated that sense of courtesy
which, for Aquinas, is a synonym for friendship.

We can never cultivate the virtue of courtesy until we look beyond
ourselves to the other and see there rights and claims equivalent to
our own. Courtesy must be learned not because we want elbows off
the table but because without it we degrade ourselves, others and the
fabric of our culture.

In a quatrain I learned as a child, Hilaire Belloc said it well, even
though he may have understated the matter:

> Of courtesy it is much less
> than greatness of heart or holiness
> But in my walks it seems to me,
> The grace of God is in courtesy.

—Notre Dame Magazine, Spring 1994

Developing a Christian Social Conscience   *Max Oliva, S.J.*

We have become increasingly aware, during the past ten years, of
the need to educate ourselves and others to the role unjust structures
and systems have in our lives, in order to be able to build a more just
social order. Efforts to bridge the gap between our faith and the
world around us have spread from establishing justice and peace centers to organizing parish social concern groups and seminars on
peace and justice. What is happening in this process is the development of personal and group social conscience.

The Second Vatican Council, in the document *The Church in the
Modern World,* has this to say about conscience:

> Conscience is the most secret core and sanctuary of a person. There
> he is alone with God, whose voice echoes in his depths. In a wonder-
> ful manner conscience reveals that law which is fulfilled by love of
> God and neighbor. In fidelity to conscience, Christians are joined with
> the rest of people in the search for truth, and for the genuine solution
> to the numerous problems which arise in the life of individuals and
> from social relationships. (No. 16)

Conscience is not only personal but social as well. It concerns love
of neighbor and the common good. It leads us as a community and

individually to seek for appropriate ways to solve problems of injustice and violence.

Traditionally, we are perhaps used to thinking of the human person in two ways: *intra-personally,* that is, focusing on the uniqueness of each individual, that which sets each one of us apart from everyone else; and, *inter-personally,* stressing the relational aspect of our personhood—to be from, toward, for and with other persons. There is, however, a third way of viewing the person: *societally.* The societal dimension involves our relationship to human environments—structures, systems, institutions and processes—for example, business corporations, the government, media, the Church, laws, and so forth.

What we are considering in the societal dimension of our personhood is *social morality.*

Basic to a discussion of social morality is the dignity of the human person. In fact it is the way economic, political and social structures affect the lives of people that make what seem to be "secular" matters, moral ones. This is so because of what we learn about the person in Scripture. In the Old Testament (Gn 1:26-27) we discover that all people are created in the image and likeness of God. In the New Testament we see that by becoming human Jesus has raised us to a new dignity.

Social morality includes terms and realities similar to what we are used to naming in personal morality, namely, sin, grace and examination of conscience. *Social sin,* according to Fr. Peter Henriot, S.J., is a category that attempts to recognize and to interpret the structural injustice experienced in contemporary society. It can be manifested in "sinful structures" or policies within a structure that violate the dignity of people, such as discrimination on the basis of race or sex in hiring practices. It can stem from individual people who are so caught up in self-interest that they ignore the interests of others by amassing power or material things to the exclusion of others. It can occur when people of good will do not act to change an unjust situation.

Cardinal Alfrink, of Utrecht, wrote these reflections on social sin:

> Unjust economic and political structures constitute a close-at-hand occasion to commit sins of individual and particularly collective injustice. An unjust situation becomes a grave sin at the moment in which one becomes aware of it and refuses to exert oneself to change it. Conversion of heart is indispensable but this should arrive at the point of strongly wishing to bring about the change of situations which are objectively unjust.

Social grace flows through structures that build up the human person and the community, that promote justice and peace, that liberate people from whatever binds them or threatens to make them less human. One can think of organizations that do this: volunteer organizations that seek to alleviate people's material and spiritual needs; church groups that reach out even beyond their immediate membership to heal the wounds of society; business corporations with a sense of social responsibility as well as the desire for profit; real estate agencies that do not discriminate or cause others to discriminate in the selection and sale of housing on the basis of sex, color, or religion; private associations that have open membership; and so forth.

The virtue of social justice is implicitly present in both social sin and social grace. According to the National Catechetical Directory, social justice is that aspect of Church teaching and Christian life which seeks to apply the Gospel command of love to and within the structures, systems and institutions of society, which are the framework in which all human relationships take place. It seeks to assess the worth of social systems in view of how they impact the lives of people and calls for personal responsibility and effective action to change those which are oppressive.

A *social examination of conscience* is precisely what the bishops of the world had in mind when they met in the 1971 Bishops' Synod and issued the statement *Justice in the World*. This document involves a careful, reflective consideration of the Christian in the world. Considered from a faith perspective are such realities as: economic injustice, lack of social participation among some groups in the benefits of our technological age, high rates of consumption in the developed countries and a corresponding unequal distribution of goods on a worldwide scale, and media manipulation.

A contemporary examination of one's social conscience might involve these kinds of questions:

> Have we allowed ourselves to become enslaved to anything which makes us less than we are called to be by God putting our worth in terms of what we own or use (consumerism) instead of in the love of God for us?

> Do we judge the worth of others in terms of what they do or do not have, materially speaking?

> Do we consider ourselves superior to others because of race (racism) or because of sex (sexism) and treat the other as inferior?

Do we enslave other people by putting pressures on them, by discriminating against them in any way, by discouraging them, by keeping them in ignorance, by denying them proper food, clothing, or shelter?

Do we follow the path of integrity and honesty in our dealings with others or the path of compromise and hypocrisy?

Am l aware of any unjust situation where I work or recreate that could be changed for the better if I were to speak up for those who are being oppressed?

Is my concern for peace in the world mirrored in the way I treat other people? Do I try to resolve conflicts in such a way that both sides win?

Are we who are parents raising our children to be citizens of the world, with a deeply committed concern for those who are treated unfairly? Does our life-style as a family witness to this global concern and to global inequality in the sharing of goods?

Do we accept our need for God and our dependence on God's power as we consider the evils in the world, or do we try to solve all the problems we face without God? Do we believe more in the power of God than in our own feelings of powerlessness as we face the reality of unjust structures and systems?

To what extent is my faith so genuine that it impels me to work for a more just and peaceful world? To what extent does my commitment to justice and peace grow out of my faith?

Conversion of the heart, as Cardinal Alfrink points out, is necessary if we are to go beyond our traditional understanding of morality as personal to include the social dimension of our lives as well. A social vision in our understanding of the faith is indispensable if we are to be able to read the "signs of the times"—the economic, political, religious and social characteristics of our day—and see them in light of the Gospel. We shouldn't be surprised, however, if we discover resistance within ourselves to accepting the social dimension of faith. Pope John XXIII, in his encyclical *Christianity and Social Progress,* noted this quite well: "If it is indeed difficult to apply teaching of any sort to concrete situations, it is even more so when one tries to put into practice the teaching of the Catholic Church regarding social affairs. This is especially true for the following reasons: there is deeply rooted in every person an instinctive and immoderate love of his own interests; today there is widely diffused in society a materialistic philosophy of life; it is difficult at times to discern the demands of justice in a given situation." Such resistances call for conversion and compassion if we are to develop a social conscience.

Compassion is a key virtue in the faith that acts for justice and peace. It is what enables us to go beyond our private interests and reach out in solidarity with those in need. There are many ways to stimulate growth in compassion. Films about the plight of oppressed peoples, books that recount the stories of those who seek liberation, and speakers who have seen oppression firsthand and poignantly describe it to others can touch our hearts and render us more compassionate. But for compassion to deepen and expand in such a way that we want to join with the oppressed in their struggle because we now truly see life through their eyes, more is needed than films, books and speakers. What is needed is personal contact with suffering people.

During the summer I conduct a program of insertion among materially poor people for Jesuit priests and brothers. The participants have had little if any contact with people who suffer from involuntary poverty, but are open and interested in experiencing the hard, everyday consequences of injustice and oppression in order to more effectively address justice and peace issues in their regular ministry. Besides the personal contact with people whose lives are marred by poverty and the effects of unjust social structures, each participant is visited twice by a facilitator whose task it is to help the man interpret his experience in the light of faith and integrate what he is seeing with an analysis of the causes of the poverty. Perhaps what I have learned in the role of facilitator in this "school for compassion" may be of help to others–laity, religious, diocesan clergy–who spend quality time with the materially poor or those who are handicapped in some way. By "quality time" I mean whatever time you are able to give. This may be once a week, every other week, once a month, a summer, and so forth. And the kind of activity could be anything from visiting the sick and shut-ins to visiting people in jail, working part-time in an urban parish to helping out in a downtown soup kitchen, and so forth. Such activity not only affects our compassion but is also the kind of experience that enables our social conscience to grow.

A very interesting dynamic that I have noticed each summer in the program for Jesuits occurs during the first couple of weeks for most participants. For those working in such a situation on a part-time basis, this dynamic would still occur but in a different time frame. We might call it a "blocking mechanism." Despite the obvious openness of each man to the summer experience, it is quite common for the man to unconsciously prohibit the poverty from affecting him any further once he is over his initial fears and uncertainties. It is a block to one's heart, to one's compassion and understanding. The following are "blocking mechanisms" that I have come in contact with.

- *spiritualism:* The participant interprets the situation almost solely from a detached spiritual perspective and finds it very difficult to conduct a structural analysis of the situation in order to understand the causes of the oppression.
- *intellectualism:* The participant intellectually understands the situation, but is unable or unwilling to engage his heart in his work or in a reflection on that work.
- *personalism:* The participant gives himself completely to the persons with whom he works, but is not interested in a re- flective and intellectual analysis of the situation.
- *blaming the victim:* The participant blames the victim of poverty for the state he or she is in. The victim is simply inferior, gen- erally defective, or morally unfit. Or the defect and inade- quacy is attributed to the malignant nature of poverty. There is no attention given to the unjust structures, such as the schools, the housing system, the lack of jobs, the police and the courts, and more, that require systemic change. (I am in- debted to William Ryan for his excellent book, *Blaming the Victim,* Vintage Books 1976, which has helped me to under- stand this phenomenon.)
- *prejudice:* A person may discover that he is morally judging and evaluating behavior in, for example, the black commu- nity, through the eyes and values of his, let's say, Italian- American background. Fr. Joe Fitzpatrick, S.J., describes this as, "the problem of culture—our tendency to identify our par- ticular culture with nature."
- *comparison:* Some participants compare the poverty they are seeing with more dismal conditions in other cities or coun- tries they have been to or read about. The result is a tendency to miss the poverty that is right in front of them. As facilita- tor, I try to point out that poverty is relative, that is, if the ef- fects of injustice—unemployment, inadequate housing, lack of

quality education, insufficient medical care, and so forth—are present, they are just as dehumanizing to the people where the participant is working as are conditions of poverty in other places, though perhaps not to the same degree.

- *personal history:* Sometimes a situation will develop that will remind a participant of something painful from his own past, for example, close contact with an alcoholic in one's past, and will cause him to shy away from, or misjudge, the people he sees in skid row or in low-income neighborhoods who are drinking a lot.

- *analysis:* Some people are very analytical by nature and after being in a placement for only a few days are quite able to analyze all the strengths and weaknesses of a parish or community center. The danger is that such a person will conclude that he has nothing to learn here because of the various deficiencies he sees. The role of the facilitator is to help the participant see what he is doing and help him to be open to learn from the very place and people he has analyzed.

These blocking mechanisms, if they remain undetected, can stifle or at the very least diminish conversion of the heart, a conversion that is necessary if we are to develop a compassionate social conscience. Access to some kind of a facilitator while one is working with the victims of injustice can be a great help to uncovering one's blocks and correcting the thinking that goes with them.

In conclusion, if we are to join in the search for genuine solutions to the numerous problems which arise in the life of individuals and from social relationships (Second Vatican Council), we must allow our social conscience to grow. If we are to overcome our ignorance as to the causes of injustice and violence and our possible apathy in doing anything constructive to change the world, we need some ongoing personal contact with our suffering brothers and sisters, a contact that changes our hearts so that whatever actions we take may be consistent and long-lasting.

Our model for being with the oppressed is the incarnate Christ, of whom St. Paul wrote in his letter to the Philippians (2:5-7):

> Your attitude must be that of Christ:
> Though he was in the form of God,
> he did not deem equality with God
> something to be grasped at.

Rather, he emptied himself
and took the form of a slave,
being born in the likeness of human beings.

—Review for Religious, July–August 1983

Conscience: Reflection Questions

1. What do you understand by the words "informed conscience"?

2. Why develop a Christian Social Conscience? How do you do it?

3. John Henry Cardinal Newman asserted that conscience is the first Vicar of Christ. What did he mean?

4. Read the entire play *A Man for All Seasons* by Robert Bolt, or arrange to see the film. Why was Thomas More considered a man for all seasons? Why would More give the devil the benefit of the law? Norfolk suggested that More violate his conscience for the sake of fellowship. How did More respond? Explain the image he uses with daughter Meg, that in taking an oath, one "holds his own self in his own hands. Like water."

5. What do you make of Cunningham's suggestion that courtesy be rehabilitated as a virtue and not merely as a refinement of manners?

3
Dying and Death

1 Corinthians 15:51-58

⁵¹Listen, I will tell you a mystery! We will not all die, but we will all be changed, ⁵²in a moment, in the twinkling of an eye, at the last trumpet. For the trumpet will sound, and the dead will be raised imperishable, and we will be changed. ⁵³For this perishable body must put on imperishability, and this mortal body must put on immortality. ⁵⁴When this perishable body puts on imperishability, and this mortal body puts on immortality, then the saying that is written will be fulfilled:

"Death has been swallowed up in victory."
⁵⁵"Where, O death, is your victory?
Where, O death, is your sting?"
⁵⁶The sting of death is sin, and the power of sin is the law. ⁵⁷But thanks be to God, who gives us the victory through our Lord Jesus Christ.

⁵⁸Therefore, my beloved, be steadfast, immovable, always excelling in the work of the Lord, because you know that in the Lord your labor is not in vain.

The Mystery of Death

18. It is in regard to death that man's condition is most shrouded in doubt. Man is tormented not only by pain and by the gradual breaking-up of his body but also, and even more, by the dread of forever ceasing to be. But a deep instinct leads him rightly to shrink from and to reject the utter ruin and total loss of his personality. Because he bears in himself the seed of eternity, which cannot be reduced to mere matter, he rebels against death. All the aids made available by technology, however useful they may be, cannot set his anguished mind at rest. They may prolong his life-span; but this does not satisfy his heartfelt longing, one that can never be stifled, for a life to come.

While the mind is at a loss before the mystery of death, the Church, taught by divine Revelation, declares that God has created man in view of a blessed destiny that lies beyond the limits of his sad state on earth. Moreover, the Christian faith teaches that bodily death, from which man would have been immune had he not sinned,[14] will be overcome when that wholeness which he lost through his own fault will be given once again to him by the almighty and merciful Saviour. For God has called man, and still calls him, to cleave with all his being to him in sharing for ever a life that is divine and free from all decay. Christ won this victory when he rose to life, for by his death he freed man from death.[15] Faith, therefore, with its solidly based teaching, provides every thoughtful man with an answer to his anxious queries about his future lot. At the same time it makes him able to be united in Christ with his loved ones who have already died, and gives hope that they have found true life with God.

[14]Cf. Wis. 1:13; 2:23-24; Rom. 5:21; 6:23; Jas. 1:15.
[15]Cf. 1 Cor. 15:56-57.

—Gaudium et spes 18

"I Am Going to Leave This World a Happy Man"
Fr. Mark Hollenhorst

This homily was delivered at the Church of St. John in Grand Marais on December 1, 1991. Fr. Mark Hollenhorst was a priest of the Diocese of Duluth, Minnesota, until his death from cancer on December 27, 1993. This homily is from More Urgent Than Usual: The Final Homilies of Mark Hollenhorst, *edited by William C. Graham (Collegeville: The Liturgical Press, 1995).*

At Easter two years ago, I played for you one of my favorite pieces of music: the last three exciting minutes of Bruckner's Fourth Symphony, one of the greatest passages in all of music. You remember that, at the time, I told you that Bruckner described it as the sun rising gloriously over the majestic mountains. Advent is a time to look forward to that same kind of light: the light of Jesus our Savior that shines in our world during the Christmas season.

I had the wonderful opportunity to hear the Minnesota Orchestra play Bruckner's Fourth Symphony in its entirety at Orchestra Hall. I listened with mixed emotions though. As the music progressed toward the powerful conclusion, the excitement kept mounting. But I also had a growing sadness that it would all soon be over. I wanted it to last forever. So the closer it got to the end, the more I appreciated each individual note. When it was over, there was great sadness in me; I did not want to leave; I wanted to hear it all over again. But I left the concert a richer person, and grateful to God for giving me such a wonderful experience.

My life has been like that concert the last couple of weeks. I have been thinking about life and death a lot lately, because my cancer has come back, and I know now that I am a lot closer to my death than I am to my birth. I found out this week that one of my ribs is disintegrating. It sounds worse than it feels. It does not hurt much. Every once in a while, if I strain it the wrong way, it feels kind of like sore muscles after a heavy workout.

When I got the news, my first response was: "Doc, you gotta be ribbin' me!" But it was strikingly easy for me to take. I was actually more distressed by the Vikings' loss to the Lions last week. I go back next week to find out what happens next, and what kind of treatment I need. Hopefully, God will give me many more good years of life, but I'm ready for whatever comes.

Life on earth is a wonderful gift to us from God. It's like listening to that Bruckner Symphony: full of beauty, tension, struggle, joy, sorrow, hope, and, at times, profound peace. I wish life could go on forever, but I know it is drawing to a close. There is a sadness in that, but consequently, every breath becomes richer and every moment is appreciated all the more. And when it comes time to die, I know that I am going to leave this world a happy man, grateful to God for having given me the experience.

We are all in the same boat, really, some of us just have a better indication of the time frame. Today's Gospel offers us a great hope in the face of our transient and all too brief existence on earth. It says that we have something to look forward to at the end of our lives. Something as glorious as the end of Bruckner's Fourth Symphony awaits us all. We will see Christ face-to-face and we will live with him forever. I believe this Gospel, and that is why I have very little distress about my condition. I am ready to take whatever comes, because I know that something wonderful lies just beyond it.

I look at it this way: if it is true that the more my cancer grows, the closer I get to death, and if the Gospel is also true in saying that we will see the glory of Christ face-to-face, then, to me, it appears that my cancer is the way through which I will get to God.

How Long Must We Preserve Life?
Catholic Ethics at the End of Life   *Thomas A. Shannon*

A year ago my wife and I spent an evening with a group of couples who had been meeting for serious discussion over a period of twenty years. We were invited to discuss ethical issues surrounding the removal of life-prolonging therapies. I was to give an overview and then discussion would follow—as indeed it did. The other salient fact about this group is that it was Jewish; my wife and I are Catholic. As the discussion proceeded and a variety of points were pursued and different perspectives vigorously argued and counterargued, one man asked me what role my religion played in developing my perspective. Starting to give the standard statement on the ordinary-extraordinary distinction made within Catholic moral thinking, my questioner interrupted. "No, no," he said, "you believe in immortality, otherwise you could not speak as you do."

My questioner was pointing to an important theological context for discussions of forgoing or terminating life-support therapies—a context that gives a particular orientation to this discussion, indeed, gives it meaning and life, as well as a certain consoling perspective. This theological context has two dimensions: belief in God and immortality, and the finiteness of human life.

As Christians we may too easily assume belief in God as a given in ethical discussions, but without taking seriously what that actually means. God is our ultimate reality. Such ultimateness is the ground of the command that we are not to have false gods before us. Nothing and no one but God is to be adored or worshiped as God. Nothing else, no matter how prized and precious, is of ultimate value. The ethical conclusion is that all values and practices must be seen as means to our journey to God, not ends. To say or suggest that anything else has the ultimate value or meaning that God has is to commit idolatry.

This includes human life. For while human life is sacred and valuable, it is created and finite and to suggest it has an ultimacy because of its sacredness is to commit idolatry. Such a point has ethical significance in evaluating medical therapies and technologies. For while life is valuable, it is neither the ultimate value nor the only value relevant to the issue at hand. Nor does life's being a basic value give it a privileged position among other values. Even though life is not a means to other ends, it is not of ultimate value. Thus, for example, some argue that the demands of justice can require the taking of human life as in war or self-defense. Were human life of ultimate value moral positions asserting the priority of other values would not be viable within Roman Catholicism.

This perspective is particularly relevant when the only outcome of a therapeutic or technical intervention is the preservation of organic or biological life. Designating biological survival as the normative or controlling value in decision making in these cases comes close to idolatry because life is given an importance beyond its created status. Life is made an ultimate good rather than remaining a finite good.

As Christians we also believe in the life of the world to come. We have all taken comfort from the belief, expressed in the funeral liturgy, that life is not taken away, but transformed. Our belief and our hope is for life in the Kingdom, revealed in its fullness in the Resurrection of Jesus.

This belief too provides strenuous challenge to those who would confer ultimate value on our present life. For indeed, if we are dust and unto dust we will return, why does biological life have such a controlling role in ethical decision making? The question grows out of my reading and reflection on "Nutrition and Hydration: Moral Considerations" (*Origins,* January 30, 1992), by the Pennsylvania Bishops' Conference, and "Nutrition and Hydration: Moral and Pastoral Reflections" by the National Conference of Catholic Bishops' Pro-Life Committee (*Origins,* April 9, 1992). The Pennsylvania bishops, for example, say: "Supplying nourishment would not be an instance of simply prolonging the dying process without actually preserving life. Life would be preserved at length and not merely temporarily prolonged while waiting for an imminently terminal condition to complete its course."

For the patient in the persistent vegetative state, biological life certainly would be prolonged at length, but what confers on a created reality the ultimate significance that would lead these bishops to their conclusion? What in human dignity is protected by maintaining the biological processes when there is no reasonable basis for expecting any change in the person's medical status? To maintain biological processes for their own sake gives priority to the impersonal rather than the personal, is death-denying rather than death-accepting.

These two core beliefs of Christianity—the ultimacy of God and the finiteness of human existence—seem to me to be given too little consideration in current episcopal teaching about forgoing or terminating therapies or technologies. Can one not argue that life is sacred without conferring an ultimacy on it that borders on the idolatrous? I am seriously concerned about the strong tendency in ecclesial discussions of these questions to absolutize biological life or, at least, to make it the privileged factor in decision making.

In the context of this theological background, I want to examine several other critical issues, particularly in relation to medically assisted nutrition and hydration.

First is cost. Here the Pennsylvania bishops make an interesting observation. They acknowledge what the church has long held: when a family reaches the limits of its resources, they have reached the limits of ordinary care. But then they go on to say "however, in the society in which we live this does not present a fully convincing argument. Resources are available from other sources, and these can often be tapped before a family reaches dire financial straits." Assuming that such resources are available, why does the fact of their availability make them ethically mandatory? Why does the use of scarce funds and resources for prolonging biological life take priority over other uses?

The NCCB's Pro-Life Committee also acknowledges that cost can be a valid factor in decisions about life support. But this issue is needlessly complicated when the committee separates the cost of providing a particular modality—for example, medically assisted nutrition and hydration—from the cost of the total care. First, the actual cost of a therapy or treatment does not in itself constitute the basis of the determination of ordinary or extraordinary. Rather it is cost in relation to the patient's values and overall prognosis. Second, if one breaks the total cost down, it may be the case—to follow the bishops' reasoning—that no one particular item considered in itself would be that expensive (though not if one has looked at itemized hospital invoices lately). However, few, if indeed any, pay for isolated items only. The totality of the cost of treatment is the point of departure for a determination of proportion or disproportion. To argue for the determination of proportion or disproportion on the basis of one or the other therapy or intervention distorts the evaluation of the actual cost of the totality of the treatment, the appropriate locus of the moral analysis.

The Congregation for the Doctrine of the Faith's "Declaration on Euthanasia" (1980), which these two statements cite approvingly, holds that disproportionate means can be refused because of a desire "not to impose excessive expense on the family *or the community*" (my emphasis). The congregation acknowledges that built into the evaluation of whether a treatment or technology is extraordinary or disproportionate is a recognition of both the individual good and the common good. While it may be the case that funds are available outside of the family, either through insurance plans or other state or federal monies, it does not follow that the availability of such funding automatically makes its use ordinary. Neither should we automatically assume an entitlement to them such that denial of access *ipso facto* is an injustice.

A second issue is the traditional distinction between ordinary and extraordinary means of treatment. As the Pennsylvania bishops correctly note, such a distinction is not to be "based solely on the commonness and availability of the means themselves, although this is taken into account." This position seems to be in contention with the prolife committee's approving citation of the 1975 Declaration of Helsinki that medical procedures are appropriate if in the judgment of the physician they offer "hope of life, reestablishing health, or alleviating suffering." The Helsinki statement implies that therapies or outcomes are ordinary by virtue of the physician's determination. Such a position is a type of medical indications policy that mandates treatment based on physician assessment of medical benefit or outcome, not the patient's values or the implications of the prognosis for the patient.

Such a position first establishes what is ordinary by categorizing the technology or procedure in the abstract. Second, it does not seek to determine the relation of benefit to burden for the patient. Third, the stance assumes that the physician is the major—or perhaps only—decision maker.

A treatment's routine or customary use in the practice of medicine or even its being lifesaving does not make such a treatment morally ordinary. One must look to the benefits and burdens to see if there is a disproportion. The terms ordinary and extraordinary do not refer to abstract classifications or categorizations of treatments or technologies on the basis of which we determine whether or not they are to be used. Rather these terms refer to the conclusion of a moral analysis of the facts of the case and the relevant values. On the basis of such an analysis we conclude that a particular treatment is ordinary or extraordinary and should be used or not accordingly. This avoids an equivocation between what is medically ordinary—meaning routine—and what is morally ordinary—meaning a favorable proportion of benefits to burdens.

Interesting examples of this meaning of the terms show up in the history of moral theology and exemplify how attuned these moralists were to the culture, the state of medicine, the economic status of the person, and personal values. These examples range from Lessius's teaching in the 1600s ("women, especially virgins, are not bound to accept from men medical treatment of this type in the more secret parts . . . but many modest virgins prefer to tolerate a disease or death rather than to be touched by men") to Patuzzi's (d. 1769) observation that discussions of ordinary means may be impractical because "people usually sin by being too solicitous of their lives rather than the other way around" (quoted in Daniel Cronin, doctoral dissertation, in *Conserving Human Life,* John XXIII Medical–Moral Research Center, 1991). These are only examples and they have the limits of examples. Nonetheless, they point to a certain common-sense approach to the problem. Their additional significance is the acceptance of the patient's values and perspectives.

A third issue is a pragmatic one. I can think of no surer way to encourage or even play right into the hands of those who are advocating euthanasia than to strongly imply that some therapies cannot be forgone or stopped once started. Please note that I am not saying this is what the bishops actually say. I am talking about what impression people can take from stories about the documents. Such an impression will be a total disaster. One of the sanest and most profoundly Christian instincts of the Catholic medical ethics tradition has been its recognition of the limits of medical intervention, grounded in a clear sense of human finitude. Such wisdom is in danger of being lost.

My reason for fearing such a loss is the growing influence of the extreme versions of the prolife movement which see euthanasia as the analogue of abortion. My impression is that in this quarter, any action that can be remotely construed as a compromise of life is to be rejected. Thus for the sake of the value of biological life, we are to maintain individuals on life support systems until they die. The ultimate or normative value is life, whether personal or biological. Nothing can compromise or qualify that value.

A byproduct of this line of argument could be a decision not to start someone on a therapy or technology for fear that it would not be stopped if and when that treatment should become inappropriate. Fear of technological entrapment could cause great harm because people who might benefit from a treatment would not receive it or would reject it. Unfortunately one often does not know whether or not a treatment is beneficial until one actually tries it.

Fourth, the prolife committee uses the terms "treatment" and "care" in a way which suggests that they are interchangeable. Thus the committee asks whether "medically assisted nutrition and hydration should always be seen as a form of normal care." I am quite leery of speaking of treatment and care as interchangeable; for though we are always obligated to care for a patient, we are not always obligated to provide treatment. Neither is a particular treatment always an appropriate way of manifesting care, that is, when the burdens are disproportionate to the benefits. My concern is not to pick linguistic nits, but to warn against an implicit begging of a critical question. For if we assume that treatment and care are mutually extensive terms, then to reject treatment is to reject care, which does not follow.

Fifth and finally, the prolife committee states: "It is not easy to arrive at a single answer to some of the real and personal dilemmas involved in this issue." Why is it necessary for us to arrive at a single answer, particularly when the issue is so complex, as the committee's statement itself documents? I think that the only way a single answer could be given would be to prohibit removal of various forms of life support, particularly medically assisted nutrition and hydration—which of course is the presumption the committee holds. Such a position, however, assumes individuals are not to be trusted in coming to such a serious decision, that answers to complex issues can be formulated in terms universally applicable to all cases, and that the magisterium is to have the final word in resolving practical moral decisions.

Many years ago when I began doing ethics rounds in various hospitals, I was asked to speak with two elderly, unmarried Irish sisters who wanted to terminate treatment for the third sister. We discussed the situation and it was clear that death was imminent and further therapies useless. Indeed, this was the classic case for terminating therapy. Toward the end of our conversation, I asked if they wanted to discuss this with their parish priest, for I was surprised that they asked to speak with the ethicist rather than him. "No," they said, "he will tell us we can't stop the treatments, but we know it's the right thing to do and we're going to do it."

I was taken aback, both because the two sisters were so firm in their assessment and because I would not think that this would be the priest's response. But the fact that this experience from so many years ago was among the first things that came to my mind on reading these documents on medically assisted nutrition and hydration suggests that maybe these elderly sisters were right on both counts. And what a tragedy to feel that the church has abandoned you at the time of deepest need.

—*Commonweal*, December 3, 1993

Richard Cory   *Edwin Arlington Robinson*

Whenever Richard Cory went down town,
We people on the pavement looked at him:
He was a gentleman from sole to crown,
Clean favored, and imperially slim.

And he was always quietly arrayed,
And he was always human when he talked;
But still he fluttered pulses when he said,
"Good-morning," and he glittered when he walked.

And he was rich—yes, richer than a king—
And admirably schooled in every grace:
In fine, we thought that he was everything
To make us wish that we were in his place.

So on we worked, and waited for the light,
And went without the meat, and cursed the bread;
And Richard Cory, one calm summer night,
Went home and put a bullet through his head.

—1896

Veritatis splendor **in Focus: Killing the Patient**
                              Richard McCormick

A particular target of the papal encyclical is proportionalism. But the Pope has not been well advised about what these theorists and other moral theologians criticized actually say, according to a Jesuit priest who is the John A. O'Brien Professor of Christian Ethics in the University of Notre Dame, Indiana.

The encyclical *Veritatis splendor,* signed on 6 August but released on 5 October, did not appear from nowhere, a kind of surprising and sudden ecclesial "Big Bang" documented. The temperature had been elevating gradually but perceptibly.

In 1983 Cardinal Edouard Gagnon, now president of the prestigious Pontifical Committee for International Eucharistic Congresses, proposed an intriguing "final solution" for the moral problems of our times: "change 90 percent of the teachers of moral theology and stop them from teaching." That is quite remarkable therapy. But what is the disease?

If one is allowed a mischievous suspicion, one might suggest that Cardinal Gagnon and Cardinal Joseph Ratzinger have occasionally shared a coffee over the subject. For in the *Ratzinger Report*—a summary of some interviews in 1984—Ratzinger identified the disease, at least in the moral sphere, as "consequentialism" and "proportionalism" and saw it as infecting especially American moral theologians. This conveniently overlooked the fact that the major contributors to this tendency were European (Peter Knauer SJ, Bruno Schüller SJ, Joseph Fuchs SJ, Louis Janssens, the late Franz Böckle, and Franz Scholtz, to name but a few). Whatever the case, there can be little doubt that the impulse towards *Veritatis splendor* has been building up for some time. Indeed, there is absolutely nothing new in the heart of the encyclical that had not been stated earlier.

In his apostolic exhortation "Reconciliation and Penance" (2 December 1984), John Paul II gave strong hints as to what would appear in *Veritatis splendor*. In the 1984 document he deplored the loss of the sense of sin in our time. He listed several influences that undermine this sense. One such influence he identified as a "system of ethics." (Another noted was the notion of the fundamental option. I cannot treat it here since it is a complicated subject.) The Pope stated: "This may take the form of an ethical system which relativises the moral norm, denying its absolute and unconditional value, and as a consequence denying that there can be intrinsically illicit acts, independent of the circumstances in which they are performed by the subject." He was, I believe, ill served by his advisers in framing the matter in this way.

Equivalently the Pope is saying that certain actions can be morally wrong from the object *(ex objecto)* independently of circumstances. As the German theologian, Bruno Schüller SJ, one of the most influential of proportionalists, has shown, that is analytically obvious *if the object is characterized in advance as morally wrong*. No theologian would or could contest the papal statement understood in that sense. But it is not the issue. The key problem is: what objects should be characterized as morally wrong and on what criteria? Of course, hidden in this question is the further one: what is to count as pertaining to the object?

That is often decided by an independent ethical judgment about what one thinks is morally right or wrong in certain areas.

Let the term "lie" serve as an example here. The Augustinian-Kantian approach holds that every falsehood is a lie. Others would hold that falsehood is morally wrong (a lie) only when it is denial of the truth to one who has a right to know. In the first case the object of the act is said to be falsehood (= lie) and it is seen as *ex objecto* morally wrong. In the second case the object is "falsehood to protect an important secret" and is seen as *ex objecto* morally right (*ex objecto* because the very end must be viewed as pertaining to the object).

If you are with me so far, hang on. Here is more. These differing judgments do not trace to disagreements about the fonts of morality (object, end, circumstances), but to different judgments about the use of human speech. Some view "falsehood to protect a secret" as permissible, others do not. In this sense one could fully agree with the Pope that there are "intrinsically illicit acts independent of the circumstances" and yet deny that this applies to the very matters apparently of the most concern to him (sterilisation, contraception, masturbation). The quite traditional Jesuit author of the popular manual of moral theology, H. Noldin, wrote:

> All those things pertain to the object of the act that constitute its *substance,* viewed not physically but *morally;* furthermore, all those things constitute the substance of an act which are so essential and necessary to it that if something is lacking or added, the act is different. Thus, the object of theft is someone's property taken against his reasonable will; for if the thing is not someone else's, or is taken with the owner's consent or not against his reasonable opposition, it is not theft.

Take masturbation, for instance. When masturbation occurs in the context of sperm testing, there are many theologians who believe that this context enters the very object or meaning of the act. In other words, they regard it as an act different from self-pleasuring, much as they would think killing in self-defence is a different act from killing during a robbery. Those who reject these differences have attributed a full independent moral character to the material event of self-stimulation that they do not attribute to the merely material event of "speaking falsehood" or "taking another's property."

But now to *Veritatis splendor.* The encyclical is divided into three parts. Chapter one is a biblical meditation on Jesus' dialogue with the rich young man (Mt 19:16-22). Chapter two critically reviews certain trends in contemporary moral theology. Chapter three addresses the importance of Christian morality for the life of the Church and world and especially the teaching responsibility of bishops.

Two brief introductory remarks. First, I must note a problem. In its key second chapter, *Veritatis splendor* is dense and technical. The Pope has joined an in-house conversation among moral theologians. To deal with the encyclical adequately, one has to plough through some heavy theological literature and language. Very frankly, few non-specialists will read the papal letter, and of those who do most will emerge with cluttered and clouded but not clear heads. I state this by way of apology for the commentary that follows.

Secondly, all Catholic moral theologians should and will welcome the beautiful Christ-centred presentation unfolded in chapter one and the ringing rejection of the false dichotomies identified by John Paul II: between autonomy and theonomy, freedom and law, conscience and truth, and the rest. These extreme positions come to a dead end in relativism, subjectivism, and individualism, and all of us repudiate such pathologies. But many theologians will protest that their work has nothing to do with these deviations.

That brings us to one of the tendencies that concerns that Pope: proportionalism. It is impossible in a brief space to give a fair summary of the developments that are described by the term "proportionalism" or an adequate account of the differences that individual theologians bring to their analyses. Common to all so-called proportionalists, however, is the insistence that causing certain disvalues (nonmoral, premoral evils such as sterilisation, deception in speech, wounding and violence) in our conduct does not by that very fact make the action morally wrong, as certain traditional formulations supposed. The action becomes morally wrong when, all things considered, there is not a proportionate reason in the act justifying the disvalue. Thus, just as not every killing is murder, not every falsehood is a lie, so not every artificial intervention preventing or promoting conception in marriage is necessarily an unchaste act.

Now let us turn to the papal letter. There we read, of proportionalism: "Such theories are not faithful to the Church's teaching, when they believe they can justify, as morally good, deliberate choices of kinds of behaviour contrary to the commandments of the divine and natural law" (76). Later in 81 we read: "If acts are intrinsically evil, a good intention or particular circumstances can diminish their evil, but they cannot remove it." In brief, the encyclical repeatedly states of proportionalism that it attempts to justify morally wrong actions by a good intention. This, I regret to say, is a misrepresentation.

I wish the Pope's advisers had been more careful here. No proportionalist that I know would recognize himself or herself in that description. The stated objection is not new. It has been discussed—and I believe successfully rebutted—for many years. I shall try to summarise here what I believe is really going on in some recent work. I realise that the matter is heavy rowing. But here goes.

In the past some have objected that certain actions are (and have been taught by the magisterium to be) morally wrong *ex objecto* (from the object). But proportionalists, it is asserted, do not and cannot say this since they insist on looking at all dimensions of the act before saying it is morally wrong. The acts in question are such as contraception and masturbation.

What is to be said of this objection (and remember, it is the Pope's objection)? I think it misses the point of what proportionalists are saying. When contemporary theologians say that certain disvalues in our actions can be justified by a proportionate reason, they are not saying that *morally wrong actions (ex objecto)* can be justified by the end. They are saying that an action cannot be judged morally wrong simply by looking at the material happening, or at its object in a very narrow and restricted sense. This is precisely what tradition has done in certain categories (contraception and sterilization, for instance). It does this in no other area.

If we want to put this in traditional categories (object, end, circumstances), we can say that the tradition has defined certain actions as morally wrong *ex objecto* because it has included in the object not simply the material happening (object in a very narrow sense) but also elements beyond it which clearly exclude any possible justification. Thus, a theft is not simply "taking another's property," but doing so "against the reasonable will of the owner." This latter addition has two characteristics in the tradition. (1) It is considered as essential to the object. (2) It excludes any possible exceptions. Why? Because if a person is in extreme difficulty and needs food, the owner is not reasonably unwilling that his food be taken. Fair enough. Yet, when the same tradition deals with, for example, masturbation or sterilization, it adds little or nothing to the material happening and regards such a materially described act alone as constituting the object. If it were consistent, it would describe the object as "sterilization *against the good of marriage.*" This all could accept.

Let me return, then, to John Paul II's language. He cites as an objection to proportionalist tendencies the notion that some acts are intrinsically evil from their object. I believe all proportionalists would admit this *if the object is broadly understood as including all the morally relevant circumstances.*

In conclusion, proportionalists are not justifying "deliberate choices of kinds of behaviour contrary to the commands of the divine and natural law." They are saying that we must look at the dimensions (morally relevant circumstances) before we know what the action is and whether it should be said to be "contrary to the commands of the divine and natural law."

My own reading of this encyclical letter suggests that an item on the agenda is unstated. It is this. I am convinced that the Pope will reject a priori any analytic adjustments in moral theology that do not support the moral wrongfulness of every contraceptive act. Proportionalism certainly does not give such support.

What will be the effect of this encyclical letter? On the public, zero. It is too technical and abstract to address anyone but specialists. How about bishops? Chapter three urges bishops to take their teaching responsibilities seriously. Will that mean refusing a forum to theologians who disagree here and there with an official judgment (usually on a matter of concrete application where disagreement should, according to Vatican II and the American bishops as well, be expected)? Nothing new here. It has been going on for years. Will it mean sackings from teaching positions? Hardly and for two reasons. First, the bishops will wisely (I hope) want to maintain the credibility of Catholic higher education by supporting its institutional autonomy.

Secondly, the vast majority of moral theologians known as proportionalists will *rightly* say that they do not hold or teach what the encyclical attributes to them. They cannot be punished for uncommitted crimes. In this respect *Veritatis splendor* differs from Pius XII's *Humani generis* (1950). Pius's encyclical sadly led to silencings and sackings (Yves Congar, Henri de Lubac, Jean Daniélou, *et. al.*). Most of the positions of these distinguished theologians were eventually accepted by the Church at Vatican II. *Veritatis splendor* at key points attributes to theologians positions that they do not hold. It will, I predict, eventually enjoy an historical status similar to *Humani generis*.

−*The Tablet,* October 30, 1993

Even I Can't Back Death Penalty: Forgiveness, Not Vengeance, Is Best Reply to a Murderer   *Antoinette G. Bosco*

A friend at the *Bigfork Eagle,* a weekly newspaper in Montana, recently sent me a fax of a newspaper clip from the Daily Inter Lake in Kalispell. The headline, in big letters, said, "Justice Is Served," and the story told of the execution of murderer Duncan McKenzie Jr. on May 10.

McKenzie had been on death row for 20 years. His death by lethal injection was the first in Montana since 1943 and the 20th in the United States this year. Officials said he was cooperative; all he asked was to be able to listen to country music through headphones as he was being legally killed. Was justice served?

I may be the only person in Connecticut who cares about an execution in Montana, but I do, and for good reason. For the past year and a half, my life has been dominated by the status of the death penalty in Montana. That's because my life was seared by murder in that rolling state of "A River Runs Through It," so tranquil, so beautiful, but also, for me and my family, so deadly. And I had to let the authorities know if I wanted the death penalty for the murderer.

On Aug. 12, 1993, I received news that no one, certainly no mother, should ever get. My son John and his wife, Nancy, were murdered, blown away by a 9mm gun in the hand of an intruder as they lay sleeping in their bed in their home in Bigfork, Mont.

It turned out that the killer was an 18-year-old, Shadow Clark, the son of the couple from whom my son and his wife had purchased their home a few months earlier. Clark confessed, but never gave a motive for this horrible crime.

This young man faced the death penalty, and I had to confront my soul.

Where did I stand now, when the death penalty would never again be an academic question for me? When you are in that pit, alone with your searing pain, that's when you can't play cat and mouse with honesty. I could easily say, "Put him away for life, he must be punished." But no matter how tempted I was to say "he deserves to die," could I say, "kill this killer"?

Very early in life, I was chilled by the thought of legal execution. It was the day my Uncle Tony's wife was physically restrained and taken to what they called the "insane asylum" in Poughkeepsie, N.Y. I asked my mother why Aunt Margie went crazy and she told me.

Her brother and two friends had robbed a store and killed the owner. All three were put to death in the electric chair in 1928. My aunt never got over it; she ended up mad. From that day on, the notion of the death penalty appalled me.

Years later, when I was getting a master's degree and taking an ethics course, the death-penalty question came up. In brash, liberal fashion, I said I opposed the death penalty. The professor then asked me, "Suppose someone raped and murdered your daughter. What would you say then?" I was stunned. I hadn't expected this ever to be a personal matter. In honesty, I answered, "I think I'd say, kill the bastard."

In 1993 I remembered that question as I felt my heart cut out, visualizing Clark's stealing up to the isolated house where my son and daughter-in-law were asleep in their bed, cutting the phone and electric wires, breaking in through a first-floor window and creeping up the stairs to their room. He shot John once in the head, killing him instantly.

Nancy woke from the explosion, reached for her glasses and put them on. She must have seen what was coming, for she crouched in a fetal position, as the next bullet went through her upper back, out her chest, up through her chin and cheek, and out her eye, breaking her glasses. He "may have touched her," he said in a chilling confession after he killed her.

When I saw his confession, I wanted to mutilate him. How could anyone do this evil thing to another person? Did anyone who could steal the lives of two good people deserve to live? Where did I stand now on my generous, altruistic, liberal opposition to the death penalty? Facing that question was one of the most intense moments of truth I ever had to struggle with. Now I was in a new place, facing the raw, real confrontation with my soul.

In Montana, I had to taste the death in that bedroom, with the bullet hole in the wall, and the blood on the floor. I fell to my knees, praying to the Lord to exorcise the evil from that room. Strangely, in that moment, I didn't want more death.

I saw so clearly that we are wrong to put the emphasis on "penalty" when it should be on unnatural "death" and all the horror this word conveys. Unnatural death, at the hands of evil, is horrendous, hateful to the life-giving Lord. My faith taught me that. But it also taught me that even worse is murder when it is sanitized by calling it official and lawful.

Some politicians have tried to capitalize on the nation's frustration with crime by advocating capital punishment. Some have trivialized an issue we should agonize over—precisely because it deals with the ultimate human question of the value of life. Some say the death penalty will reduce violent crime and punish people who kill others.

But never have I seen any statistics or studies validating the argument that the death penalty reduces crime or deters potential killers.

When I read of Duncan McKenzie's death, I kept wondering just how justice was served by this premeditated killing of a man 20 years after his crime? I was glad that my family and I had made it clear to the Montana authorities that we did not want Clark, facing the death penalty, to be killed. One year after the murders, he pleaded guilty, thus avoiding a trial. He was sentenced to 220 years in prison, with no parole until he reaches age 60.

The bottom line in my personal story may be that I opposed the death penalty for Clark for selfish reasons. I remember once reading of a rabbi who had lost his family in the Holocaust. He forgave Adolf Hitler because he did not want to bring Hitler to America with him.

It's hard to forgive. Not forgiving keeps us angry and anger makes us feel more powerful. But if we don't forgive, we stay emotionally handcuffed to the person who hurt us, as the rabbi understood. Now I am free enough to pray for Clark, hoping he will one day be able to respond to the touch of grace we are all given by God, and find redemption. His act of killing reinforced my commitment to affirming life—and, forever, my opposition to the death penalty.

—Hartford Courant

Declaration of Life

I, the undersigned, being of sound and disposing mind and memory, do hereby in the presence of witnesses make this Declaration of Life.

Background

1. I believe that the killing of one human being by another is morally wrong.

2. I am opposed to capital punishment on any grounds whatsoever.

3. I believe it is morally wrong for any state or other governmental entity to take the life of a human being by way of capital punishment for any reason.

4. I believe that capital punishment is not a deterrent to crime and serves only the purpose of revenge.

Therefore, I hereby declare that should I die as a result of a violent crime, I request that the person or persons found guilty of homicide for my killing not be subject to or put in jeopardy of the death penalty under any circumstances, no matter how heinous their crime or how much I may have suffered. The death penalty would only increase my suffering.

I believe it is morally wrong for my death to be the reason for the killing of another human being.

I request that the Prosecutor or District Attorney having the jurisdiction of the person or persons alleged to have committed my homicide not file or prosecute an action for capital punishment as a result of my homicide.

I request that this Declaration be made admissible in any trial of any person charged with my homicide and read and delivered to the jury.

I request the Court to allow this Declaration to be admissible as a statement of the victim at the sentencing of the person or persons charged and convicted of my homicide; and, to pass sentence in accordance with my wishes.

I request that the Governor or other executive officer(s) grant pardon, clemency or take whatever action is necessary to stay and prohibit the carrying out of the execution of any person or persons found guilty of my homicide.

This Declaration is not meant to be, and should not be taken as, a statement that the person or persons who have committed my homicide should go unpunished.

I request that my family and friends take whatever actions are necessary to carry out the intent and purpose of this Declaration; and, I further request them to take no action contrary to this Declaration.

During my life, I want to feel confident that under no circumstances whatsoever will my death result in the capital punishment of another human being.

I request that, should I die under the circumstances as set forth in this Declaration and the death penalty is requested, my family, friends and personal representative deliver copies of this Declaration as follows: to the Prosecutor or District Attorney having jurisdiction over the person or persons charged with my homicide; to the attorney representing the person or persons charged with my homicide; to the judge presiding over the case involving my homicide; for recording, to the Recorder of the County in which my homicide took place and to the Recorder of the County in which the person or persons charged with my homicide are to be tried; to all newspapers, radio and television stations of general circulation in the County in which my homicide took place and the County in which the person or persons charged with my homicide are to be tried; and, to any other person, persons or entities my family, friends or personal representative deem appropriate in order to carry out my wishes as set forth herein.

I affirm under the pains and penalties for perjury that the above Declaration of Life is true.

WITNESS   **DECLARANT**

_____   _____

_____   _____

Printed Name   Printed Name

_____

_____

Printed Name

STATE OF _____)

                                                              SS:

COUNTY OF _____)

Before me, a Notary Public in and for said County and State, personally appeared the Declarant and acknowledged the execution of the foregoing instrument this _____ day of _____ 19_____.

WITNESS my hand and notarial seal.

My Commission Expires:

_____   _____

                                                              NOTARY PUBLIC

County of Residence: _____

_____   Printed Name

Please return your signed, notarized Declaration of Life to:
    Convent of Mercy
    273 Willoughby Ave.
    Brooklyn, NY 11205

(If you did not have your Declaration notarized, please include a stamped, self-addressed envelope so that a notarized copy may be returned to you.)

Dying and Death: Reflection Questions

1. Is the concept of "eternal life" easy or difficult for you to accept?

2. Does the reality of death make each moment of your life more important?

3. Do you find Mark Hollenhorst believable when he asserts that he'll leave this world a happy man? Why or why not? What prompts his suggestion?

4. How does the funeral hymn "May saints and angels lead you on" make evident what Christians believe about life after death?

5. Because the issue of prolonging life is so complex, is there any hope of arriving at a single answer for every situation?

6. Why do you think Richard Cory went home and "put a bullet through his head"? Is it fair to say that Richard Cory is a typical modern human being?

7. Should we kill killers? If you answered "no," would your opinion change if the killer had murdered a member of your family?

4
Faith

Hebrews 11:1-39

Now faith is the assurance of things hoped for, the conviction of things not seen. [2]Indeed, by faith our ancestors received approval. [3]By faith we understand that the worlds were prepared by the word of God, so that what is seen was made from things that are not visible.

[4]By faith Abel offered to God a more acceptable sacrifice than Cain's. Through this he received approval as righteous. God himself giving approval to his gifts; he died, but through his faith he still speaks. [5]By faith Enoch was taken so that he did not experience death; and "he was not found, because God had taken him." For it was attested before he was taken away that "he had pleased God." [6]And without faith it is impossible to please God, for whoever would approach him must believe that he exists and that he rewards those who seek him. [7]By faith Noah, warned by God about events as yet unseen, respected the warning and built an ark to save his household; by this he condemned the world and became an heir to the righteousness that is in accordance with faith.

[8]By faith Abraham obeyed when he was called to set out for a place that he was to receive as an inheritance; and he set out, not knowing where he was going. [9]By faith he stayed for a time in the land he had been promised, as in a foreign land, living in tents, as did Isaac and Jacob, who were heirs with him of the same promise. [10]For he looked forward to the city that has foundations, whose architect and builder is God. [11]By faith he received power of procreation, even though he was too old—and Sarah herself was barren—because he considered him faithful who had promised. [12]Therefore from one person, and this one as good as dead, descendants were born, "as many as the stars of heaven and as the innumerable grains of sand by the seashore."

[13]All of these died in faith without having received the promises, but from a distance they saw and greeted them. They confessed that

they were strangers and foreigners on the earth, [14]for people who speak in this way make it clear that they are seeking a homeland. [15]If they had been thinking of the land that they had left behind, they would have had opportunity to return. [16]But as it is, they desire a better country, that is, a heavenly one. Therefore God is not ashamed to be called their God; indeed, he has prepared a city for them.

[17]By faith Abraham, when put to the test, offered up Isaac. He who had received the promises was ready to offer up his only son, [18]of whom he had been told, "It is through Isaac that descendants shall be named for you." [19]He considered the fact that God is able even to raise someone from the dead—and figuratively speaking, he did receive him back. [20]By faith Isaac invoked blessings for the future on Jacob and Esau. [21]By faith Jacob, when dying, blessed each of the sons of Joseph, "bowing in worship over the top of his staff." [22]By faith Joseph, at the end of his life, made mention of the exodus of the Israelites and gave instructions about his burial.

[23]By faith Moses was hidden by his parents for three months after his birth, because they saw that the child was beautiful; and they were not afraid of the king's edict. [24]By faith Moses, when he was grown up, refused to be called a son of Pharaoh's daughter, [25]choosing rather to share ill-treatment with the people of God than to enjoy the fleeting pleasures of sin. [26]He considered abuse suffered for the Christ to be greater wealth than the treasures of Egypt, for he was looking ahead to the reward. [27]By faith he left Egypt, unafraid of the king's anger; for he persevered as though he saw him who is invisible. [28]By faith he kept the Passover and the sprinkling of blood, so that the destroyer of the firstborn would not touch the firstborn of Israel.

[29]By faith the people passed through the Red Sea as if it were dry land, but when the Egyptians attempted to do so they were drowned. [30]By faith the walls of Jericho fell after they had been encircled for seven days. [31]By faith Rahab the prostitute did not perish with those who were disobedient, because she had received the spies in peace.

[32]And what more should I say? For time would fail me to tell of Gideon, Barak, Samson, Jephthah, of David and Samuel and the prophets— [33]who through faith conquered kingdoms, administered justice, obtained promises, shut the mouths of lions, [34]quenched raging fire, escaped the edge of the sword, won strength out of weakness, became mighty in war, put foreign armies to flight. [35]Women received their dead by resurrection. Others were tortured, refusing to accept release, in order to obtain a better resurrection. [36]Others suffered mocking and flogging, and even chains and imprisonment. [37]They were stoned to death, they were sawn in two, they were killed by the sword; they went about in skins of sheep and goats, destitute, persecuted, tormented— [38]of whom the world was not worthy. They wandered in

deserts and mountains, and in caves and holes in the ground.

[39]Yet all these, though they were commended for their faith, did not receive what was promised, [40]since God had provided something better so that they would not, apart from us, be made perfect.

Obedience of Faith

5. "The obedience of faith" (Rom. 16:26; cf. Rom. 1:5; 2 Cor. 10:5-6) must be given to God as he reveals himself. By faith man freely commits his entire self to God, making "the full submission of his intellect and will to God who reveals,"[4] and willingly assenting to the Revelation given by him. Before this faith can be exercised, man must have the grace of God to move and assist him; he must have the interior helps of the Holy Spirit, who moves the heart and converts it to God, who opens the eyes of the mind and "makes it easy for all to accept and believe the truth."[5] The same Holy Spirit constantly perfects faith by his gifts, so that Revelation may be more and more profoundly understood.

[4]First Vatican Council, *Dogm. Const. on Cath. Faith,* c. 3 (on Faith): *Denz.* 189 (3008).
[5]Second Council of Orange, can. 7: *Denz.* 180 (377). First Vatican Council, *loc. cit.: Denz.* 1791 (3010).

—Dei verbum 5

Does College Kill Faith?   *Lawrence S. Cunningham*

In the department of religion at the state university where I began my college teaching career, I was, as I liked to characterize myself, the token Roman Catholic. Others, unhappy with the whole idea of religious studies departments in tax-supported universities, might have characterized me in less kind terms.

Religious studies departments appeared in the early 1960s, after a Supreme Court decision affirmed the right to teach about religion in public institutions. That upset two distinct groups. Some parents, preachers and campus ministry types would warn students about the perils of being in the classroom with "pinko, atheistic, faith-destroying professors"; meanwhile, academe's cultured despisers of religion saw us as crypto-evangelists seeking to shore up religious beliefs that they lumped with the tenets of the Flat Earth Society.

What disconcerted critics of both stripes was the fact that students flocked to elective religious classes. A class I taught on the academic study of religion often enrolled up to 300 students. Religion, the critics should have known, is an intensely interesting subject. Any old grad will remember that dormitory bull sessions always revolved around politics, sex or religion—or a combination of the three.

When I left Florida five years ago to direct the undergraduate theology program at Notre Dame, it was like coming to a new world. Students here must take two theology classes. The Notre Dame faculty is not overly suspicious of the theology faculty because, by any fair estimate, its members include some of the most distinguished biblical, liturgical and theological scholars in the English-speaking world. And unlike my more pluralist classes in Florida, students at Notre Dame are overwhelmingly Catholic.

Parents, however, still worry that the study of theology will "destroy" the faith of their youngsters. Each semester I get a few calls wondering if Professor X is "orthodox" or "safe" for their child. Other parents write to ask if we can help bring an already errant son or daughter back into the church. And some parents still question—often in letters to University President Father Edward Malloy—whether Notre Dame bears responsibility for their child's lapse from religious grace.

As one who came to this campus from a secular environment, I can state baldly that those who have spent their lives here cannot begin to appreciate how Catholic this place is. You see it in its atmosphere (the net result of tradition, liturgical life, core faculty, the presence of the Holy Cross community, the kinds of issues discussed, the attitudes of the alumni, even the kinds of letters printed in the campus newspaper) and in its stated educational philosophy. I think it was Norman Mailer who once said that Notre Dame is the kind of place where one can say the word "soul" and nobody blushes. Exactly.

Part of the Catholic atmosphere comes from its department of theology (note "theology"—not "religious studies"), which is, people will be surprised to learn, a relatively new phenomenon in U.S. Catholic universities. Apart from a visionary program at Saint Mary's College begun after World War II, lay people could not get advanced work in theology in this country until Marquette and later Notre Dame started such graduate programs in the 1960s. Undergraduate theology before that usually consisted of apologetics and, perhaps, a course in ethics with a heavy emphasis on marriage preparation.

Theology is an academic discipline. It is not an extension of the parish CCD program, nor are its professors in the business of persuasion or moral uplift. Its primary task is helping students to see that the faith in which they were raised also can engage their intelligence. We try to heed seriously the old definition of theology—*fides quaerens intellectum* ("faith seeking understanding")—in the setting of a contemporary university.

Such an enterprise is not without risk. If a student comes to Notre Dame with a grammar-school picture of the religious cosmos (God up there; we down here; bad folks below) and we ask: What happens when we realize that in the post-Einsteinian world there is no "up there" or "down here"?—certain naive pictures of the world begin to splinter. How does the world of the Bible have relevance to the world described in classes like biology and physics? What happens when the instructor says, correctly, that the early church did not know there were seven, and only seven, sacraments?

For some students, raising such questions can be a shattering experience. That experience is also called growing up. When I was in college, I thought I had all the religious answers—and could, precocious lad that I was, intellectually beat up on my atheist or fundamentalist peers. Now, after an entire adulthood in the service of theology, I am beginning to see, dimly, what the questions are. Ironically, my questioning now leads me back, lovingly, to engage the old texts—the Fathers, the mystics, the saints and, above all, the scriptures—with a fresh eye. This is the passage from what the philosopher Paul Ricoeur has called "first naiveté" into "second naiveté." Most of our students have not tried to get beyond first, but if they are to become adults, they must.

So what do I want my students to learn?

Religious literacy, for starters. I want them to know that this reality we call Catholicism has a long history to it, a history that has had its ups and downs as we very imperfect people try to learn what it means to be a follower of the man named Jesus whom we call the Christ. I want them to know that the way the following of Christ gets enfleshed—incarnated—is far richer than just saying "yes" to creeds, although that is also important. I want them to know that fidelity to the Word can be detected in more than doctrines; you can learn an awful lot of theology by strolling through an art museum or reading poetry or watching people in church.

I also want to trigger in my students a love of learning. It is part of the authentic Catholic way of being that we value learning; if not, what are we doing sponsoring a university in the first place? Jean Leclercq, in his classic work *The Love of Learning and the Desire for God,* demonstrates that the old monastics did not study the classics and manage scriptoria as a penance but rather from a deep conviction that lifelong learning is a path to God. The monks used a shorthand formula: Reading leads to meditation; meditation leads to prayer; prayer leads to contemplation.

If students read/think/inquire more after they've been with me a semester, I am a happy person. If some who call themselves "non-practicing" or "ex-Catholic" are a tiny bit worried after they have been in my class, I am happier still. If they move beyond reading to something more, I am happiest of all.

Finally, I want students to mature as Christians in the same way they mature as biologists or economists. I want them to see that going to church may derive from a decision of faith, but it may also derive from habit, like flossing each evening. I prefer them to commit to the church for the first reason.

Are they going to be a bit more critical and unsettled after they get out of my class? God, I hope so. If they leave my classroom with the same things they entered with, then what have I been doing all term besides packing information into their brains?

A final observation: Many people allege that the famous but fictive person in the pew runs the risk of losing his or her faith from reading contemporary theologians. However, as my colleague Richard McBrien and others have said, you could put all the people who have left the church after reading Hans Küng or Charles Curran into a phone booth. By contrast, you could fill Notre Dame Stadium with Catholics who've listened to the siren song of the fundamentalists (as has happened among Hispanics in this country and farther south) or who get caught in impossible canonical situations (divorce and re-marriage) or who simply have found the church lacking in that hospitality the Gospel demands of us.

The very word "theologian" tends to mystify people. When I'm asked what my occupation is—say, on a plane—and I answer "theologian," there is almost always a sharp intake of breath followed by a profession of faith or apostasy ("I'm a Baptist but not a very good one, but, what the heck, we're all going to the same place"). After I reassure my seatmate that no tract is about to be thrust upon him, things relax.

What we theologians do, basically, is this: We teach classes, talk to students, read theses, prepare seminars. Because we are also responsible for the needs of the larger community, we give talks at everything from parishes to conferences, write background papers for bishops, help in the preparation of ministerial students. Some of us decipher ancient manuscript fragments found near the Dead Sea;

others prepare critical editions of early writers; still others write articles and books for both the public and the academy.

More than 30 years ago I heard the great Canadian Jesuit theologian Bernard Lonergan say he'd spent his whole life "reaching up to the mind of Aquinas." The phrase has stayed with me. I don't want students to reach up to my mind (well, actually I do, but that's the old ego showing up), but I sure want them to reach.

Sometimes that is a risky thing to do in matters of faith. But we dare do no less since, as a pretty good theologian once said, "When I was a child, I spoke like a child, I thought like a child, I reasoned like a child; when I became an adult, I gave up childish ways" (1 Cor 13:11).

−Notre Dame Magazine

A Way Through, Not a Way Out   *Don Talafous, O.S.B.*

Anxiety is inevitable in an age of crisis like ours. Don't make it worse by deceiving yourself and acting as if you were immune to all inner trepidation. God does not ask you not to feel anxious but to trust in him no matter how you feel.   −Thomas Merton

(Encouraging his followers at Jonestown to drink the poison:) It's hard only at first. Living is much, much more difficult.   −Rev. Jim Jones

Too often, people have felt Christianity was a miracle drug to make life miraculously easy without suffering and pain. The purpose of Christianity is not to avoid difficulty, but to produce a character adequate to meet it when it comes. It does not make life easy; rather it tries to make us great enough for life. It does not give us escape from life's burdens, but strength for meeting them when they come.

−J. Christensen

The great American vice, utilitarianism: everything has to pay, produce results, immediate visible results including God: produce or shut up! That's why so many people are more interested in getting his help in "miraculously" passing a test or meeting a girl or losing weight than in asking for the kind of character which would be able to work with perseverance, be unselfish enough to attract a girl or have enough self-control to pass up the chocolate cake.   −Anonymous

To those who want salvation cheap, and most men do, there is very little comfort to be had out of the great teachers.   −Walter Lippmann

"Why should I shave when I can't think of a reason for living?" (attributed to an authority with the self-effacing name of Jack Smith). As if in answer to that question and in comparably down-to-earth terms, Frederick Buechner writes: "Faith is what gets you out of bed in the morning"—and we could add: helps you make the coffee, brush your teeth, put on a clean shirt. If these present no problem, the moment of truth may come later when we ask: why eat? why go to the office? why greet anyone? why attend another meeting? why be careful about the traffic? In some mental cases, of course, we do see an inability to handle such elementary situations, a kind of failure of nerve. At some time most of us, I imagine, even the apparently sane and physically vibrant, are attacked by some hesitancy about these matters, some weakness in the knees. A bad cold, a little depression, a failure can do it. Whatever else it is in its higher reaches, faith is, on the elemental and practical level, an attitude, a conviction, that assures us it's worth getting up in the morning, worth carrying out the demands of daily life.

Needless to say, in the case of the unquestioned life the demand for any kind of faith may not be all that obvious. We *do* seem capable of moving and living quite well for greater or lesser periods of time simply on the power of some instinctual concern for our hide. Varying with the individual, a new restaurant, a shopping spree, or a high-speed ride can fortify our sense of well-being, of being alive. It's only when the tedium and circular nature of Monday, Tuesday, Wednesday, Thursday, etc., gets to us that we feel the need of a justification for it all or recognize with Albert Camus "that there is but one truly serious philosophical [we might say, human] problem, and that is suicide. Judging whether life is or is not worth living amounts to answering the fundamental question of philosophy [we could say, of life]" (*The Myth of Sisyphus* [New York: Vintage Books, 1960] 3).

But, though such moments or days may come, we can still balk at facing basic questions about whether life is or is not worth living. We may try, instead, to fortify failing instincts with a more conscious bravado. In the following excerpt from an interview with a woman of forty who had her days in the television of the early seventies is illustrated a battle between declining vigor and the will to put up a good front. It seems close to what most of us would call despair:

> At forty, without a husband, you realize you only have a few years left when you are vital and able to take care of yourself. . . . I'm scared of old age; all of us are; it's very frightening to be on your own. But it's very challenging. Your body goes to pieces, you get arthritis or cancer, or your liver is going to go to hell. Everything's just going

down the tubes. And you're not married anymore; you're alone. But you hope, when it comes for you, you have some money to pay the doctors and nurses. You hope when it's over, you've had the guts to do your number. . . . that's all there is. You only have yourself to fall back on. I enjoy life immensely. When you hit my time of life, you have to grit your teeth and say, "To hell with it, here I come." But sometimes in the dead of night, it's so very hard. You're alone, and you get scared, and, God, it would help to have somebody to throw an arm around. A warm body, yeah, that would help. Still, you know, you have to fight it yourself.

"It's very frightening." "But it's very challenging." "You only have yourself to fall back on." "I enjoy life immensely." Give or take a few years, a few changes in our situation, and that might be any of us—desperate, close to an overdose at the bed and an overdraft at the bank. Trying to believe and telling ourselves, against the evidence, that everything we need is at the beck and call of whatever bluster we can muster.

"The warm body" she speaks of may sound a bit minimal in its anonymity, but the context contains an implicit plea for much more. To give adequate importance to faith does not require that we downgrade that love which the woman sees as part of the solution. Yet here, too, she is perceptive enough to see the limitations. "Still, you know you have to fight it yourself" is close to classic statements that, no matter how many friends and loves we might have, we all suffer alone, we all die alone.

Most who are reading this, it can be presumed, are believers in some sense of the word. Equally, many of us just do not see our faith as capable of giving us sufficient enthusiasm and courage to live in its light through all of life's difficult moments even if we are not driven to think of suicide. And, if we do see faith as an all-round antidote to despair, to lack of nerve, to simple boredom, or as the source of our courage and perseverance, we should not endanger it by illusions. Faith will *not* guarantee uninterrupted painlessness or absolute joy. Such a presumption would be unrealistic, contrary to New Testament teaching. Faith can and must grow but never with the un-Christian expectation that after a certain level we will be immune to unhappiness and suffering. How can people talk that way when Jesus, the model of faith and of our relation to God, suffered misunderstanding, hatred, crucifixion, and an untimely death?

What our faith, our trust in Jesus Christ and his Gospel can do, it seems to me, is this: (1) enable us to live, i.e., motivate us for persevering and energetic living; and (2) save us. That is, faith strengthens our adhesion to and trust in Jesus Christ, who has gone through all the events of our life, passed through the worst—suffering and death—to resurrection and eternal life. Joined to him by baptism and faith, we share his relation to the Father and the ability, through him, to ultimately overcome the evils of our life.

But before all this becomes plausible we often need to grow very much in our faith. Our faith needs vigor and central convictions, the latter partly an intellectual matter. It needs some certainties, and these deeply founded. A telescoped model of the necessary growth, a paradigm of the believer, is put before us in that intriguing story of the blind man in chapter 9 of St. John's Gospel. (A complete retelling is no good; read it.) As the blind man is questioned by his hostile interrogators he progresses by degrees to a fuller understanding of and faith in who Jesus is.

In verse 11, after being questioned, he says he was cured by "the *man* called Jesus." In verse 17, in answer to "What do you say about him?" he replies that he is a *prophet*. When his prosecutors raise the objection that they don't know where this Jesus comes from, he answers that *he must come from God* (v. 33). In verses 35 to 38 the blind man confesses belief in the *Son of Man* and calls him *Lord*, titles reserved in John's Gospel for the eternal Son of God and Savior of his people. The man's faith in and understanding of Jesus have moved from the necessary belief that he shared our condition to trust that he is the loving Lord of the universe and his people's salvation, from the conviction that Jesus was human enough to have had "diaper rash as an infant" (Martin Marty's phrase) to the full Christian belief that he is also the unique Son of God in whom we can put our final trust.

That we instinctively look for and require persons and institutions that we can depend upon has been grotesquely dramatized in recent years in such phenomena as Jonestown and a huge assortment of groups cashing in on this need. True religion, most would agree, should leave room for human freedom and risk. But no religion and none of its representatives are automatically free of the temptation to try to be more to people than they should be. And in the incipient believer the correlative tendency is often found: we can be so hungry for certitude and support that we put our trust in any number of only relatively valuable enterprises and people. We put our trust in the free enterprise system, in a group of friends made in high school or college, in a neatly packaged moral system, in a slick promise of peace of mind. We put our trust in music, business, science, a career, achievements, and, most often and above all, in that one person with whom we hope and believe we can grow and live in lasting love, who will always be there.

In most lives a combination of several of these serves as support for us. All have some value, especially the last, another person or persons. And all are open to loss and destruction through failure, change, accident, disease, and death. Mental breakdowns, poor health, depression, changed attitudes, and new interests all show us that persons and achievements and elements outside ourselves can fade or be dissolved. Our need for them tells us also that we are not our own footing.

It is no simple matter of saying that all human and earthly consolations are so much refuse and, because of their shortlivedness, unworthy of our devotion. We should, therefore, simply put all our trust and confidence in Jesus and find ourselves overwhelmed with joy, peace, and tranquility. Possibly—just possibly—some few mystics have found the solution to life's problems in such absolutes, but generally we do not have the option of resigning from the universe and instantly finding ourselves in constant and beatific union with God. Transcendental Meditation and similar groups have promised that adhesion to their program will end all pain and evil and, in effect, take one out of this existence insofar as it is imperfect, full of risk, and open to pain. But if there is one great and universal lesson to be drawn from the incarnation of the Son of God, it is that his way is not a *way out* of the conditions of human existence but a *way through* them which leaves them basically intact. Unlike the devotees of flashier faiths, the follower of Christ asks to be saved from the contamination of evil, not to be delivered from the world or matter or the human condition. Karl Rahner's statement of the core of Christian belief puts it beautifully and realistically:

> Jesus Christ, faith and love, entrusting oneself to the darkness of existence and into the incomprehensibility of God in trust and in the company of Jesus Christ, the crucified and risen one, these are the central realities for a Christian.   —*Foundations of Christian Faith,* 324.

Faith in Jesus means belief that he truly lived our life, went through genuine and awful suffering, died horribly, and rose again. Joined to him, the difficult circumstances of human life are transformed by the fact that as we go through them *he is with us* (or, we are in him—different ways of stating the basic point). Just as Jesus did not cure every sick person in the Palestine of his time—he was not out to render physicians and human care obsolete—neither does he in exchange for faith remove us from the ordinary challenges, uncertainties, and worries of human life. He transforms them, puts them in *the* meaningful context and points to the goal beyond them. Faith consists in our trust that he is with us and can transform life; it tells us that if we test our belief by living it, we can come to the adult decision that this is indeed how life should be lived. The living, the testing, will tell us that, in a very profound way, it fulfills, not that it necessarily thrills.

To expect some imperturbable euphoria to follow from belief in Jesus is to expect more for ourselves or something different for ourselves than what, for example, his mother received. In the New Testament and in early Christianity she is depicted as the model disciple. Much contemporary scriptural scholarship confirms also the conviction that she was, as recent Catholic piety had it, the "mother of sorrows," that she did not sit quietly through all the vicissitudes of her Son's life secretly comforted by the sure knowledge that he would come out of every difficulty unscathed. She worried about his "behavior" and she sorrowed over his suffering and death.

Jesus' own promises, as presented to us in the words of the Gospels, contain references to the cross and the necessity of routine day-by-day faithfulness and obedience, e.g., "If anyone loves me, he will keep my words" (John 14:15). Indeed, he does say: "If anyone loves me, my Father will come to him and we will make our dwelling with him" (John 14:23). But not: "If anyone loves me, he will experience untold and constant bliss." Certainly some joy, even some great joy, may be generated as a by-product of our faith. We should be thankful for such occasions but regard them as grace, not something to be presumed any more than we open the morning paper expecting to read all sorts of evidence for humankind's essential lovableness. With growth in faith we should expect some abiding trust to sustain our lives like a deep and relentless bass tone undergirding the often erratic melody of our life.

Woody Allen, that explorer on the edges of serious thought about life and death, is quoted somewhere as saying: "There's no religious feeling that can make any thinking person happy." Granted the dogmatism apparent in such a sweeping statement, it is, in a sense, what I've been trying to say. But Allen's phrasing implies that he is, like so many of us, under the misapprehension that happiness in an empirical and this-worldly sense should be the end-product of religious belief.

Too many pop religious books entitled *Jesus, the Way to Joyous Living,* etc., have taken their toll. "No religious feeling can make a thinking person happy," but belief in Jesus (which is not simply feeling, though composed partly of that) does give us a great hope, does help us get out of bed, put on our clothes, eat, and realize that efforts to alleviate suffering are worth making. It does tell us that even if the universe is expanding infinitely—a cosmological theory which brought all activity to a standstill in the youthful and precocious Allen, according to one of his films—there is still a point to our human life, independent of any theory of cosmology.

Faith tells us that human life can be lived with dignity and meaning. Or we can say in response to remarks like Allen's: happiness, no; salvation, yes. All we've been talking about is really what we mean by salvation: a way to live this life with purpose, dignity, and honesty, assured that the struggle and effort are all part of ultimate victory.

C. S. Lewis addressed the same problem with his usual perceptiveness and quiet wit in an essay printed in *God in the Dock*. Asked the same old question in a slightly different form—"Which of the religions of the world gives to its followers the greatest happiness?"— Lewis responded:

> While it lasts the religion of worshipping oneself is the best. I have an elderly acquaintance of about eighty, who has lived a life of unbroken selfishness and self-admiration from the earliest years and is, more or less, I regret to say, one of the happiest men I know. From the moral point of view it is very difficult! I am not approaching the question from that angle. As you perhaps know, I haven't always been a Christian. I didn't go to that religion to make me happy. I always knew a bottle of port would do that. If you want a religion to make you feel more comfortable, I certainly don't recommend Christianity. I am certain there must be a patent American article on the market which will suit you far better.
>
> —Walter Hooper, ed. (Grand Rapids: Eerdmans, 1970) 58–59.

Despite its topicality, that was said some forty years ago. The only amendment we might make would be to say that while America remains fertile ground for religions that promise to make one happy, many of them are imported from the Orient.

Founding and Preserving Faith

If, then, faith in Jesus Christ does not guarantee us constant elation, an enduring "high," thereby "proving" its worth and encouraging us in its practice, what, then, will help to fortify and preserve this faith? And, further, how do we move from a limited and elementary faith to a more complete kind? To trust that our world is in the hands of a God who loves us with a love that cannot fail, who is always there: to commit ourselves to such a faith cannot be simply a matter of wishful thinking. Too many experiences militate against an easy acceptance of "God loves me." If we are to believe that God truly does love us and save us, how is that faith to be justified?

Jesus Christ must become more for us than some figure like Plato or Henry Ford; his word must be more to us than any word of Khalil Gibran or John Denver. But to know him as the Savior who is there in the dead of night or the heat of day, no matter where we have been, to know, believe, trust this—how does this come about or become convincingly real?

Ordinarily, it will be of little help to be told that God must give this grace, true as that is. That is somewhat like being told to go out and inherit a million dollars. The truth that faith is a gift cannot, of course, be underestimated. And the reader I am presupposing undoubtedly feels he or she has received that gift in some measure—if we use somewhat materialistic terms. Some receptivity on our part, being open to what is beyond and other than ourselves, must be there for faith to commence and to grow. As is indicated elsewhere in these pages, that is undoubtedly the most elemental prerequisite on our part, the only preparation we can make, itself a gift, for the grace of faith. But, more actively, what can we *do* once faith is initiated?

What activity on our part can help give this faith a suitable nurture, the right formula for growth? A little reflection will, I think, persuade most of us that it must, first of all, be practiced. . . . We must allow its demands to influence the way we live. The teaching of the Sermon on the Mount, for instance, to take a fairly obvious example, by helping to soften the harshness of ordinary human society, demonstrates the wisdom of the teaching and example of Jesus. Adhesion to the priorities of the Gospel can save us from participation in some of the mad pursuits of our culture, world, milieu, and, in the process, show us how truly Jesus Christ is the way through the jungle, the truth about living and the life amid death and decay.

Beyond living the truth, there is prayer and reflection, two matters which easily merge in practice. C. S. Lewis calls it "training the habit of faith" and says that the content of one's belief must be kept before the mind regularly. We do this by reflective reading, prayer, participation in the church's liturgy. Without such persistent attention our belief or any belief, for that matter, will not endure. We speak so often of people losing their faith but no one really loses it in the sense that almost inadvertently we discover it is no longer alive. We kill it, perhaps, or starve it or neglect it and so it may fade away. But since we are responsible for some voluntary and human acts to sustain it, it is much more correct to say that we throw it away rather than lose it.

Prayer and reflection. After the basic attitude of receptivity, of awareness of need and insufficiency, along with the effort to test faith by living it, there must be these two "activities," prayer and thinking. Praying is, for our relation to God, what conversation, a few words, a letter, or a phone call is in any human relationship. Without something of that nature, friends fade out of our lives, are forgotten. For most of us a daily few moments, speaking directly to God, to Christ, about our life and its circumstances and daily content of joys and difficulties makes the relationship real, acknowledges the presence and reality of God. Liturgy (worship) does the same thing in a more formalized and communal way. Even if our conversation, our praying, starts out as almost a sort of talking to ourselves about our life, it can easily slip into speaking to God about it and asking his help, guidance, strength. We will grow in our faith to the point where it gets us out of bed with some zest and through the day only if we consciously practice it by at least adverting through prayer to the one in whom we believe. Faith understandably roots itself in thinking beings only if they consciously reflect on it, give it some time and place comparable to what they spend on gardening, money-making, perfecting their golf game.

As Lewis wrote, faith is not really lost. It slips away or we throw it away by indifference, lack of attention and care. It is not simply a matter of time, obviously, but we must ask ourselves how we expect it to live when the amount of time and attention we give it is so minimal in comparison with the attention we give to television, the daily paper, balancing our checkbook, the care of our skin or hair, our professional and personal ambitions, etc. Faith is a gift that we must believe God is ready to give to anyone. But on the human side it is like the gifts we speak of in human nature—a gift for music, for instance. Without some education and practice, the gift can remain for all practical purposes unborn. Lord, through your gift, I believe; now, help my unbelief (cf. Mark 9:24).

Plainly, this essay has amounted to a restatement of the conviction, developed elsewhere in these pages, that the only proof of faith is in the doing and the participation, that some serenity and confidence come only through prayer and doing the word we have received and thought about. We have been saying also that there is no proxy way to faith or towards building it up. Apart from *our* receptivity and *our* effort, no one else or anything else is going to provide it for us. While faith is not our creation, it will not survive without our nurture.

—The Risk in Believing

Faith: Reflection Questions

1. What effect does faith have on your life?

2. Who or what is primarily responsible for your faith life?

3. Does college kill faith?

4. What do you make of Fr. Don Talafous's conviction that "the only proof of faith is in the doing and the participation"?

5
Feminism

Galatians 3:26-28

^{26}[F]or in Christ Jesus you are all children of God through faith. ^{27}As many of you as were baptized into Christ have clothed yourselves with Christ. ^{28}There is no longer Jew or Greek, there is no longer slave or free, there is no longer male and female; for all of you are one in Christ Jesus.

Freedom from the Curse of Ignorance

60. Man is now offered the possibility to free most of the human race from the curse of ignorance: it is, therefore, one of the duties most appropriate to our times, above all for Christians, to work untiringly for fundamental decisions to be taken in economic and political affairs, on the national as well as the international level, which will ensure the recognition and implementation everywhere of the right of every man to human and civil culture in harmony with the dignity of the human person, without distinction of race, sex, nation, religion, or social circumstances. Hence it is necessary to ensure that there is a sufficiency of cultural benefits available to everybody, especially the benefit of what is called "basic" culture, lest any be prevented by illiteracy and lack of initiative from contributing in an authentically human way to the common good.

We must do everything possible to make all persons aware of their right to culture and their duty to develop themselves culturally and to help their fellows. Sometimes conditions of life and work are such as to stifle man's cultural efforts and destroy this urge for culture. This holds true especially for those living in the country and for manual workers who ought to be provided with working conditions not unfavorable, but rather conducive to, their cultural development. At present women are involved in nearly all spheres of life: they ought to be permitted to play their part fully according to their own particular nature. It is up to everyone to see to it that woman's specific and necessary participation in cultural life be acknowledged and fostered.

Gaudium et spes 60

What Keeps Women "in Their Place"?   *Anthony Layng*

During the decade of the 1970s, women in numerous nations called for the elimination of sexual discrimination. In the U.S., this latest feminist resurgence ambitiously attempted to end all inequalities between the sexes—including those involving employment, political participation, property rights, recreation, language, and education—and some reforms were achieved. An increasing number of women began to act like they were socially equal to men; there has been much talk about teaching girls to be more assertive; and there is now considerable confusion about what constitutes appropriate sex roles. Yet, judging by the fact that the Equal Rights Amendment did not pass and that it presently shows little promise of being resuscitated in the near future, many seem to have concluded that most American women are, by and large, content to remain where they are in relation to men. Further, since women in other industrialized nations have remained essentially "in their place," it appears that there are other formidable obstacles to overcome if we are to bring about such fundamental social change.

Why do sexual inequalities persist in the face of concerted feminist challenges? Is there any realistic basis for us to hope that sexual discrimination ever will be eliminated? What must be done to bring about full emancipation of women? What is it that keeps women "in their place"?

To understand fully how women have been kept "in their place," we first must learn how they came to be there. This requires consideration of the course of human evolution. Prior to 4,000,000 years ago, there was probably little social differentiation based on gender, because the two sexes were not economically interdependent; one could survive quite well without assistance from the other. It is likely that economic interdependence developed only after the evolving human brain reached a size that necessitated earlier birth, before the cranium of an infant was too large to pass through the birth canal. Giving birth earlier meant that the babies were less mature and would be more dependent on their mothers for a longer period of time. Prolonged helplessness of infants eventually created a need for mothers to depend on others for food and protection.

At the same time, more evolved brains enabled us to invent and use tools that resulted in our becoming effective hunters, in addition to being scavengers. Females with helpless infants still could gather and scavenge a variety of foods, but they were likely to be relatively handicapped hunters and so came to depend on males to provide them with a more reliable source of meat.

Increasing brain size and improved hunting skills also meant that some of our ancestors could begin to occupy northern regions where successful hunting was necessary for survival, since those foods that could be gathered were insufficient during some seasons. In such an environment, females with infants would not live long without food provided by others. Under these circumstances, a sexual division of labor made very good sense.

Although biological factors created the especially long dependency of human infants, the solution to this problem may have been entirely cultural. There is little evidence to suggest that any instinct developed at this time which led females to restrict their economic activities to gathering roots and fruits and men to go off in search of game, but doing so was sound strategy. Such specialization—encouraging females to learn and concentrate on gathering, and teaching only males to be hunters—was an efficient and realistic adaptation requiring only a change in our ancestors' learned behavior and attitudes.

So, a sexual division of labor emerged, but what about sexual inequality? The subordination of females was not brought about by this economic change alone, for, although economic specialization by sex made women dependent on men, it also made men dependent on women. Where human populations subsist entirely by what can be hunted or gathered, most of the food consumed is provided by the gatherers—women. Meat acquired by hunters may be given a higher social value than nuts and berries and the like; but, if the technology employed in hunting is very primitive, meat is difficult to acquire and frequently absent from the menu. Thus, when men began to concentrate on hunting, an interdependence between the sexes emerged, each relying on the other to provide food that made survival possible.

Beliefs and Customs

The development of a sexual division of labor may have preceded and even facilitated social inequality, but it did not create male dominance. Although male dominance would be very difficult to achieve in the absence of a sexual division of labor, it takes firm beliefs and customs as well to retain a higher status for men. The following examples illustrate how societies in various parts of the world have directed the socialization of their children to assure that women will be kept "in their place."

- Mythology which justifies maintaining female subordination. Mythology and folklore are used in tribal societies to explain and justify the social *status quo*. The story of Adam and Eve illustrates how sexist myths can be, but some are even less subtle than Genesis in rationalizing male preeminence. Frequently found tales of Amazons or an era when our ancestors lived in matriarchal communities may be functionally equivalent to the Adam and Eve account; although they serve as inspiring models for some women, they may be far more instrumental in reminding men why they must be ever-vigilant in protecting their favored status. So, such tales become an important part of the conservative social learning of children.

- Seclusion based on the concept of pollution. In many horticultural societies, women must retire to a special hut during menstruation, since it is believed that their condition magically would jeopardize the well-being of the community. Their economic inactivity during these and other periods of seclusion serves to indicate symbolically that their economic contributions are of secondary importance. This subconsciously may suggest to children in the community that the labor of men is too important to be so restricted by taboos.

- Segregation of male domains. Many tribal societies have a men's house in the center of each village in which nearly all important political and ritual plans are made. Women are not allowed to enter this house, under the threat of severe punitive sanctions such as gang rape. Since this form of segregation effectively precludes the participation of women in the political arena, they are not likely to develop any political aspirations while growing up.

- Exclusion from sacred public rituals. Tribal societies custom-
  arily devote much energy to elaborate religious events, believing that the health of the community depends on these.
  With very few exceptions, men direct these rituals and play all
  the key roles; commonly, women merely are observers or participate only in a support capacity. A primary function of these
  public rituals is to reinforce social values. Since they even attract the full attention of young children, tribal members learn
  early that men are far more important than women, for they
  are the ones charged with magically protecting the people.

- Exclusion from military combat. As in the case of religious ritual in tribal societies, war is considered necessary to insure
  the survival of the community and almost always is conducted
  exclusively by men. Success as a warrior brings conspicuous
  prestige and admiration from women and children alike. Here
  again, the socialization process, instilling norms and attitudes
  of correct conduct, leads easily and inevitably to the conclusion that everyone's welfare depends on the performance of
  the men, and that the women should be suitably grateful.

- Exclusion from high-status economic roles. Women in most
  tribal societies are important producers and consumers, but
  their economic role is restricted largely to domestic concerns,
  producing food and goods for kinsmen. When it comes to
  regulating the exchange of goods between kin groups or with
  outsiders, men usually dominate such activities. This division
  of economic roles is fully consistent with the assumption that
  men are more important socially and more skillful politically.
  Given such an assumption, the economic differences between
  the behavior of men and women are likely to seem both
  proper and inevitable.

- Veneration of female virginity. If the religious, political, and economic activities of women are of secondary importance, then
  what, besides producing children, is their real value? One might
  be tempted to speculate that, because children in primitive societies are taught to venerate female virginity, this indicates that
  the status of women is not so lowly as might otherwise be assumed. However, it seems far more likely that this concern
  with virginity is an extension of the double standard and a re-

flection of the belief that the major value of women is their sexuality and fertility, their unexalted role as wife and mother.

- Preference for male children. When parents usually prefer that their next child will be a boy, this attitude may be considered as both a consequence of and contributor to the higher status of men. Before young children are mature enough to appreciate that one sex socially outranks the other, they can understand that their parents hope to have a boy next time. Impending childbirth in a home is given much attention and takes on real importance; this often may be the earliest opportunity for children to learn that males are more valued than females.

- Sexist humor and ridicule are used as important socialization methods in all societies and lend themselves quite effectively to maintaining a sexual hierarchy. Girls who behave like boys, and boys who behave like girls, almost inevitably inspire ridicule. Sexist jokes, particularly when they are considered to be good-natured, are especially effective in this regard. Women who take offense or fail to find such jokes amusing are accused of having no sense of humor, thus largely neutralizing their defense against this social control mechanism.

- Sexual stereotyping. Stereotypes of any sort are likely to be of little use in teaching social attitudes to children unless they are accepted by the children as true images of nature. To believe that women and men behave differently because it is the way they were created helps to prevent misgivings from arising about the social inequality of men and women. To the extent that such status differences are believed to be imposed by human nature, the cultural supports of such inequality are not likely to be recognized and, therefore, will not be questioned.

Do Women Accept Subjugation?

A society which effectively keeps women "in their place" need not employ all of the above techniques to do so; just a few will suffice, so long as there is general agreement throughout the population that the *status quo* of sexual inequality is both appropriate and natural. It is just as necessary that women accept this view as it is for men. Although some reformist writers argue that the subjugation of women was instigated by a male chauvinist plot forced upon unwilling victims, it seems amply evident that these social control mechanisms could not work effectively without the willing cooperation of women. They, too, must believe that they were designed by their creator to be subordinate; religious, political, and economic leadership are less suitable for them; and they have their own domains and should not be so immodest as to attempt to interfere where they do not belong. They, too, must consider military exploits as unsuitable for themselves.

Is this asking too much? Do not women value their virginity and that of their daughters as much as men do? Do they not condemn promiscuous women and at the same time tolerate promiscuous men? Is it not common for women to hope to have male children, in preference to daughters? Most women accept sexual stereotypes as an accurate reflection of nature to some degree, and they continue to encourage sexist humor by their laughter.

It seems clear that the "lowly" status of women was not brought about by a conspiracy, nor is it perpetuated only by men. There is no reason to view the above social controls as sinister or perverse where women willingly, even enthusiastically, teach their sons to be "real" men and their daughters to admire such men without wanting to be like them. In other words, in tribal societies, it is not male suppression which makes women subordinate.

It is only when we assume a missionary mentality, viewing such societies in light of our own society's values, that we think these women long for emancipation. Such an ethnocentric view fails to recognize that inequality, where it is accepted by all concerned as inevitable and proper, can be advantageous to lower-status individuals as well as to those who outrank them. Dominance hierarchies, like pecking orders, establish and maintain social order, a condition which tribal societies understandably prefer to disorder and uncertainty. Women in traditional societies do not contribute to their own subordination because they do not know any better or because they are forced to comply with the wishes of the men; they do so because they are socialized appropriately in an orderly society which is culturally well-adapted to its environment.

In tribal societies, sexual inequality is relatively high and protest against such inequality is relatively low. However, an increasing number of women in other societies are protesting sexual discrimination and their subordinate position. Most of this dissent comes from stratified and heterogeneous populations, where gossip, ridicule, and taboos are relatively ineffectual social control techniques. Social order in these more complex societies tends to be enforced by laws and specialized agencies, rather than depending upon voluntary compliance. Even in such complex societies, women need not necessarily feel unjustly deprived, for here, too, as in tribal societies, most may be wholly supportive of the social *status quo,* in spite of their own lowly status. Nevertheless, most of the discontent about sexual inequality comes from these populations.

In spite of such feminist discontent, sexual hierarchies still survive in even highly modernized societies like our own. American women have gained important rights in recent years, but many Americans continue to find Biblical justification for sexual discrimination. Many still think that our nation's economy appropriately remains under the domination of men, and, although the number of exclusively male domains (athletic teams, lodges, clubs, etc.) have been reduced greatly in recent years, a large number still find general endorsement and remain very much intact. Sexual stereotypes continue to enjoy robust health, the double standard is far from moribund, and sexist humor and ridicule seem to have recovered from their recent bout with militant feminism in the 1970's.

Today, in spite of a recent Gallup poll indicating that more than half the women in the U.S. consider themselves to be feminists, the most ambitious goals of the feminist movement have not been realized. However, it has grown increasingly difficult to convince American women that it is proper for them to be socially inferior to men, or that they should behave submissively. It seems that those customs and beliefs which deny opportunity to women in America are going to continue to be questioned by some who are very persuasive. Since a sexual division of labor has become largely anachronistic for our technologically advanced society, we may anticipate that efforts to preserve exclusive privileges for either sex will encounter increasing resistance.

Although tribal societies need to depend on a system of ascriptive statuses to maintain an orderly social structure, we do not. Tribal populations are not at risk in assigning economic roles strictly by sex, because not basing such assignments on individual aptitude and inclination is of little importance where the economy requires only a narrow range of tasks. In modern industrial society, however, where much highly skilled specialization is essential, selecting candidates for such positions from a limited talent pool, from only half of the adult population, places such a society at an unnecessary disadvantage, one which shows up very clearly if that society must compete with other nations which do not handicap themselves in this fashion. Also, traditional American values which exalt equality, opportunity, and achievement (matters of relatively little concern in tribal societies) are bound to give us increasing difficulty if we continue to deny equality to women and so restrict their ability to achieve the success that they desire and that our economy requires.

Since men have been politically dominant in all human societies, it is not surprising that many scholars have concluded that it is our nature, not our nurture, that has necessitated this inequality. Still, if sexual inequality is inevitable, given our nature, why must tribal populations resort to so many cultural methods to keep women subordinate and submissive?

Knowing how women have been kept "in their place" so long is essential if attempts to combat sexual inequality are to have some success. Just as the most effective medical cure is based on accurate causal diagnosis of an illness, so must social reform efforts take into account the nature of that which we would alter. If we recognize the various ways that our society uses cultural means to perpetuate differential socialization for boys and girls, we are prepared better to redesign that process to foster equality between the sexes. Similarly, if we are aware of the customary practices which encourage women to be submissive, we are more able to challenge and change such customs effectively. To fully understand how and to what extent women are kept "in their place" in the U.S., it is important that we understand how various societies effectively accomplish stable inequality.

Before all of this can enable us to eradicate male dominance, it may be that we first must learn why our society continues to deny equality of opportunity to women, for it is unlikely that we do so only as a result of cultural inertia. It may be that inequality is socially functional in ways that we do not understand fully.

Nevertheless, if women are to achieve total equality, if such a fundamental change can be brought about, it will require far more than passing the Equal Rights Amendment or changing discriminatory laws piecemeal. Since longstanding customs which encourage inequality thoroughly are ingrained in our culture, sexual equality will not be achieved until we face up to the fact that inequality is a product of our own behavior and attitudes. Only then might we discard this vestige of our tribal heritage.

−USA TODAY MAGAZINE, May 1989

Sojourner Truth and Women's Equality

During the Women's Rights Convention of 1851, an unscheduled speaker approached the podium and asked the president if she could "say a few words." The bold woman, known as Sojourner Truth, was an emancipated slave who captivated the audience with her now famous speech about women's equality. Her homespun wisdom and passionate delivery captured the imagination of all who heard the brief but convincing presentation.

Sojourner Truth's "Ar'n't I a Woman" Speech

I want to say a few words about this matter. I am a woman's rights. I have as much muscle as any man, and can do as much work as any man. I have plowed and reaped and husked and chopped and mowed, and can any man do more than that? I have heard much about the sexes being equal. I can carry as much as any man, and can eat as much too, if I can get it. I am as strong as any man that is now. As for intellect, all I can say is, if women have a pint, and man a quart—why can't she have her little pint full? You need not be afraid to give us our rights for fear we will take too much,—for we can't take more than our pint'll hold. The poor men seem to be all in confusion, and don't know what to do. Why children, if you have woman's rights, give it to her and you will feel better. You will have your own rights, and they won't be so much trouble. I can't read, but I can hear. I have heard the bible and have learned that Eve caused man to sin. Well, if woman upset the world, do give her a chance to set it right side up again. The Lady has spoken about Jesus, how he never spurned woman from him, and she was right. When Lazarus died, Mary and Martha came to him with faith and love and besought him to raise their brother. And Jesus wept and Lazarus came forth. And how came Jesus into the world? Through God who created him and a woman who bore him. Man, where is your part? But the women are coming up blessed be God and a few of the men are coming up with them. But man is in a tight place, the poor slave is on him, woman is coming on him, he is surely between a hawk and a buzzard.

—*Anti-Slavery Bugle,* June 21, 1851

What's Right with the Catholic Church? *Joan Chittister, O.S.B.*

There are two stories that form the framework of these remarks. The first is from personal experience:

It was the spring of 1984. I was sitting on a stage at Stanford University. The hall seemed like a black cave to me. All I could see were high-wattage Klieg lights and, far in the back, the outline of exit signs over the auditorium doors. I had just delivered a kind of summary closing address to the public session of a three-day symposium on "Communities of Women." The symposium had been organized by the research arm of *Signs,* a journal then located at Stanford University and entirely devoted to interdisciplinary scholarship on questions of women in culture and society. Women from all over the bay area were in attendance and the vibrations of feminism were running a very heady high.

It was as if the outside world with all of its institutionalized sexism no longer existed; that this was the real world where competent women recognized and respected competent women; that the millennium had finally come.

And there sat I in the midst of it, sisterhood brimming over until suddenly a voice out of the darkness on the other side of the lights called me very quickly and very firmly back to the real world.

"Sister Joan," the voice said, "I would like to ask you a personal question. How and why does a woman like you stay in the Catholic Church?"

The message was very, very clear. I had heard many times before all the tones of passion and anger and pain that underlay the question. And then the woman's voice went on:

"I was a Catholic once," she said, "and the misogyny was so bad I knew it was either get out or have a breakdown. I would like to know how and why," she repeated, "someone like you stays in a church like that?"

The second story from Sufi religious literature is, I believe, an answer to the first. This story tells that a seeker arrived at the monastery in search of a spiritual guide.

"People say that you have found wisdom," the seeker said to the Holy One, "and I have come to ask if that is true?"

"You could say so," the Holy One said in a matter-of-fact kind of way.

"But what makes one wise?" the disciple asked.

"Wisdom," the Holy One said, "is simply the ability to recognize."

"I know that," the disciple said, "but the question is to recognize what?"

"Spiritual wisdom," the Holy One said, "is the ability to recognize the butterfly in a caterpillar, the eagle in an egg, the saint in the sinner."

I know intuitively—at least where women and the Church are concerned—that the Holy One is right. I find myself, as a Christian feminist, in the peculiar position of someone who sees the unseen. Like a boater out of sight of land, I have been taken—and by the very same current—away from one shore to the edges of a distant other, in storm and in darkness, but with confidence and a good compass.

The fact is that I am a feminist precisely because I am a Catholic—not as a reaction to what is wrong about the Church, but actually as a response to what is right about the Church. My Christian feminist commitment to the equality, the dignity and the humanity of all persons and the need to change structures to make that so does not come as a result of my rejection of what I see as bad in the Church. It comes as an inevitable recognition of what I see as the great, the magnetizing, the empowering, the energizing good that is inherent for women in the Church and promised for women in the Church, even when I cannot see it yet being brought to fullness, even in the Church.

The fact is that what is right about the Church for women is the vision of Jesus. And everything it manifests. And everything it mandates.

Jesus, we must always remember, was a good Jew. Jesus went up to the temple, and taught the Torah, and kept the high holydays, and went on pilgrimage to Jerusalem, and studied the law. Jesus knew what was expected of him and Jesus did it. Except, of course, when an even greater revelation of the will of God demanded change. It is in those very departures by Jesus from Jewish revelation to new insights about the mind of God that we see most clearly the Christian dispensation.

So, to understand the impact of what Jesus does we must understand what Jesus is expected to do. We must remember well that Jesus' Jewish culture and Jewish religion were very clear about women. The culture and religious code in which Jesus was formed—and which we can expect him to honor unless, of course, it is those very concepts that must be challenged with a fuller notion of the will of God—left little doubt about the role and place of women.

"Better that the Torah be burned than placed in the mouth of a woman," the rabbis preached. Woman's place is in the home or in the outer court of the temple, the Law said. Women's bodies were polluted and polluting, the Torah taught. Women were not to speak to men in public—not to their husbands, not to their fathers, not to their sons.

Women were for childbearing, not for thinking, the scholars said. Women were domestic servants, not developed adults. Women were for inheritance and for convenience—not for religion, not for law. "When a boy child comes, peace comes," the rabbis taught; "when a girl child comes, nothing comes."

Oh, yes, Jesus knew church law about women, all right. And then despite it all, in great, grandiose, graphic gestures, Jesus came and swept it all away. Jesus spoke to women in public, Jesus let women follow him out of the house, Jesus discussed theology with women, and sought out their companionship, and valued their friendship, and Jesus told women—and only women—that he was the Messiah. And Jesus sent women to give testimony to his Resurrection; Jesus sent women as apostles to the apostles.

It was women who anointed him, and women who proclaimed him, and women who prepared him for burial, and women who pronounced his return.

It was women, in fact, whom Jesus put at the very center of the only two mysteries of the faith that are basic and essentially differentiating to the faith—the Incarnation and the Resurrection. And not only were women there at the Incarnation and the Resurrection, but only women were there.

Jesus taught women: "Mary has chosen the better part and it shall not be denied her," he said of the woman learning at his feet.

"Go and tell the others what you have heard," he missioned the Samaritan woman as first evangelist to the non-Jew.

"Arise and walk," he said to the corpse of a dead and worthless woman.

"Do whatever she tells you," he instructed the men servants.

"And there were women in the crowd," Scripture reads. "And women followed him, ministering to him," Scripture reads. "Woman, your faith has made you whole," Scripture reads. "And power went out of him to her," the Scripture reads.

Oh, yes, if you are a woman, the images are strong, and bold, and clear, and empowering, and life-giving and preserved by the Church. Etched on our minds forever, thanks to the Scriptures of the Church, are the figures of the strong, present, prophetic women of the Gospels.

Never forget:

• A woman with the same power to say NO to God as the power given to Abraham and Moses;

- A woman turning God into the body and blood of Christ;
- A woman, Anna, proclaiming the birth of the Messiah;
- The woman evangelist sent from the well to convert an entire city in Samaria;
- Women demanding miracles and getting them;
- Women anointing him and preparing him for burial;
- Women waiting faithfully at the empty tomb;
- Women clinging to the Risen Christ;
- Women sent "to tell Peter and the others."

Indeed, when the Church and its documents and its structures and its symbols and its language and its laws and its liturgies forgets or foregoes or forswears the place of women in the Christian dispensation, there in its Scriptures the vision of Jesus with women stays vibrant and vital and unable to be forgotten. And without it, so much the poorer the Church.

What is right about the Church, then, is that whatever else it does or does not do, the Church sustains the memory of Jesus with women and always recalls it and has often heeded it, at times in genuinely significant ways.

There are at least six contributions of the Church to Christian feminism that flow from the vision of Jesus. In the first place, the Church has from the earliest times preserved the notion of an alternative lifestyle for women. The admission of women to recognized religious orders in the Church and the confirmation of the single state as a recognized call from God to women as well as to men has been and continues to be a strong affirmation of the integrity and spirituality of women.

The posture implies that women can receive a call from God that is uniquely theirs and have the soul and the grace and the mind to respond to it.

Women, in other words, do not have to be defined by a man, owned by a man, coupled to a man, identified by a man, or controlled by a man to be a fully adult and right-functioning human being. Women, it seems, are fully rational and equally spiritual beings in their own right. The implications are awesome. If women, like men, can be called alone and separately to God's service, then God's grace is simply not sexist. God's grace simply cannot be trusted to limit itself. But if grace is not gender specific, then God may ask the same things of women that God asks of men, or else it is not the

Church which is being held hostage to sexism. It is God who is being held hostage to sexism. God may want absolutely outrageous things of women. God may have absolutely outrageous plans for women. Grace once released is a dangerous thing.

There is a second contribution of the Church to Christian feminism: Consider, too, that female role models have always been defined and upheld in the Church as much models for men, surely, as John and Sebastian and Francis of Assisi, for instance, are for women. All the saints have been given to all the Church for emulation. Sainthood–the fullness of service and the fullness of self–is accepted and applauded and expected of women as well as of men in the church. Teresa of Avila, doctor of the Church, and Catherine of Sienna, counselor of the pope, and Therese of Lisieux, seeker of priesthood, and Joan of Arc, leader of men, and Gertrude and Mechtilde and Hildegarde, abbesses of great dual monasteries, and Hilda, convener of Church synods, and Jane Frances de Chantal, wife and mother with a second career, are indeed holy hopes and worthwhile ideals to be aspired to by women as well as by men.

If the Litany of Saints in the Catholic Church says anything at all, it says that women's lives have made a difference, both to the Church and to the world–a position, incidentally, rarely conceded by other institutions in their history books.

There is a third contribution of the Church to Christian feminism. There is no doubt that the Roman Catholic concept of sacramentality– the notion that divine grace is given without prejudice to sex–marks women as well as men as channels of God's grace. Sacramentality is, therefore, an important contribution to the recognition of the full humanity of women. Why some graces work on women–Baptism, Confirmation, Eucharist, Penance, Sacrament of the Sick and Marriage, for instance–and some do not, why women are impediments to some graces but not to others, is yet to be explained, of course. But there is at least a clearly developed theology of Baptism, Grace, Incarnation and Redemption that legitimate the question.

Women, it is now argued, can get grace. They simply cannot give it. God's grace goes powerless when it gets to women–blocked apparently by some deficiency of nature–but ironically and gracefully enough, it is the best doctrines of the Church itself which continue to challenge that thought.

There is a fourth contribution that the Church makes to Christian feminism. Feminine spirituality, from the time of the nonviolent Jesus who instructed Peter to put away his sword and the apostles to feed the famished five thousand, continues to mark the Church to our own time.

It is interesting to note that the two more prophetic, more troublesome documents of our own day, the Bishop's Peace Pastoral and the Bishop's Pastoral on the American Economy, are also the most feminine. In a world that calls for power and superiority and control and order and domination and a logical approach to an enemy world, these pastorals call for cooperation and flexibility and support and a feeling of concern for the poor and oppressed. And it is precisely on those grounds that they are being criticized as "foolish" and "incompetent" and "weak" and even "ridiculous." Women have known that kind of criticism for eons.

At the same time, no documents of the American Catholic Church sound more like the Gospel unglossed, unwarped, and undistorted. The Church, it seems, affirms the feminine and needs it for the fullness of the Gospel, and suffers when it realizes that. Strange. Interesting. Disturbing. Hopeful.

There is a fifth contribution of the Church to Christian feminism. Beyond all these other things, there is in the Church a sense of sin, a call to conversion, a consistent reach for reconciliation in the work of righteousness.

Paul confronted Peter for rejecting the vision that lifted Jewish dietary laws from Christianity, and Peter repented. Peter confronted the early Church for rejecting Gentiles in the Jewish Christian community, and the early Church repented. (Acts 11) Vatican II confronted the contemporary Church with its anti-Semitism and its failure to respond to the Protestant reformers, and the Church is attempting to repent.

If the Church is true to its own best doctrines, and its own best insights, and its own best graces, and its own best definition of Church, and to the vision of Jesus that it preserves, sustains and preaches, it is inevitable that one day it will also confess and repent the sin of sexism.

Finally, there is an overarching contribution of the Church to Christian feminism that defies the diminishment of half of the human race. The image of Mary, the Mother of God, and Mary, the Mother of the Church, is a strong affirmation of the independence, the fullness of grace, and the necessary participation of women in the divine work of salvation.

Some years ago, one of the pillars of Marian piety was a book entitled, *A Woman Wrapped in Silence*. Somehow, in that approach, Mary came across as remote and ethereal, unreal and unreachable. She swept on and off its pages in gossamer and shawl. She was docile and bowed and passive. Strong in suffering, yes, but not like women who had to bend their wits to live and bear and survive. Not like women who gave their entire lives for the salvation of others.

Mary, it seemed, was simply a pawn in the will of God. But a "pawn in the will of God" is a contradiction in terms. There simply cannot be a "pawn in the will of God." The will of God is something that must be chosen and that costs. The will of God is not a trick played on the unsuspecting. The will of God is always an offer of co-creation. Mary was asked, and Mary said Yes.

Mary was a partner in the plan, not a pawn. Mary was free to say no, not enslaved in a pseudo yes. Mary was invited to depart from the system in order to fulfill it. If we understand that, then we begin to understand Mary in a new way. And we also begin to understand the role of women in Church and society in a new way.

It wasn't that Mary was "a woman wrapped in silence." It was simply that her actions spoke more loudly than any number of words could ever do.

We, all of us, women and men, need to understand those actions now. The fact is that Mary is not simply "Mary, the Mother of God." No, on the contrary. The Mother of God is the image of women everywhere. The Mother of God is Mary, independent woman; Mary, the unmarried mother; Mary, the homeless woman; Mary, the political refugee; Mary, the Third World woman; Mary, the mother of the condemned; Mary, the widow who outlives her child; Mary, the woman of our time who shares in the divine plan of salvation; Mary, the Bearer of Christ.

Mary, you see, could withstand and confront every standard of her synagogue and of her society, and take the poverty and the oppression and the pain to which that led because the will of God meant more to her than the laws of any system. That's the kind of woman God chose to do God's work. That's the kind of woman that the Church raises up for women to be. That's the kind of woman who made the *Magnificat* the national anthem of women everywhere. Indeed, God was with her. And because of Mary, God is also with us. How can we possibly do less?

The Church has preserved the vision of Jesus, and an alternative life-style for women, and the witness of women saints, and the concept of sacramentality, and a consciousness of conversion, and the call to feminine spirituality, and the model of Mary–Mother of God and Mother of the Church. How can we possibly do less?

What is most right about the Church to a feminist is that moment in time when Jesus said, "Woman, you are healed of your infirmity," and straightened to full-size the woman too stooped to stand. And he did it while he was teaching the Torah, in the middle of the synagogue, in the presence of the Pharisees, on a Sabbath, and despite the law.

So to the question, "Why does a woman like you stay in the Catholic Church?," I say, "Precisely because I am Catholic." What is spiritual wisdom? Spiritual wisdom is the ability to recognize the butterfly in a caterpillar; the eagle in an egg; the saint in the sinner.

Are these women trying to destroy the Church?

"I have no idea what tomorrow will bring," the disciple said, "and I don't know how to prepare for it."

"You fear tomorrow," the Holy One said, "not realizing that yesterday is just as dangerous."

It is not on novel doctrine that Christian feminists depend. On the contrary. It is on yesterday's dangerous vision that Christian feminism stakes its hope.

And that is very right.

—WomanStrength: Modern Church, Modern Women

Feminism: Reflection Questions

1. In what ways should the Church actively participate in helping women achieve more social equality?

2. After reading Chittister's article, what would you say is "right with the Catholic Church"?

3. How do you react to a recent national poll that suggests that boys are more traditional than girls in their expectations of family life?

4. How do you evaluate Sojourner Truth's role as a pioneer for equal rights?

6
Homelessness

Luke 16:19-31

[19]"There was a rich man who was dressed in purple and fine linen and who feasted sumptuously every day. [20]And at his gate lay a poor man named Lazarus, covered with sores, [21]who longed to satisfy his hunger with what fell from the rich man's table; even the dogs would come and lick his sores. [22]The poor man died and was carried away by the angels to be with Abraham. The rich man also died and was buried. [23]In Hades, where he was being tormented, he looked up and saw Abraham far away with Lazarus by his side. [24]He called out, 'Father Abraham, have mercy on me, and send Lazarus to dip the tip of his finger in water and cool my tongue; for I am in agony in these flames.' [25]But Abraham said, 'Child, remember that during your lifetime you received your good things, and Lazarus in like manner evil things; but now he is comforted here, and you are in agony. [26]Besides all this, between you and us a great chasm has been fixed, so that those who might want to pass from here to you cannot do so, and no one can cross from there to us.' [27]He said, 'Then, father, I beg you to send him to my father's house— [28]for I have five brothers—that he may warn them, so that they will not also come into this place of torment.' [29]Abraham replied, 'They have Moses and the prophets; they should listen to them.' [30]He said, 'No, father Abraham; but if someone goes to them from the dead, they will repent.' [31]He said to him, 'If they do not listen to Moses and the prophets, neither will they be convinced even if someone rises from the dead.'"

A Consequence of Original Sin

2448 "In its various forms—material deprivation, unjust oppression, physical and psychological illness and death—*human misery* is the obvious sign of the inherited condition of frailty and need for salvation in which man finds himself as a consequence of original sin. This misery elicited the compassion of Christ the Savior, who willingly took it upon himself and identified himself with the least of his brethren. Hence, those who are oppressed by poverty are the object of *a preferential love* on the part of the Church which, since her origin and in spite of the failings of many of her members, has not ceased to work for their relief, defense, and liberation through numerous works of charity which remain indispensable always and everywhere."[247]

[247]CDF, Instruction, *Libertatis conscientia*, 68.

—*Catechism of the Catholic Church*

Lazarus in Our City?   *Anne Buckley*

It was just a couple of days after Catholics heard the Sunday Gospel about the beggar Lazarus and the rich man who ignored him that a Federal District Court judge in Manhattan ruled a ban on street begging unconstitutional.

Judge Robert W. Sweet, deciding that the law violates the First Amendment guarantee of free speech, said Sept. 30, "A peaceful beggar poses no threat to society. If some portion of society is offended, the answer is not in criminalizing those people . . . but addressing the root cause of their existence."

In the Gospel for Sept. 27, the rich man, tormented by the flames in "the abode of the dead," sees Lazarus, whom angels had carried from his suffering to the bosom of Abraham, and begs for a drop of water from the tip of his finger. Abraham reminds the rich man that he was well off in his lifetime, while Lazarus was in misery, which appeared to explain why the rich man was now in torment and Lazarus had found consolation. Abraham also had a little zinger to the effect that if the rich man had listened to the prophets he would have behaved differently.

It's coincidental, of course—that the legal defense of beggars in New York City in 1992 came on the heels of the reading of Jesus' parable about the rich man and beggar. But it made me think a lot about the ways the messages of God get through to us.

Among reminders in the press of the public's objections to street beggars—it lowers the quality of life in the city, it's embarrassing, annoying—I thought of an encounter a friend had with a beggar. I'm going to tell the story on CNY's general manager, Arthur L. McKenna.

He'd been inspired by conversations with Msgr. Thomas Modugno, who directs the office of the Society for the Propagation of the Faith, across the hall from CNY's offices. Msgr. Modugno has a whole clique of homeless people on his walk home from the Catholic Center at First Avenue and 55th Street to St. John the Martyr on East 71st Street. He has conversations with them, explaining, "It's not the quarter or dollar you give them so much as the human exchange."

When Art McKenna came upon a legless man in a wheelchair holding a paper cup on a cold, rainy evening, he decided to give it a try. He asked the man if he was cold, to which he replied, "Yes." Was he hungry? "Yes." Would he like some food? His wheelchair was handily located in front of a supermarket, a pricey gourmet establishment. Some peanut butter would be nice, the man told Art with a smile. And maybe some jelly. Art said he'd get bread, too, and the man said that would feed him for several days.

Would he like some coffee? No, but what he'd really like, hadn't had in a long time, would be a can of sardines. Done, said Art, promising crackers to accompany the beggar's canapés.

Well, in the elegant market, a block from Sutton Place, what Art called his "simple person-to-person gesture" cost him $9.45. "I honestly didn't intend to spend that much," Art told me later. His explanation: "He never asked me outright. He kind of *invited* me to be generous. His style was to make me want to help him."

Art told the story as a joke on himself. But I know he got more out of the encounter than a feeling of being conned. So can we all, when we have a chance to help someone in need, whether from their own fault or not.

One panhandler told a reporter, "I hate having to do this. But what are people supposed to do who have no money whatsoever?" Doesn't that prompt one to offer a little help to "a peaceful beggar"—along with a smile and a few pleasant words?

And have you noticed now many street people say, "God bless you," when you give them something? I'll bet Lazarus would have said that to the rich man, had he noticed him. And things might have turned out differently for the rich man.

—*Catholic New York,* October 8, 1992

For Pete's Sake: Our Homeless Parishioner   *Pastor Urbanus*

Recently, like every priest on every Sunday after Mass, I was greeting people on the church steps when a woman broke into my morning routine with a vexing matter; our "resident" homeless man. "I don't want to interfere," she said, starting to do just that, "but who is this man and what are you going to do about him?"

She listed her solutions, but didn't want to hear that we had already tried these with no result. Critical of our actions, she dismissed justifications. How could I have explained such a complex problem in so brief a conversation? Would she have cared to learn that while half of the parish wants this fellow pushed out, the other half wants more help for him than he receives now? She wasn't even from our state, but she demanded an immediate response. But what she did mostly was put me on the defensive. That makes sense, since I've been there for almost five years, every day trying to deal with a most atypical case.

Sometimes I try to generalize about the homeless from this particular situation, but it's difficult to comprehend a systemic problem. So I simply try to help this one fellow, whom I'll call Pete. Frequently, I resign myself to the fact that, as we advance technologically, our country appears to be coming apart sociologically. I'm frustrated—with myself, with my homeless friend, with buttinskies who think I'm a hypocrite. All of us—my parish, my staff, the community and myself—are trapped in ambivalence. I often think our whole society is reacting in much the same way. Like a partially completed jigsaw puzzle, some pieces of the issue of homelessness fit together, but most are in disarray.

I don't think that I alone have to help the homeless, because I don't feel that the problem is mine personally. It's ours. I agree that more attention must be paid to the homeless, but just who should do what is an unresolved question. I believe this is a question so vast that no one individual can address it. In my previous parish, I led a team that opened a community shelter. My current parish supports a shelter elsewhere in our county. In Pete's case, however, I've been frustrated by proposing resources that he constantly refuses to tap. Pete is usually quite selective about what type of help he'll accept, but he still likes to sleep under our rectory's side portico and sit in our church all day long—and he knows when to knock on the kitchen door.

There are many contradictions here and they start with Pete. He certainly doesn't always look "homeless." Parishioners give him L. L. Bean clothes for Christmas; he visits a nearby relative to shower and pick up mail. He has plenty of food (mainly hand-outs) and a top-line sleeping bag. He plays chess and reads an upscale newspaper. His conversation is clear and lucid; there is no sign of drugs or alcohol. After a little digging, I discovered that his parents were divorced when he was a child and that he has since lived with several relatives who eventually asked him to leave.

Pete also creates anxieties. I once received a complaint that he had followed a girl home. What if he were to start a fire in the church and injure himself or others? Things seem to get broken when Pete doesn't have his way. Several days after he argued with one of our lay staff, who now regularly gives him a few dollars, the man's tires were slashed. We once called in a psychiatric professional specializing in the homeless who told us Pete was no immediate danger to himself or others. That put me a little at ease, but not totally.

Our parish is really concerned both to help Pete and to protect itself. It's my job as pastor to address not only Pete's needs, but also those of the parish. Our lawyer has repeatedly told the parish council that if we gave Pete access to a room or to the church vestibule for sleeping, we would be in specific violation of some city ordinances and subject to liability for what happens there. What if Pete were to bring someone in and molest him or her? The thought of these possibilities and their moral ramifications creates anxious knots in my stomach. Our legal responsibility is best handled by getting rid of Pete, but our Christian duty to help is best taken care of by bringing him even closer.

I'm challenged as a priest in several ways, not the least of which is the personalization of the Gospel. How can I preach a caring Gospel, I ask myself, when I can't do anything for Pete? Am I absolved if my attempts are spurned? I find myself in the position of those who give money to a beggar to buttress their own self-image. They have met their own needs, but have they effectively helped the beggar?

I'm also confronted as a priest by my parishioners. Most of them are middle-class owners of their own homes in an area that so far shows only the first early hints of decay. More homeless people are moving closer to our neighborhood and there is a tightening ring of other signs of decline: an unremoved car wreck, the gutted storefront.

Some householders and heads of families react very strongly to Pete's presence. They call anonymously to say they will pull their kids from our school or stop attending Mass here unless we get rid of Pete. These parishioners who reject Pete and other homeless persons do not see themselves as rejecting the Gospel but as defending their homes, families and neighborhood. Their reaction can be voiced in an un-Christian and antagonistic way. Yet it's a very real, honest and understandable reaction with which I can sympathize to some degree. All the same, it's my job to get our parishioners to understand that Pete's situation is one to which the Gospel message must be especially applied. This can be difficult.

When Pete was suspected of vandalizing a neighborhood business, the manager called to see what I would do about "my man." Recently, it was I who had to tell Pete that his father had died. In fact, many people consider Pete my personal problem, but I reject that view. Pete is not my child from a biological or sociological standpoint nor even from a religious one. The spiritual title "Father" does not mean *in loco parentis*. Yet I know that I am part of Pete's life story and that we are all accountable for each other to some degree. This conviction is nagging enough to keep me trying.

Pete refuses to go to that small nearby shelter the parish supports, but he will work at local odd jobs. However, the rhythm of regular employment seems to frighten him off. He'll comply with certain requests, yet he has used parts of the church area as a toilet and has collected stray cats. Where can I draw the line? At the risk of appearing as harsh as Scrooge, I will not allow him to hang tarps to close off the portico where he sleeps. I have my reasons. That device would not only suggest a shanty-town but it would probably alienate some in the community who are disposed to help Pete.

If I ask him to come inside a heated garage on an especially wintry night, he'll refuse with the boast that he likes the cold. News reports of homeless people shivering in parks take on a very personal dimension for me when I'm in my warm bed and Pete is in his wind- and snow-battered sleeping bag, minimally protected by the portico below my window. One of my main fears, in fact, is that he will freeze to death. I visualize a newspaper with a picture of Pete's frozen body on the church steps splayed across the front page. All the words in the world would not be able to explain away that one picture, even though it would suggest a story quite opposed to the facts of our concerned parish community.

In spite of my ambivalence, I am certain about three small sections of this jigsaw puzzle. First, there is not just one homeless problem. There are many types of homeless problems and making universal statements about them is not a step forward. Second, solutions, otherwise workable, often fail because they are unacceptable to the one most concerned, the homeless person. Finally, we should remember that "needs" is a word requiring definition whenever it is used. Whose needs are in question—the needs of the homeless person, the needs of the community or one's personal need to maintain the image of a concerned Christian?

Talking about Pete might be a step toward further clarifying my own thinking and actions. Perhaps I've just reached the end of my rope and I'm casting about for ideas. Or could it be that I want to explain myself to those who see me as cold-hearted and don't appreciate where I'm coming from?

All I'm attempting to do is live the way Jesus taught. I'm grateful that the Gospel does not ask us to succeed, but only to try.

—America, April 10, 1993

Advocacy for the Homeless   *Kim Hopper*

A decisive change has taken place in the circumstances that spawn and perpetuate homelessness in the United States. . . .

Decisive changes have occurred in the economy at large, in the housing market, and in governmental programs which provide for the disabled and dependent, which have had the net effect of marginalizing an ever-growing segment of the U.S. population. Homelessness is but the extreme instance of this process of marginalization.

The driving dynamic behind it is a widening gap between subsistence needs on the one hand and the resources with which they can be met on the other. Specifically, our analysis suggests that the growing scarcity of housing in the low- and middle-income range operates in reciprocal fashion with the progressively worsening situation of individual household economies to produce a dearth of housing as a procurable good.

The indicators of this new marginalization are many: rising rent income ratios, a growing reliance on soup kitchens to stretch household food dollars, a rising incidence of such makeshift accommodations as doubling-up, and the silent, undocumented misery of those who just manage to scrape by. At the extreme edge is homelessness.

I can put it simply: homelessness in my view is not so much a new problem as it is the contemporary mode of expression of a number of traditional problems—problems which themselves have worsened of late. Specifically, *homelessness today is not the alien face of the skid row alcoholic, so much as it is the familiar countenance of poverty.*

That said, it is still the case that relief efforts are at a level not seen for 50 years. What kind of success does this represent?

Soup kitchens, shelters, drop-in centers and outreach efforts–along with the public and private funds to support them–stand at a post-Depression high. Equally impressive has been the slow erosion of inherited images of the homeless poor as synonymous with skid row denizens. Everywhere, the press has been forced to confront the detailed particulars of the lives of today's homeless; stereotypes have been shattered.

Litigation is a third area of success: most lawsuits resulting in favorable rulings or settlements have sought recognition of a right to shelter or the removal of barriers to the offer of shelter; a few have won recognition of certain qualitative standards to be met by "decent" shelter; several have secured the right to vote for homeless citizens; and one in New York currently seeks appropriate housing for ex-psychiatric patients as part of their right to treatment.

Fourth has been the tentative awareness that, whatever their special needs, the mentally disabled among the homeless share a need for accessible, safe refuge (see, for example, the American Psychiatric Association's Task Force report on The Homeless Mentally Ill, 1984).

A fifth and final area of success–albeit a limited one–has been the growing recognition of the centrality of decent, affordable housing to any long-term solution to homelessness, and a parallel awareness of the importance of preventive measures (see, especially Catholic Charities USA's position paper on housing). New York State's Homeless Housing and Assistance Program (which provides capital funding to not-for-profit organizations and municipalities seeking to house the homeless); Massachusetts' revised welfare regulations (removing residency barriers to General Relief, extending medical coverage to G.R. recipients, and providing for rental or mortgage assistance for families under threat of eviction or foreclosure); Minnesota's housing demonstration program; the pending of seven bills in Congress this spring to provide emergency shelter and housing–all, in part at least, may be justly read as responses to the growing crisis of homelessness.

Perhaps the most significant development in advocacy recently– aside from recent efforts of the homeless to organize themselves (in Philadelphia, Washington, D.C., San Francisco, and New York)–has been the alliance of advocates for the homeless with the low-income housing movement at large. Especially fruitful has been the growing incidence of collaboration at local and national levels concerning such matters as inclusionary zoning provisions, housing development funds, opposition to federal cutbacks, and new models of supportive housing.

Again, the successes of advocacy must be understood within the context of the cluster of factors that have influenced public receptivity to the issue. Homelessness has proven a powerful focal point for the convergence of a wide array of dissatisfaction with contemporary social policy. In many cities, it is a highly visible phenomenon, again, in marked contrast to that poverty chronicled by Harrington in the early '60's: "invisible . . . hidden . . . off the beaten track" were his descriptions. Even in localities where the problem is less apparent, extensive media coverage has made awareness of the issue commonplace. Vignettes recounting the travails of homeless individuals and families have come to sound more and more like the stories one might hear within the confines of kin and friends. And, in recent years, the issue itself has evolved as a touchstone for opposition to the Reagan administration's efforts to dismantle the legacy of the New Deal. Governor Cuomo's keynote address to the ill-fated Democratic Convention of 1984 was notable for its sounding of the Victorian "two cities" theme, in which the hungry and homeless figure prominently.

Limitations and Setback

What, then, are the shortcomings of such efforts? The most dismaying failure to date is also the most obvious: There are still legions of homeless people making do without any but the most rudimentary, jerry-rigged shelter. Despite all the effort, even this most basic and least disputed goal has yet to be realized.

And where shelter has been provided, almost without exception, its unerring tendency has been to become—not a way station en route to permanent, affordable housing—but an enduring makeshift way of life.

There are three additional areas of development that are worrisome. Because they have not received much attention, they merit mention here: the local character of entitlement; the emergence of "backlash" programmatic initiatives; and a new ideological twist on the notion of the "deserving poor."

Survival as a Local Entitlement

In Pennsylvania, a court case challenged the 1982 revision of the Welfare Code restricting benefits to able-bodied individuals to three months in any calendar year. Before the court challenge, 68,000 were removed from welfare rolls. The initial favorable ruling was overturned by Third Circuit Court in 1983—even though the court fully recognized that penury was the likely outcome of its decision. By early fall 1983, a fifth of those quartered in Philadelphia shelters were thought to be casualties of the new regulations.

Programmatic Setbacks

Signs of a return to the workhouse model of the 19th century are emerging. New York City's Work Experience Program for shelter residents mandates 20 hours a week in exchange for shelter, food and a stipend of $.63/hr. Those who refuse are sent to flophouses.

Similar, but more extreme, is the case of Sacramento which, in October 1982, eliminated all cash grants to able-bodied adults who were offered bed and board in a barrack-like facility in exchange for seven days work each month for the county (clearing brush or cleaning drainage). This stipulation is now being challenged in court and the ruling is pending. But during the months it was in effect, new applications for relief fell by 50 percent.

Institutional Anomalies

During the current transitional period, the generic functions of shelter and asylum are being redefined and redistributed in a seemingly ad hoc fashion. Traditional domains of responsibility no longer correspond to actual fields of practice: Hospital emergency rooms function as stations of temporary respite, offering security, heat and a place to put up one's feet for a while. Skid row institutions, on the other hand, have in certain areas taken on the character of open asylums, so pronounced is the presence of obvious disability.

It is the new products of this period that I mean to designate by the term "institutional anomaly." For example, former psychiatric buildings in New York have been pressed into service as emergency shelters and, in an ironic twist of fate, homeless ex-patients have found themselves shuttled back to the sites of their former confinement, this time as shelter clients rather than patients. The converse has also occurred: A psychiatric in-patient unit in a Boston hospital found that it could cut operating costs by 14 percent if it converted to day-hospital status. Patients without an address of their own, or any friends or relatives to care for them, were quartered in a former hospital gymnasium, hastily converted into an emergency shelter.

Is it to be the case that the only feasible solutions to (at least some part of) the problem of homelessness will be those which salvage otherwise discarded resources to house the otherwise discarded?

Blame-the-Victim to Pity-the-Casualty

Ideologically, a shift in the official view of what kind of social problem homelessness represents should be noted. Not long ago, in the winter of 1982–83, it was not uncommon for the Reagan administration to dismiss concern for the homeless poor as misplaced hand-wringing. "Some of those people," in the president's own memorable words, "are there, you might say, by their own choice." Eccentric it may be, so the apparent logic went, still their exercise of free choice should be tolerated.

But by the spring of 1984, in at least some corridors of government, a different theme had surfaced. In the words of former Secretary of Health and Human Services, Margaret Heckler, homelessness is not a new problem, but one "connected to the problem of alcohol or drug dependency," whose victims have wound up on the streets "throughout the years, maybe centuries." If there is one novel feature to the contemporary picture, it is the presence of the mentally disabled among the homeless. "But the problem is as old as time and with this new dimension complicating it, it's a serious problem; but it always has been."

Thus is the reality of homelessness simultaneously recognized and reduced to the proportions of vice and disease. Not outraged indignation at gratuitous harm, but weary resignation to a pre-ordained scheme of things; not analysis of contributing policies, but adumbration of Biblical injunctions ("the poor ye have always"); not a focus on the problem of homelessness, but one on the problems of the homeless—these, suggested Heckler, are the proper antidote for an easily aroused and all-too-American impulse to rescue the unfortunate.

Is this, then, the bitter fruit of three years of vigorous advocacy? Will homelessness be recognized as a genuine public policy issue only to be assigned to that remorseless engine of pity and contempt that has historically governed society's response to the abject poor? Will this maneuver, in turn, quell the anxiety created by a growing mass of people who, as one leading liberal daily put it, "continue to consume tax dollars and demoralize society" (*New York Times,* 4/9/84)?

And what of the role we advocates ourselves have played? An old formula for successful advocacy runs as follows: continuous renewal of the terms of the demand coupled with unremitting criticism of all efforts to accommodate it without significant change. Might not some advocacy efforts have let vigilance flag in the interest of incremental success? Haven't we fallen prey at times to the trap of packaging a difficult and disturbing reality in terms which are both non-stigmatizing and designed to elicit public sympathy at large?

"Homeless" may be a welcomed substitution for a variety of earlier epithets, but might not one of its unanticipated consequences be the artificial simplification of a host of problems, the collective import of which runs much deeper than mere lack of shelter?

And although advocates have with growing frequency insisted upon the larger, systemic linkages that the problem has, is it clear that that insistence has had much impact? Indeed, is it not the case that the urgency and immediacy of the existing need have overshadowed what else it may portend about the fundamental needs satisfying structures of our economy and government?

Some Counsel from Forebears

Descendants of the great documentary tradition of the thirties, present-day advocates for the homeless are also heirs to its hazards. Chief among these is a reflexive, paternalistic impulse to eradicate the surface misery while leaving untouched the underlying structures of impoverishment. The signs are all around us: the proliferation of emergency shelters and soup kitchens, the enormous outpouring of popular support for the cause, and extensive voluntary participation in relief efforts. In short, the large part of the apparatus of support that agitation and litigation have caused to come into existence.

In an assessment of the emergence of homelessness as a social problem and its acquisition of a new-found legitimacy, Mark Stern has argued that the phenomenon may well spell the demise of the welfare rights movement of the 1960s (Stern, 1984). Not entitlement, but benevolence is the watchword of much of the contemporary response to homelessness. In this, Stern discerns a return to the Victorian tradition of voluntary charity and personalized relief. The substance of need is taken to be obvious, the style of assistance is direct and immediate, and—whether intended by those who offer food and shelter or not—humiliation of the recipient is its usual accompaniment. By extension, it is possible to argue that in this guise, homeless relief functions as a disciplinary measure, one effect of which is to deter potential applicants for assistance and force the needy to fashion makeshift accommodations on their own (Hopper and Hamberg,

1984). Inadvertently, then, and over the objections of their champions, "the homeless may actually have functioned to reduce the willingness of Americans to explore the complexities of need in the 1980s" (Stern, 1984, *Social Service Review,* p. 299).

This is a harsh judgment. The necessary corrective, while onerous, is not mysterious. What it will mean is a re-examination of tools and approaches to which we advocates have found ourselves naturally drawn. And it derives, appropriately enough, from a neglected strain of the same documentary tradition of the thirties.

The truth is that homelessness is the sort of historic fault that reveals once again just how heedless of human need the normal operations of a well-functioning system can be. It also suggests, by virtue of its own complexity, just how complex and thoroughgoing an *adequate* governmental response must be. Little wonder, then, that the latest audit of the federal response to homelessness characterized it, in the course of four sentences, as "unresolved . . . uncertain . . . unanswered" (General Accounting Office, 1985).

There is nothing quite like a stint at a soup kitchen or shelter to convince one both of the urgent need for such endeavors *and* of their utter insufficiency. This, I think, is a broadly enough reported experience to be counted as a truism today. Those who volunteer at such places are not mindless, captive drones. They are people who do not allow themselves the uninformed detachment that passes for tacit approval of so much social policy today. And once exposed to the lived realities of street life—and the desperately impoverished nature of the relief that is available—these people are much less likely to fall for the bloodless abstractions and nimble dodges that are regularly trotted out in official pronouncements on the problem. They are much more likely to see shelters and soup kitchens for what they are—or, at best, can be: minimally decent, stop-gap measures, whose only legitimate function is to enable people who might perish to hang on a bit longer, while the larger decisions as to their ultimate fate are made.

On occasion, such an experience takes root and produces a sudden, unbidden moment of shared kinship—the sort of recognition reported by a Presbyterian elder at a Salt Lake City soup kitchen:

> I look at these people and I think: I am one job and one divorce away from them (*Iowa City Press-Citizen,* May 7, 1983).

And, as I see it, it is from such people—alive to the precariousness of everyday life for so many people, and insistent that more than mere shelter be provided to remedy the situation of the homeless poor—that the political constituency of support for long-term solutions to homelessness might one day be forged.

In the meantime, building bridges for the homeless must have an anchor in two bulwarks. The first is human gesture: the only instrumentality through which dignity and respect can be conferred (much to the dismay of the social engineers). William Blake, in his poem *Jerusalem,* makes the point nicely:

> He who would do good to another must do it in Minute Particulars:
> General good is the plea of the scoundrel, hypocrite and flatterer.

If the first is remarkable for its subtlety, the second is so ordinary and pervasive as to be missed altogether. Let me quote from George Cook, writing in the pages of the *American Journal of Insanity* in 1886:

> It is not well to sneer at political economy in its relations to the insane poor. Whether we think it right or not, the question of cost has determined and will continue to determine their fate for weal or woe.

In the tension between those two recognitions lies the task for building bridges for the homeless.

> *I look at these people and I think: I am one job and one divorce away from them.*
> —*Charities USA,* April 1986

The Catholic Church and Homelessness   *Timothy A. Mitchell*

In a major document on the plight of the homeless in the world, the Pontifical Commission for Justice and Peace said that homelessness "is a scandal and one more indication of the unjust distribution of goods, originally destined for the use of all."

According to the social teachings of the Church the right to own private property is limited by what the document refers to as its "special social function subordinated to the right of common use."

That is, this "special social function" limits the right of individuals to buy and own property and to reap a profit from it. Hence, since "housing constitutes a basic social good," it "cannot simply be considered a market commodity."

The reasoning here is purely scriptural. For as the Sabbath was made for man, not man for the Sabbath, it follows that both property and the market commodity were made for man, not man for them. On this point, the document is precise and concise.

"Property," it points out, "is at the service of the human person. Any speculative practice which diverts property from its function of serving the human person should be considered an abuse."

Touching on many aspects of the Church's social doctrine, Pope John Paul II, in the Preface, emphasizes the familial and social harm that housing shortages and homelessness cause. It upsets normal family life and creates a social condition where the streets house the homeless.

The document, which is the result of information supplied by bishops' conferences and other Catholic organizations from over sixty countries, was issued on Dec. 27, 1987, on the occasion of the International Year of Shelter for the Homeless. It runs for 29 pages and is entitled: "What Have You Done to Your Homeless Brother? The Church and the Housing Problem." (For text, see *Osservatore Romano*, Weekly Engl. ed. [Feb. 8, 1988] 9–13.)

In a special to the *New York Times* Robert Suro, writing from Rome, points out that in "its most basic conclusions the document reflects several ideas that the Pope has emphasized in recent years: that injustices are built into all economic systems, that ethical direction must be given to market economies, that there should be a mix of public and private solutions to social problems and that local initiatives should be pursued" (quoted from *Common Good* 10,1 [1988] 4).

These four ideas adequately sum up the social teachings of the Catholic Church. And because they do, they constitute the major reasons why extremists on both the left and the right view Her as being extremely in the other camp. Yet, when properly understood, they reveal two things, namely, on economic matters they put the Church in neither camp and, more importantly, they make good common economic sense.

To begin with, all economic systems are produced by man, who is a morally flawed creature. Because of this (what the moral philosophers call concupiscence), men as a rule are guided by self-interest and, even though protected by the grace of God, are prone toward wrongdoing. Thus, a socialist economy, where economic decisions are the proper purview of a tightly controlled state, and a laissez-faire capitalism, where the only rule is no rules, both end up with economic structures in which power resides in the hands of a relatively few like-minded thinkers.

Hence, the market economies, which are diametrically opposed to socialism (which has been severely condemned by the Church because it inverts the relationship of the state to man by proclaiming that man was made for the state, not the state for man), cannot of themselves constitute an ethical alternative to it. For they, too, are prone to invert the priority of man over created goods. As such, they must be given ethical direction, lest they subordinate man to a man-made system of producing and distributing goods. For the goods were made for man's good.

Accordingly, social problems which are man-made cannot be solved exclusively by the state in a socialistic economy nor by any market economy which excludes the intervention of the state, which does ethically exist to serve the common good. The state must intervene in the public interest when the economic power of the few in a market economy threatens the welfare of the many. And the market economy must serve as a check upon the state before it becomes a behemoth-like monster with totalitarian control. Needed simply is the mix of the public and private sectors.

Finally, local initiatives, guided by the principle of subsidiarity, must be pursued to paradoxically broaden and limit the power of the state. For this principle, which states that any initiative that can effectively be pursued at a lower social level must be pursued at that level, limits the role of centralized government while leaving open a role for government at all levels to become involved in the resolution of a nation's social problems.

In a word, since housing was made for man and not man for housing, it follows that homelessness "is a scandal" and another "indication of the unjust distribution of goods" which were made by God "for the use of all." And since all economic systems are made by man and in need of ethical direction, it follows that the Church (which examines these systems in terms of the higher law and the common good) must intervene wherever this "scandal" and "unjust distribution for goods" persist. Not to do so would be an abandonment of the real meaning of separation of Church and state. For there is a scriptural command to render to Caesar the things that are Caesar's and to God the things that are God's.

—Social Justice Review, July/August 1992

Oh, Give Me a Home   *Douglas D. Watson*

Ben Stein who is a lawyer, actor, writer and economist says his words are fact. "The cities and towns of America are rapidly becoming unlivable because of the infestation of pathetic, often dangerous homeless people."

Mayor Tony Senecal of Martinsburg, West Virginia, tends to agree with Mr. Stein. "Bums. They refuse to work in a fast-food restaurant for $4 an hour because they can make twice as much an hour panhandling."

The one-two punch has really hit home for Anthony Johnson of Chicago. First Anthony lost his job then was evicted from his apartment. These days Anthony and his mother call two vacant cars "home."

Ted Lindsy of Chicago has been homeless for 20 years. Ted describes his life as "walking the streets a lot" and eating from garbage cans.

Charlotte, North Carolina, Mayor Sue Myrick believes that "Many people are becoming less patient with the people on the streets. We've become a very selfish nation."

The homeless still exist in America but the working public are showing an ever increasing apathy toward them. Just a few years back the hearts of Americans yearned to help the disadvantaged and homeless. Now the attitude of America seems to be, "I have to work for *my* home and food; let them do the same."

An Oakland City, Indiana, man gave away most of his possessions so that he would be completely homeless and then went to Chicago to learn about the homeless. He lived on the streets of Chicago for two weeks. Two weeks of going from one shelter to another, and at times no shelter at all. The man related the story of an off-duty policeman threatening to arrest him when he tried to go to Mass at St. Peter's Church.

The Indiana man said the only way to beat the cold Chicago winter was to ride trains and buses. Homeless people are leery of sleeping for more than an hour at a time because they fear someone will mug them. The Chicago homeless get their 40 winks when the libraries open for business. One group of homeless will leave the library when another group enters. If there are too many homeless people in one place they will all be chased out. That's how they watch out for each other.

There are good and bad shelters for the homeless. Because of the bad shelters, many homeless people avoid all shelters. In a bad shelter what starts out as a peaceful sleep could end in a rude awakening with all of a person's valuables being stolen while he was fast asleep.

Today people are repulsed by the grimy hands reaching out toward them and a voice begging for "spare change." People are tired of giving. The more they give the more homeless people come out of the woodwork.

The following statement is attributed to Seneca. "However degraded or wretched a fellow mortal may be, he is still a member of our common species."

The 1990 census count of homeless people was 228,621. Homeless activists say the true number is between 200,000 and 3 million. No matter what the *actual* number of homeless people is, any number above zero is too many for a Christian nation such as the United States.

The New York Times reported that the Census Bureau used decoys posing as homeless people for the counting of the homeless. The number of decoys missed were calculated as actual people who were missed. In New York City it is estimated that the homeless count is off by 45%, in Los Angeles 59%–70% and in Phoenix between 57%–80% of the homeless were missed.

Tony Reinis of the California Homeless Coalition in Los Angeles remarked: "People want the homeless problem to go away. But instead the problem is getting worse and worse."

I can't judge if a person is a bum who won't work or if he's a person who has lost everything through no fault of his own. Christians as a whole need to help the homeless and let the judgment of each recipient rest with God. If I am to love my fellow man then I must aid him and refrain from judging him. I guess the bottom line would be that when I'm ready for mankind to judge me then I can judge mankind.

Some naysayers would quickly point to the Scriptures in defense of not aiding the homeless. Their fingers would rapidly turn the pages of the bible until coming to 2 Thessalonians 3:10, "For even when we were with you, this we commanded you, if anyone would not work, neither should he eat." That is all well and good for the sluggard but what about his family? What about the wife and kids he deserted? What about the children?

A young woman who has three children was deserted by her husband. She is working and bringing home $600 per month. Her rent takes $495 and electricity runs about $150. Those two items alone add up to $40 over her monthly income. She is looking for a cheaper place to live but she can't afford the deposit required at most places.

There is an elderly single grandmother trying to raise her 8-year-old granddaughter. The woman's adjusted income is less than $300 a month and yet she is only eligible for $10 worth of food stamps.

America is a giving nation that sends food to Africa and Ethiopia, Bibles to Russia and supports missionaries world-wide while *5.5 million American children under the age of 12 are going hungry.* While at the same time *6 million other children under 12 are living on the edge of poverty.* The children not only experience the gnawing empty feelings in their stomachs but they are also at risk of health and learning problems.

Vermont Senator Patrick Leahy stated that, "When the richest country in the world stands aside as children go hungry, it is a moral outrage."

USA Today asked former surgeon general C. Everett Koop why so many children were starving in a country as rich as the USA. He answered: "Distribution. The trouble in our country is that 85% of us have everything we need and 15% of us don't. And the 85% of us who have it don't spend much time worrying about how the 15% that don't might be able to get it."

America is opening up its pocketbook to people overseas while at the same time closing its heart to the poor and homeless in the U.S. In the editorial section of the *USA Today* issue of March 29, 1991, are these words. "When a parent has no answer for the child who says 'I'm hungry,' the answer must come from the rest of us."

In order for me to become a more loving individual I've got to get out of the *me* frame of mind and into the *us* frame of mind. I need to put my wants on the back burner and put the needs of the homeless and the hungry on the front burner. The same food I take for granted may be a lifesaver to a starving child.

Seeing the problem is the easy part. Solving the problem is the hard part. The responsibility of taking care of the poor and needy should not only fall on the shoulders of the government. When government becomes the lone resource for aid to the poor many will fall between the so-called cracks. The care and well-being of the poor and homeless should also come from the church. But alas, the churches are still paying off their huge building debts and the other debts not related to taking care of those who are forced to do without.

Maybe churches could help those in need in exchange for work to be done on the church grounds. After all it would save church funds if the poor would cut the grass, shovel snow, clean the Church building and the parking lot. Are there not buses to be cleaned and windows to be washed?

By using the 1990 census figure of 248 million as the base and if Mr. Koop is right in that 85% of us have what we need then that number of people is 210.8 million. Using the same figures, the needy people in the USA would be about 37.2 million. If the 210.8 million gave $5 per week to the needy that amount would be $4,216,000,000 per month. That would average out to be about $113.33 per needy person a month. Not a lot of money but food on the table nonetheless. A single person would receive the $113.33 per month, a married couple would receive twice that amount, a family of five would be eligible for 5 times the $113.33.

Now the problems arise. Only volunteers could be used to take care of collecting and distributing the money. The paying of an overseer or anyone else would be defeating the purpose. I have often wondered why there are so many volunteers at hospital and nursing homes that charge the patients an arm and a leg and yet the volunteers for the needy are at a minimum.

The volunteers can't be poor or middle-classed because the temptation to keep some of the money would be tremendous. The volunteers can't be wealthy people because the temptation of greed would be on their mind constantly.

What if a board made up of Christian leaders were elected to take care of the money? That would work except that the *ACLU* would argue that the board is discriminating against all atheists. If atheists and Christians are on the same board there would be less monies meted out and more arguments taking place.

The committee would end up in the same shape that America is in today. With everybody being so busy talking about the poor and homeless that nobody has the time to help alleviate the problem. These are the so-called *good intentions* that often pave the road to hell.

I have spent time writing this article. The reader has spent time reading this article. And the homeless people and the starving youngsters still exist.

The homeless and undernourished need constant help, not just a money raising benefit once a year. The 15% need help that goes beyond food and water. They need love, compassion, education and a need to feel good about themselves and their lives.

Athletes make millions of dollars playing the games of childhood. The poor and homeless are starving to death in the adult world. America tends to put the rich and famous on a pedestal while the poor and homeless are swept under the rug.

It is well past the time for well-meaning cliches to point out the plight of those who are physically suffering for the bare necessities of life. Pleading and talking about the less fortunate will not fill one of their stomachs. Cliches, pleading and talking are of the yesterdays. The todays and tomorrows must be filled with actions, anything less is failure.

An unknown source made the following statement that seems to bring this entire article into focus. "It would be extremely helpful if the poor were to get half the money that is spent on studying them."

—Social Justice Review, July/August 1992

Helping the Homeless:
How Individuals Can Make a Difference   *Gary M. Stern*

Is there anyone left in the world who hasn't been accosted by a homeless person for a spare quarter or peso? Residents of Washington, D.C., San Diego, Tucson, New York City and metropolises, medium-sized cities, and smaller towns across the country have become inundated by the hundreds of thousands of homeless who roam the country's streets, too poor to afford housing, ravaged by alcohol or drug abuse, or released from mental institutions. As the number of homeless has grown, many people feel overwhelmed by the problem, believing that there is nothing that they can do to help. Certain individuals nationwide, however, motivated by their own conscience and concern for others, have been proving that individuals can make a difference in the lives of the homeless.

At the same time that more and more people have been helping the homeless, a backlash against the homeless has been brewing. As Robert Hayes, counsel to the National Coalition for the Homeless, asserts, "Everyone has extreme reactions to the homeless. Typically, it's compassion and sympathy. But lurking right beneath that is fear and loathing. It doesn't take much for it to shift from one to the other." Recently in the resort town of Hollywood, Florida, after a homeless man was accused of homicide, ordinances were passed by the city legislature ordering the homeless out of town. The City Commissioner declared that, "When I grew up in the Depression, we didn't call these people homeless; we called them bums. I don't see any reason not to still call them that."

How can people show their compassion to the homeless? Is giving them your spare change the right thing to do? How can an individual make a difference in the lives of homeless people? Why has the backlash developed?

Other people wonder why, with so many help wanted signs around and so many jobs available in stores and businesses, so few homeless don't work and help themselves? Patricia Burton-Eadie, director of Shelter Development for the New York City-based Partnership for the Homeless, asserts that many homeless do work, often at construction jobs or lower-level jobs such as messengers. Yet she adds that it's difficult to maintain steady work unless you have a permanent place to live. "It's a big issue not having a home," she says. "Trying to concentrate on work when you're thinking about where you are going to spend the night, how to take a shower, where to store your clothes, and finding a place to eat is difficult."

Moreover, she adds that most low-level jobs pay minimum wage and make it impossible for a homeless person to save money. To rent an apartment, tenants must pay at least one month's security, often a brokers' fee, and even renting a room at a modest hotel involves a deposit. "It would be nice if you could work two weeks, save money, and then find a place to live, but that's impossible," she says.

Knowing how difficult it is for the homeless to survive has motivated volunteers to help them. For example, Megan Tingley, a 24-year-old Boston children's book editor at Little Brown was troubled by seeing countless numbers of homeless people, particularly families and children, on Boston's streets. Tapping her own strengths as a children's book editor and her past experience working at a day care center and teaching autistic children, she started a small library at Boston Family Shelter where homeless families with their children reside.

Supported by a grant from Time Inc. and enlisting the support of four of her colleagues, Tingley organizes once a week library sessions at the Boston Family Shelter with homeless children. She will read stories to children, have them read aloud, and at day's end, allow them to borrow books for their own reading. "Reading can empower young people and help them to get a head start," Tingley says. Giving change to a homeless person was a form of tokenism, she suggests, but now she feels that she is making a tangible contribution to many children's lives.

Tingley sees establishing this children's library as her "personal" response to the homeless. A quarter, she says, will likely not change the life of a 55-year-old homeless man, but with children there's always a sense of hope that reading will alter their lives. "It makes a difference that we come every week," she declares, sensing that glimmer of excitement in a homeless child's face when Tingley would read a Dr. Seuss book to her.

Washington, D.C., professional photographer Jim Hubbard who specializes in taking photographs of the homeless decided that he wanted to do something to publicize the plight of homeless people. Just as Megan Tingley tapped her own interests, he drew on his own photographic skills to create *Shooting Back,* which teaches homeless children who temporarily reside at welfare hotels and motels in D.C. such as the aptly named Pitts Hotel and Capital City Inn to take photographs on their own. Each week, helped by some of his colleagues, he accompanies six to eight homeless children through the streets of D.C. to photograph whatever the children want.

Shooting Back aims to teach the children basic photographic skills by documenting where they live, but Hubbard says that an important by-product is raising their self-esteem. The children decide what they want to photograph, and Hubbard notes that ironically, the children tend to reject images of decay and instead shoot "joyful" situations, children leaping into swimming pools, playing in the water spray from fire hydrants, faces of other children. Mastering the camera and seeing their own images in prints have been boosting their confidence.

Shooting Back's effort this year will culminate in late 1989 in a photo exhibit at the prestigious Washington Project for the Arts. Nor is Hubbard willing to rest on his laurels. He is aiming to raise funds for Catalyst, a permanent media center dedicated to training homeless people, teaching them video and writing skills.

Why teach the homeless how to use a camera when what they really need is shelter? Housing, he notes, provides only a partial answer to the homeless situation. Homeless people require practical skills, an ability to see an alternative, and a foundation for building self-esteem.

"It's amazing how people find what they do best to help the homeless," asserts Keith Summa, advocacy director for the New York-based Coalition for the Homeless. A concerned glove manufacturer distributed gloves to homeless people in the wintertime, a stockbroker used his computer knowledge to monitor the homeless situation, and a filmmaker has spent time videotaping homeless people to document their situation. Coalition for the Homeless volunteers, as varied as postmen, retired firemen, actors, freelance writers, distribute over 900 meals a day seven nights a week at New York's busy Grand Central Station.

Gary Blasi, director of the Homeless Litigation Unit at the Legal Aid Foundation of Los Angeles, which secures legal rights for poor people and the homeless, notes that volunteering helps the volunteers as much as the homeless. "It's important," he points out, "for people to have some human understanding of the homeless, instead of abstract, intellectual, televised understanding."

But he cautions that volunteering has built-in limitations. "We used to view soup kitchens as signs of national shame; now we see them as thousands of points of light. There is no other industrial European society which thinks that whether people live or die should depend on the charity of strangers," states Blasi. He's troubled by the fact that the homeless are becoming an acceptable part of the American landscape—and worldwide scene—like pollution and trash.

While he acknowledges that working in soup kitchens helps, sweeping changes from Congress and governments worldwide are necessary to improve the lives of the homeless on a larger scale. Producing affordable housing, employment opportunities and training will result from pressuring Congress to change priorities. "The notion of whether people live or die being dependent on volunteers isn't acceptable," Blasi says.

But to Patricia Burton-Eadie, director of Shelter Development for the Partnership for the Homeless based in New York City, volunteering achieves more than a BandAid solution to the homeless' woes. Believing that government is responsible for making primary changes, she says that "We can't just stand back and say the government isn't doing anything. You have to advocate, fight for government changes. The fact is if you're only taking care of a few people that means a lot."

People can help in a variety of ways: corporations are paying for homeless people's Christmas parties, Democratic and Republican political clubs are raising money, school children are involved in poster contests, letter writing campaigns to Congress have applied pressure on legislatures.

Homeless advocates have varying views on whether people should give their spare change when asked. Mary Ellen Hombs, acting director of the Washington, D.C. office of the National Coalition for the Homeless, admits that she doesn't give change to someone whom she thinks looks intoxicated or on drugs. She will give money to most people who are begging whom she says wouldn't be asking for money unless they were "desperate" and unable to exist on welfare benefits or minimum wage. The Coalition for the Homeless recommends that people try not to ignore a homeless person's plea for help. Do something–buy them a sandwich, provide a clean blanket, refer them to a place where they can stay.

Hombs says that handing over a dollar can be more than tokenism; it can provide an opportunity to extend yourself to a homeless person. "I don't think there's anything as important as having names and faces; to take the time out and find out why someone is in that situation," she says. Providing an old coat to someone who is homeless, buying them a sandwich, doing something personal for them registers strongly.

Diane Williams, a 24-year-old Brooklyn, New York, social worker, tired of seeing people annoyed by requests for spare change and tired of those who blame homeless people for their condition, decided to take action on her own. Working as an intern in a city councilwoman's office, she wanted to develop something that might bring together what she calls the "haves and the have-nots." Williams developed a "contact card," a business-type card that can be distributed to the homeless that contains phone numbers for soup kitchens, legal action centers, emergency assistance, and homeless associations.

Through her own initiative, she convinced the DuPont company to donate paper, JRS Press to print the cards, and designer Charles Larcou to design the card. Within two months over 50,000 cards were printed and distributed and a second press run, printing over 100,000 cards, is planned.

What did Williams learn from developing the contact card? "Everyone has power. We're the people who decide who is going to hold office. We all have a voice and if we band together with the homeless we can make a difference," she says.

Despite the efforts of many people to help the homeless and see the homeless as victims of governmental polices, a backlash has developed against them. Patricia Burton-Eadie of the Partnership for the Homeless attributes this growing backlash as a way that individuals have of distancing themselves from the homeless. "We want to think you have to do something wrong to be homeless. The person did it to themselves; they did something wrong. It couldn't happen to us." But the truth is, she reminds us, that as Walt Whitman might have said in his poem "Song of Myself," we are the homeless. Lack of affordable housing is contributing to the growing number of people on the streets. Ten years ago if someone wasn't doing well, they would move in with their family, friends or pay for a modest room in a single-occupancy room hotel, but societal changes have withdrawn many of those options today.

And Gordon Packard, who with Nancy Bissell, started the Prima Vera Foundation in Tucson, Arizona, a non-profit organization that feeds and counsels the homeless, notes that "When people don't even have shoes to pull them up by the bootstraps, the minimal obligation would be to help people understand that people care." Soup kitchens, he says, do much more than serve soup since most homeless people can scrounge a meal for themselves, but the homeless want to know that other people care about them. The homeless, Packard concludes, are merely people "who have the misfortune of being poor. We can go to a health spa, alcohol rehabilitation, have Blue Cross pay. But the first crisis that comes up, poor people are out on the street."

"If people really care about the homeless, you have to get beyond stereotyping them and take them to a place that will empower them," says Packard.

Empowering people is exactly what motivated Michael Leven, chief executive officer of the Days Inns motel chain, headquartered in Atlanta, Georgia, to establish a special program to hire homeless people as reservation clerks. In February of 1988, Leven had lunch with Bill Hodges, a Days Inn executive who encouraged him that the homeless could be trained to fill reservation jobs. Leven doubted that possibility until Hodges convinced him to visit an Atlanta shelter where Hodges had done volunteer work. Upon meeting many of the homeless, some of whom were wearing tattered clothes, Leven was impressed by many of the homeless' desire to change and hold down a full-time job. He agreed to try out the program.

The Days Inn human resources department provided social security cards, work permits to the homeless who met certain criteria, and special one-on-one training to teach them how to use computers proved effective. Formerly homeless workers are not only given a job, but provided with housing at a local hotel/motel at a cost of $20 a day. The homeless pay half, and the company pays the rest. Reservation workers earn from $5 to $5.50 per hour, receive health benefits and are eligible for promotions. Over 20 people have maintained their jobs since the program's inception, and only a handful have dropped out. Turnover is higher with other workers than it is with the formerly homeless. The program has proven so successful that Leven has invited other c.e.o.'s to meet the homeless and to use the Days Inn program as a model for theirs.

Leven feels that businesses have a moral obligation beyond writing a check to help solve human issues. He admits, however, that hiring the homeless has helped his business. Finding responsible, motivated workers willing to accept low-income jobs has not been easy for many employers.

You don't have to be a c.e.o. to help the homeless. Jimmy Novak, a 72-year-old retired Con Edison supervisor, serves as coordinator of volunteers at the Holy Apostle Soup Kitchen in Manhattan, which serves 950 meals a day, five days a week. The homeless, he notes, are served full meals—veal patties and tomato sauce, string beans, chocolate pudding, bread and butter and iced tea, for example. Why does he volunteer?

"I remember the big depression of the thirties. I stood in breadlines and soup lines. If I ever get a good job, I'm going to pay back," he says. Does volunteering help people? "For a great many people this is the one hot meal they get during the day. It has to be of some help," he says succinctly.

Who should volunteer? Says the Partnership for the Homeless' Burton-Eadie, "Anyone can volunteer." Some people who volunteer are living a subsistence life on their own, but others are bankers, actors, storekeepers. If people, she says, are given a structured, safe place to help, they can make a difference.

—Social Justice Review, July/August 1992

Homelessness: Reflection Questions

1. Do you feel any personal responsibility for the homeless?

2. What are some specific ways that you've observed the Church's preferential love for the poor?

3. What does it mean to suggest that homelessness is not so much a new problem as a contemporary mode of expression of a number of traditional problems?

4. React to Anne Buckley's story about Art McKenna.

7
Homosexuality

Psalm 145:8-18

⁸The LORD is gracious and merciful,
  slow to anger and abounding in steadfast love.
⁹The LORD is good to all,
  and his compassion is over all that he has made.
¹⁰All your works shall give thanks to you, O LORD,
  and all your faithful shall bless you.
¹¹They shall speak of the glory of your kingdom,
  and tell of your power,
¹²to make known to all people your mighty deeds,
  and the glorious splendor of your kingdom.
¹³Your kingdom is an everlasting kingdom,
  and your dominion endures throughout all generations.
 The LORD is faithful in all his words,
  and gracious in all his deeds.
¹⁴The LORD upholds all who are falling,
  and raises up all who are bowed down.
¹⁵The eyes of all look to you,
  and you give them their food in due season.
¹⁶You open your hand,
  satisfying the desire of every living thing.
¹⁷The LORD is just in all his ways,
  and kind in all his doings.
¹⁸The LORD is near to all who call on him,
  to all who call on him in truth.

Chastity and Homosexuality

2357 Homosexuality refers to relations between men or between women who experience an exclusive or predominant sexual attraction toward persons of the same sex. It has taken a great variety of forms through the centuries and in different cultures. Its psychological genesis remains largely unexplained. Basing itself on Sacred Scripture, which presents homosexual acts as acts of grave depravity,[140] tradition has always declared that "homosexual acts are intrinsically disordered."[141] They are contrary to the natural law. They close the sexual act to the gift of life. They do not proceed from a genuine affective and sexual complementarity. Under no circumstances can they be approved.

[140]Cf. *Gen* 19:1-29; *Rom* 1:24-27; *1 Cor* 6:10; *1 Tim* 1:10.
[141]CDF, *Persona humana* 8.

—Catechism of the Catholic Church

Hair of a Different Color   *Molly Stein*

It has been a year since my cousin, Anna, told me that she is not a true blonde. In fact, her hair is green.

I have no idea how difficult it was for her to admit this to me. I'm still struggling with how difficult it was for me to hear it.

I'm not sure why she chose May 1993, after all these years, to leak this piece of intelligence to me during one of our frequent AT&T marathons. But now I know that this is a truth she has known—and kept from the family—since high school. Anna started to realize she was different during her sophomore year. At first she wasn't sure what was going on, but she was too embarrassed to discuss it with anyone. When the first jade-colored strands appeared near the nape of her neck, she plucked them out one by one. By her senior year, she was dying her hair every other month, touching up the roots as needed.

Today, a few bold young adults might be brave enough to flaunt this difference. But in the suburbs of 1969, teenage girls felt uncomfortable if they so much as wore the wrong color of nail polish. Imagine having green hair.

I listened as Anna explained what her life had been like, but I couldn't respond. What could I say? I was shocked. I don't care if my cousin has green hair or purple toes or three ears. But I couldn't believe that we had known each other and loved each other for so many years and she had never told me. Not even a hint.

Anna caught me indulging in a little long-distance sniffle and she bristled. "Why are you crying? Is it so awful? It's just the way I am.

I'm used to it. How dare you feel sorry for me? I knew I shouldn't have told you."

Now it was my turn to be angry. "You're used to it because you've known about it for 25 years. I've known for a minute and a half," I said struggling to put my feelings into words, wishing we could talk face to face . . . wishing I could give her a hug or a punch in the nose. "Anna, I'm not upset because you have green hair, for heaven's sake. I'm upset because you've had to live with it all this time and you never felt you could tell me about it."

Wherever we lived, Anna was the sister I never had. We have had long (expensive) telephone heart-to-hearts about religion, finances, men, parents, music . . . I thought we could tell each other anything. Geez! I had told her about my recurring nightmare of playing doubles tennis with Pavarotti. It hurt deeply that she had not trusted me with the truth.

"C'mon, Mol," she insisted. "You must have guessed."

I swear I had no idea. Anna's hair was always a slightly different shade whenever I'd see her. I had often told her I thought the dye would ruin her hair. When we were younger, I thought she was trying to look more like our favorite rock and roll singer. When we hit 35, I thought she was trying to look less like her mother.

"Have you told your mother?" I asked.

"I'd like to," Anna said. "I'm afraid she might freak and blame herself for eating too much spinach when she was pregnant or letting us swim in that scummy pond. But I do want her to know. It's been a stupid secret for too long."

We were pretty deep into the conversation by now, so I had to ask, "Are you thinking of letting it grow out?"

There wouldn't be much support for it. Some of her friends would quietly and politely start ignoring her. Her boss might not be so quiet or polite about his reaction.

"Maybe it's a secret best kept," she said, "but I want to be who I am."

When she stopped, I stepped in with emotions at full boil. "You know I love you no matter what. All those years you were trying to deal with it and keep people from finding out. It must have been exhausting. I just wish I could have been there for you."

"In many ways you were," she said. "Just knowing that helped. I don't know what to do about Mom. Maybe I'll just keep coloring my hair when I go home." Another deep sigh. "At least now I have someone to talk to about it."

This conversation did take place, though Anna does not have green hair; she is gay.

Sometime you, too, will learn that someone you care about is homosexual. Maybe a son or daughter, niece or nephew or grandchild. Or the child of a close friend or neighbor. She, or he, may feel little or no support from community, friends, employer or church.

Like Anna, she is trusting you with the truth because she expects to receive the same compassion and unconditional love you've shown throughout other stages of your lives together. Will you still be there?

−The Senior Reporter, August 1994

Homosexuality
Richard C. Friedman, M.D., Jennifer I. Downey, M.D.

The deletion of homosexuality from the *Diagnostic and Statistical Manual* of the American Psychiatric Association in 1980 marked a dramatic reversal of the judgment that homosexuality is a behavioral disorder. In the practice of medicine, especially psychiatry, it is important to distinguish between that which is abnormal and that which is not.[1] Reviewing the present state of knowledge about homosexuality is of interest not only for medical and historical reasons, but also because of the central role of this sexual orientation in the adaptive psychological functioning of countless people.

The studies reviewed here are largely studies of white, middle-class people. Space does not allow for a discussion of cultural and ethnic diversity with regard to sexual orientation.[2]

Definitions

The term *homosexual* entered common usage in 1869.[3] The word *gay*, used to signify "homosexual," took on that meaning over the past 25 years in the context of the gay-rights movement. In common parlance, *gay* refers to males and sometimes to females, whereas *lesbian* is reserved exclusively for females. *Sexual fantasy*, in contrast to *sexual activity*, refers to private psychological imagery associated with feelings that are explicitly erotic or lustful and with physiologic responses of sexual arousal. The term *sexual orientation* refers to a person's potential to respond with sexual excitement to persons of the same sex, the opposite sex, or both. *Ego identity* refers to the sense of connection between a person and a particular social group whose values that person shares. Identity is formed during adolescence and early adulthood from experiences earlier in development.[4] The sense of being gay or lesbian is a facet of ego identity.[5] It may be entirely private, or it may be communicated to others, in which case it becomes part of one's social role.

Sexual Behavior

About half a century ago, Kinsey et al. collected sexual histories from thousands of Americans who, though diverse, were not a representative sample of the general population.[6,7] Kinsey reported that 8 percent of men and 4 percent of women were exclusively homosexual for a period of at least three years during adulthood. Four percent of men and 2 percent of women were exclusively homosexual after adolescence. Thirty-seven percent of men and 20 percent of women reported at least one homosexual experience that resulted in orgasm.[6,7]

Subsequent studies of subjects more representative of the general population have yielded lower estimates of homosexual behavior.[8,9] Fay et al. compared data obtained from national surveys of male sexual behavior carried out in 1970 and 1988 with the data originally collected by Kinsey. In 1970, according to Fay et al., 20 percent of men had had at least one homosexual experience resulting in orgasm but only 7 percent had had such experiences after the age of 19.[10] Only 3 percent of the adult male population studied had homosexual contacts either occasionally or more often. In both the 1970 and the 1988 studies, the proportion of men with homosexual contact during the preceding year was approximately 2 percent.[10] In a recent review of studies conducted in the United States on sexual behavior, Seidman and Rieder estimated that 2 percent of men are currently exclusively homosexual and that an additional 3 percent are bisexual.[11]

Data on the current prevalence of homosexual behavior among women are scant. In a review of the literature on male and female homosexuality and bisexuality throughout the world, however, Diamond concluded that approximately 6 percent of men and 3 percent of women have engaged in same-sex behavior since adolescence.[12]

Homosexuality may be underreported because of social prejudice. Also, many homosexually arousable women may be included in the population reported as heterosexual, since women may engage in sexual intercourse without sexual arousal. Studies that assess the frequency of intercourse but not sexual fantasy may therefore be misleading in this regard.

By the age of 18 or 19 years, three quarters of American youth, regardless of their sexual orientation, have had sexual relations with another person.[11] Gay males are more likely than heterosexual males to become sexually active at a younger age (12.7 vs. 15.7 years) and to have had multiple sexual partners. The ages at the time of the first sexual experience with another person are closer for lesbians and heterosexual females (15.4 vs. 16.2 years).[13]

Of heterosexually active adults in the general population, about 20 percent of men have had 1 sexual partner during their lives, 55 percent have had up to 20 partners, and about 25 percent have had 20 or more partners.[11] Some older studies conducted before the epidemic of the acquired immunodeficiency syndrome (AIDS) indicated that homosexual men were more likely than heterosexual men to have had a very large number of sexual partners.[14] More recent population-based studies have found this to be relatively uncommon. For instance, Fay et al.[10] found that of men who had homosexual contact after the age of 20, almost all had 20 or fewer homosexual partners in their lifetimes. Of 1450 men in the sample only 2 were reported to have had 100 or more same-sex partners.[10] The inconsistency in the data on the number of sexual partners of homosexual men probably reflects flaws in the sampling techniques of the earlier studies (e.g., recruiting subjects in gay bars) and their completion before the human immunodeficiency virus (HIV) epidemic. The overlap between gay and heterosexual men with respect to the number of partners is considerable, although a small subgroup of gay men have had sex with a great many more partners than almost any heterosexual men. Women have been studied less than men, but the existing data show that lesbians resemble heterosexual women more than gay men in their sexual behavior.[15] For instance, women of any sexual orientation are more likely to view sexual desire as a function of emotional intimacy and to value romantic love and monogamy. Almost all married women are sexually active only with their husbands, and unmarried women are very unlikely to have more than one partner in a given three-month period.[11] Blumstein and Schwartz reported that women in lesbian couples had fewer outside partners than women in heterosexual couples. Lesbian couples generally have less sexual activity than their heterosexual counterparts but report higher levels of intimacy and as much or more satisfaction with the sexual relationship.[16]

A substantial minority of adults in the United States abstain from sex, regardless of sexual orientation. In one study, 13 percent of homosexual and bisexual men reported having no sexual partner in the previous year, and in another, 43 percent of lesbians had been abstinent for a year or more.[17,18] Among unmarried heterosexual adults, women are also more likely to be abstinent than men.[11]

Diverse sexual practices occur in different groups regardless of sexual orientation, although with variable frequency. Thus, recent studies suggest that the majority (over 75 percent) of heterosexual and homosexual adults in the United States engage in oral-genital sex.[9,16] Homosexual couples may do so more frequently, however. Kanouse et al. reported that about 55 percent of homosexual men and 26 percent of heterosexual men and women had engaged in oral sex in the month before the survey.[17,19]

Although anal sex is practiced by 10 percent of heterosexual couples at least occasionally,[11] male homosexual couples engage in it more frequently. A recent study in Los Angeles reported episodes of anal sex in the four weeks before the survey to be six times more frequent among homosexual men than among heterosexual men studied at the same time.[16,17,19]

The high risk of contracting infection with HIV among homosexual men is usually attributed to contact with semen during unprotected receptive anal intercourse or other practices associated with the exchange of body fluids. Efforts to educate gay men in safe-sex practices to prevent HIV infection have been only partially effective in changing behavior.[20] Those who continue to engage in unprotected anal intercourse with multiple partners tend to be younger, to belong to minority groups, to engage in sexual acts more frequently, to use drugs or alcohol in connection with sex, to have psychiatric disorders, and if previously tested for HIV, to be seronegative.[21,22] Such men may have adequate cognitive information about HIV transmission but may entertain a false notion that they personally are "safe" when they engage in high-risk sexual behavior. Lapses in safe-sex precautions by men who ordinarily do practice safe sex are also common—in 45 percent over the previous six months in one study.[23]

A small number of lesbians have been reported to be HIV-positive, almost always as a result of exposure to risk factors other than contact with a partner of the same sex.[24] However, since vaginal secretions and menstrual blood are known to be implicated in female-to-male transmission of the virus, lesbians in relationships with seropositive women or who have multiple partners, including men or women of unknown HIV status, are routinely advised to use safe-sex practices. Nonetheless, no medically tested strategy for women to avoid contact with body fluids of same-sex partners has been developed that adequately addresses the particular issues presented by female anatomy and physiology.

Homosexual males have an increased risk of a variety of sexually transmitted diseases other than HIV infection. These include gonorrhea, syphilis, and human papillomavirus infection, as well as hepatitis B.[25,26] Perianal carcinomas also occur more frequently in this group.[27] Lesbians do not have a higher risk of any sexually transmitted diseases than heterosexual women.[28]

Homophobia

The term *homophobia* was coined in 1967 to signify an irrationally negative attitude toward homosexual people.[29] In the United States, two particularly prominent influences fostering antihomosexual attitudes have been religious fundamentalism and heterosexism, the belief in the moral superiority of institutions and practices associated with heterosexuality.[30]

A widespread tendency to view homosexuality as a stigma and to depict homosexual people in terms of negative stereotypes has only very recently begun to lessen. A majority of respondents to a national poll in 1987 indicated that they would prefer not to work around homosexual people.[31] Studies of homophobic people indicate that they are likely to be authoritarian, conservative, and religious; to have resided in areas where negative attitudes toward homosexuals are viewed as normal; and not to have had personal contact with gay or lesbian people.[32] Most gay and lesbian people have been harassed or threatened because of their sexual orientation, and a sizable minority have been assaulted.[33] Many negative beliefs about homosexual people are similar to those associated with other prejudices, such as racism.[31,34]

In some respects, however, irrationally negative attitudes toward homosexual people are different from other forms of prejudice. For example, a young gay or lesbian person may grow up passing as heterosexual in an environment in which his or her family and friends are all heterosexual and homophobic. A recent national survey of gay men and lesbians revealed that the average time between a person's recognition of his or her own sexual orientation and its disclosure to someone else was more than four years.[35] Many gay and lesbian people never reveal their sexual orientation, even to family members.[35-37]

Antihomosexual attitudes are prominent in many sectors of the American medical community, and numerous physicians find it necessary to hide their sexual orientation from colleagues and patients.

There are no accurate data on the frequency of such "closeting," but it is undoubtedly common.[38] Homophobic attitudes have been reported among physicians, medical students, nurses, social workers, and mental health practitioners.[39-45]

It is likely that many students enter professional schools with anti-homosexual values that go unchallenged during their education. A recent survey of American medical schools, for example, found that on average only 3½ hours were devoted to the topic of homosexuality during the four-year curriculum.[46] This is notable, since there is evidence that experience with gay and lesbian faculty members and participation in educational activities such as small-group discussions may influence students to develop more favorable attitudes toward homosexual people.[47]

AIDS

By December 1993, the number of cases of AIDS diagnosed in adolescents and adults in the United States totaled 355,936. Among the 311,578 men with AIDS, 62 percent had as their primary risk factor sex with other men, whereas only 2 percent contracted AIDS from heterosexual activity. Women accounted for a much smaller number of AIDS cases (44,357). When AIDS in women was related to sexual activity, it was most often associated with heterosexual contact with an HIV-positive man (35 percent of cases).[48]

Like the deadliest epidemics and wars, the AIDS crisis affects all members of society, not just those immediately at risk. Although it is not confined to homosexual men, the epidemic has increased their degree of stigmatization. Lesbians are at no increased risk of AIDS, but they are also stigmatized, because the public often wrongly assumes that all homosexual people are at high risk. Gay patients with AIDS are exposed to antihomosexual bias from employers, social service agencies, insurance carriers, and health care providers. Because of bias and fear of contagion, some persons and organizations may be reluctant to provide entitlements or carry out indicated medical procedures.

Undergoing a serologic test for HIV is often deeply frightening. Despite this, rates of psychiatric symptoms and syndromes have not been shown to be generally increased among HIV-positive patients as compared with those who are HIV-negative. Vulnerable subgroups, however, may have psychiatric symptoms and disorders, triggered by HIV testing or other vicissitudes of HIV infection. HIV itself and the opportunistic infections and cancers associated with it may directly cause a variety of neurologic syndromes (e.g., AIDS encephalopathy) that affect cognition, motivation, social judgment, and mood.[49–51]

Homophobia and the tendency to stigmatize the chronically ill may lead to deleterious social isolation by influencing those in the patient's support system to shun him or her. When internalized, these attitudes may motivate the HIV-positive person to avoid others. That person must decide whom to tell and may again experience conflicts about coming out as a gay person. The nuclear family sometimes first learns that a person was HIV-positive or even that the person was gay when they are notified of his or her death.

Seropositive gay patients are likely to live in a community of the bereaved.[52] In the AIDS epidemic, many people endure serial losses. Those who have lost lovers often try to establish intimate sexual relationships with others while they are still grieving. The new partners may also be seropositive. HIV-positive partners who become involved with each other when both are asymptomatic experience mutual apprehension about when one or both will become ill. An HIV-positive person who has an HIV-negative partner often fears that he or she will infect the partner, and this fear may be reciprocated. The vitality of a sexual relationship can be compromised by the constant vigilance needed to engage in sexual practices that are reasonably safe.

People who die of AIDS are often cared for by their lovers, and the strain placed on intimate and sexual relationships is substantial. Losing the sexual dimension of a partnership may be associated with shame at the loss of bodily functions, attractiveness, and sexual interest. The partner who remains well must sometimes cope with choices regarding celibacy or infidelity in situations in which the sexual activity of the couple is curtailed. There is no specific social niche for lovers, as there is for husbands and wives. For example, there is no English word comparable to "widower" for one who has survived the loss of a same-sex lover.

Many of these issues also pertain to bisexual men, particularly those who present themselves as heterosexual while they are secretly involved with other men. A wife's first awareness that her husband has been homosexually active may come when she learns that he is HIV-positive or has AIDS.

One study showed an increased frequency of completed suicide among homosexual men with AIDS.[53] Studies of suicidality in patients with AIDS and those tested for HIV have not found an increased incidence, however.[49,50] The population at risk for suicide seems to be composed of those whose history and psychiatric status had already increased their risk of suicide before the development if AIDS. The complex topic of rational suicide is beyond the scope of this article.

Helpful medical and psychological interventions for seropositive people and their affected family members and friends include self-help groups, counseling and psychotherapy, and pharmacotherapy. For many, coping with being HIV-positive includes maintaining involvement in life's activities, connectedness to others, and hope.[49-51]

Psychopathologic Issues

Independent studies with diverse designs have failed to find any increased frequency of various forms of psychopathology among homosexual people as compared with heterosexual people.[54] If identifying data on projective tests are deleted, it is impossible to distinguish homosexual from heterosexual people.[55] This finding is compatible with clinical reports that emphasize similarities in psychodynamic motivations despite differences in sexual orientation.[56,57] Studies testing the hypothesis that homosexual people have phobic anxiety about heterosexuality have had negative results.[58] Research on specific disorders, such as sexual abuse of children, has not revealed an increased frequency of homosexual perpetrators.[59] These data, in conjunction with research on the family, have invalidated the once popular idea that castrating mothers and detached or hostile fathers are necessary and sufficient causes of male homosexuality.[60] The origins of sexual orientation appear to be multifactorial and diverse.[57]

Internalized Homophobia. Developmental issues pertaining to sexual orientation are somewhat different in the two sexes. Usually boys follow an orderly sequence in which sexual feelings occur during childhood, followed by masturbation with sexual fantasies during early adolescence, sexual activity with others in mid-to-late adolescence, and a sense of identity as heterosexual, homosexual, or (in rare cases) bisexual during late adolescence or early adulthood.[60] Those who are on a developmental path toward predominant or exclusive homosexuality often feel homosexual attraction during childhood even though they may never have met a homosexual person and do not actually know what homosexuality is. The developmental pathways leading to a homosexual orientation are more varied in girls and women, although in one subgroup the pathway is similar to that described for boys and men.[61]

Gay adults often describe themselves as having felt "different" from other children.[56] The factors leading to a sense of difference are diverse and include both homosexual feelings and cross-gender interests and traits. In boys these tend to be aesthetic and intellectual; in girls, they are athletic. Beginning in childhood, many gay and lesbian people have feelings of shame at being considered deviant, as well as feelings of self-hatred because they identify with those who devalue them.[36,62] Such feelings arise from identification with the aggressor, a mental mechanism experienced by many victims of abuse.

Many gay and lesbian people have had painful childhoods. Perhaps for this reason, lifetime rates of major depression and abuse of or dependence on alcohol and other drugs have been reported to be increased among homosexual men, although their current rates of psychiatric disorders are not.[63,64] The disparity between the current and the past incidence of psychopathology awaits explanation. One hypothesis is that homosexual men ultimately develop effective ways of coping with stressors.

Suicide and Gay Youth. Three psychological postmortem studies conducted in different areas of the United States have not demonstrated an increased frequency of people identified as homosexual among those who committed suicide. On the other hand, some studies of youths who have attempted suicide have revealed a disproportionately high number of homosexual persons.[65-69] In a study of 137 homosexual youths, Remafedi et al. found that 41 had attempted suicide.[70] More than half the attempts were of moderate-to-severe lethality and involved inaccessibility to rescue—variables associated with completed suicide. The literature suggests that conflicts about the disclosure of sexual orientation (coming out) may influence young people to attempt suicide if they are otherwise predisposed. Many of those who attempt suicide have not yet disclosed their sexual orientation to anyone. Some people who have committed suicide and have not been identified as homosexual may have taken their lives because of conflict about a homosexual orientation that had been hidden from others.

Suicide attempts in all young people, regardless of sexual orientation, are associated with a common set of predisposing influences. Among vulnerable gay and lesbian young people, the physician should be particularly sensitive to self-hatred arising in response to homosexual feelings, conflicts about coming out, and homophobia among those in the patient's social support system.[35,36] A dysfunctional family often scapegoats a young person who is identified as unacceptable and attempts to recruit medical authorities to make that person conform to the family's norms.

Alcoholism and Substance Abuse. An increased frequency of alcoholism among lesbians as compared with heterosexual women has been reported in some studies.[63,71] Some researchers have reported a trend toward an increase in alcoholism or problem drinking among homosexual men.[63,72,73] The use of illicit drugs, at least occasionally, has also been reported to be more frequent among homosexual women than among heterosexual women, and a similar trend has been observed among men.[63] Because such data are sparse and studies have been confounded by the inclusion of subjects recruited in gay bars, it is impossible at this time to reach definitive conclusions about the frequencies of alcoholism and substance abuse in relation to sexual orientation.

Normal Development in Homosexuals

By the time of adolescence, some people's erotic feelings and attractions are predominantly or exclusively homosexual. The American Academy of Pediatrics has developed guidelines for physicians treating such patients.[37,74] Ideally, complex developmental processes culminate in positive gay or lesbian identity and self-acceptance.[5] Although gay and lesbian groups are diverse and no single developmental line can summarize developmental issues, pathways leading to durable, loving sexual partnerships are common among lesbians and gay men.[16,75,76]

Confusion about sexual orientation is common during adolescence, however, and most adolescents who participate in homosexual activity or have homosexual feelings do not become gay or lesbian adults. Careful history taking often makes it possible to identify patients with predominant or exclusive homosexual responsivity and to support those who need assistance in establishing a gay identity. These patients must be distinguished from the many others who are confused by concurrent homosexual and heterosexual feelings. Here, the physician can often assist the patient in avoiding the premature foreclosure of homosexual or heterosexual identity until further development has occurred.

A sizable minority of lesbians and gay men are married, or once were,[77,78] and many are parents. Conservative estimates exceed 1 million each for lesbian mothers[79,80] and gay fathers.[80,81] At least 6 million children have gay or lesbian parents.[80,82] The literature on children of

lesbian mothers indicates no adverse effects of a homosexual orientation, as evidenced by psychiatric symptoms, peer relationships, and
overall functioning of the offspring.[79,83–85] The frequency of a homosexual orientation has not been greater in such children than in children of heterosexual mothers. The data on children of gay fathers are
more scant. No evidence has emerged, however, to indicate an adverse effect of sexual orientation on the quality of fathering.[80,86]
Enough information has accumulated to warrant the recommendation that sexual orientation should not in itself be the basis for psychiatric and legal decisions about parenting or planned parenting.

Ever-increasing numbers of homosexual persons and couples are
requesting medical assistance in achieving parenthood through new
reproductive techniques, including the donation of gametes (both egg
and sperm) and the use of gestational surrogates. The data reviewed
above support the judgment that medical decisions about the use of
such techniques should not be based on sexual orientation alone.

Change in Sexual Orientation

Most people who seek to alter their sexual orientation consider
themselves homosexual and wish to become heterosexual. Studies of
changes in sexual orientation have varied in quality, and there are no
adequate long-term outcome data. Many men who view themselves
as homosexual have actually been attracted to women at some time
during their lives. In this group, the homosexual–heterosexual mental balance may sometimes shift during therapy. The meaning attributed to sexual fantasies in determining the sense of identity may also
change, so that the person may come to believe that his or her sexual
orientation has changed. Homosexual fantasies often persist, however,
or recur. Among homosexual men who have never experienced sexual
attraction to women, there is little evidence that permanent replacement of homosexual fantasies by heterosexual ones is possible.[87–93]

The data on women, though extremely sparse, suggest that there
is more variation with respect to the plasticity of sexual fantasies than
with men.[61,94] Many women seem to be able to experience bisexual
fantasies or to participate in bisexual activity without necessarily con-
structing an identity or a social role as bisexual or lesbian. A subgroup has been described, however, whose pattern of psychosexual
development is similar to that of many men. In these women, exclusively homosexual fantasies have been present since childhood, and
their total replacement by heterosexual fantasies is unlikely.[61]

Patients who seek a change in their sexual orientation are diverse with respect to sexual attitudes, values, and psychopathological features. Some are motivated by homophobia, and the wish to change subsides as this is addressed. Others reject their homosexual orientation for other reasons, often religious. Sometimes the incompatibility between sexual desires and personal values cannot be resolved by therapeutic interventions. Those who deliver health care have a continuing role in helping such people preserve self-esteem and avoid anxiety and depression as much as possible.

Psychobiologic Aspects

Genetics. In a recent study using DNA linkage analysis, Hamer et al. concluded that a gene that influences homosexual orientation in males is contained on the X chromosome.[95] Thirty-three of 40 homosexual pairs of siblings were found to be concordant for five markers in the distal region of the X chromosome, and the remaining 7 were discordant at one or more of these loci. Since certain types of families in which homosexuality was aggregated were selectively studied, no inference about the frequency of X-linked male homosexuality in the general population was possible.[95]

Bailey et al. reported increased concordance for homosexuality among male and female monozygotic twins, as compared with dizygotic twins.[96–98] Their data were consistent with results from a number of other studies of sexual orientation in twins[99,100] and of familial aggregation of homosexuality.[95,100,102] One recent study found no difference in rates of concordance for homosexuality between monozygotic and dizygotic male and female twins, but the zygosity and sexual orientation of the co-twin were determined from the index subject's self-report.[103] A genetic influence on homosexual orientation is also suggested by a few cases of identical twins concordant for homosexuality who were separated early in life and reared apart.[99,104]

Sex Hormones and Psychosexual Development. Neither plasma hormone values nor other endocrine tests reliably distinguish groups with regard to sexual orientation.[105–107] Studies of mammalian sexual behavior led to the hypothesis that a prenatal androgen deficit results in male homosexuality and that a prenatal androgen excess results in female homosexuality.

Another reason for hypothesizing that prenatal sex-steroid hormones may influence sexual orientation derives from behavioral antecedents of homosexuality. During the childhood of gay men, aversion to play that involves fighting and rough-and-tumble team sports is common.[60,63,109] The opposite pattern—vigorous tomboyish-ness—is common among girls who later become lesbians. In humans and many other mammals, prenatal sex-steroid hormones influence prepubertal nonsexual behavior, including rough-and-tumble play.[107] This raises the question whether a childhood predilection for or aversion to rough-and-tumble activities could be related to differences in prenatal androgen secretion.

Homosexual men and women report more "cross-gender" behavior (often considered to be nonconformity with sex roles) during childhood than heterosexual men and women.[63,109–112] Most boys with psychiatric disorders of gender identity who have been followed become homosexual as adolescents or adults, although most homosexual adults have not had this syndrome as children.[113-115] No follow-up studies of females have been carried out. However, childhood gender-identity disorder has not been demonstrated to be influenced directly by biologic factors.[116]

Further Implications of Intersex Studies.   Important general principles if psychosexual development have been derived from studies of patients with unusual intersex disorders.[117–119] Although each syndrome is of interest, studies of females with congenital adrenal hyperplasia treated early in life illustrate a point of general relevance. Whereas the evidence for an effect of prenatal androgens on childhood sex-role behavior is robust in these patients and in others exposed to masculinizing hormones during gestation, the evidence for an effect on later-occurring sexual orientation is modest.[107] Although homosexual responsivity develops in more of these patients than in controls, most report exclusively heterosexual behavior as adults.

Brain Differences Associated with Sexual Orientation.   Unreplicated reports have been published of the increased size of the superchiasmatic nucleus of the hypothalamus, decreased size of the third anterior interstitial nucleus, and increased size of the anterior commissure in homosexual men.[120–122] Studies of left- and right-sided dominance[123–126] and of cognitive functioning[127,128] have not been conclusive. Finally, a number of studies indicate that homosexual men tend to be born later in groups of siblings than do heterosexual men. Neither the reason for this nor its importance is yet apparent.[129]

Preliminary evidence suggests that to some extent sexual orientation is influenced by biologic factors, although the intermediate mechanisms remain to be described. Since sex differences in behavior appear to be influenced by prenatal sex hormones, the hypothesis that complex changes in prenatal androgen secretion influence sexual orientation remains viable, although unproved.[106,107,121,122,130]

Some prenatal hormonal events may be under genetic influence, whereas others may occur as a result of environmental factors. An example is prenatal stress, which inhibits the secretion of testosterone, influences the sexual behavior of rats, and may influence sexual orientation in humans (although it has not been proved to do so).[131-134] In some people neither genetic nor prenatal hormonal influences may determine sexual orientation. Diverse lines of psychosexual development could lead to the same behavioral end point with regard to sexual orientation.

Conclusions

Although there has been rapid growth recently in our knowledge about human sexual orientation, fundamental questions remain.[105,135] Enough data have accumulated to warrant the dismissal of incorrect ideas once widely accepted about homosexual people. Many areas of law and public policy are still influenced by views discarded by behavioral scientists.[30,83,136] Thus, homosexual acts are still considered criminal in many states. Decisions about custody, visitation, and adoption are frequently made on the basis of sexual orientation. Homosexual partners are not afforded the same protection as marital partners. In addition, homosexual people receive unequal treatment in the military. There are no data from scientific studies to justify the unequal treatment of homosexual people or their exclusion from any group.

—*The New England Journal of Medicine,* Vol. 331, No. 14

1. Bayer R. Homosexuality and American psychiatry: the politics of diagnosis. New York: Basic Books, 1981.

2. Herdt G. Cross-cultural issues in the development of bisexuality and homosexuality. In: Perry ME, ed. Handbook of sexology. Vol. 7. Childhood and adolescent sexology. Amsterdam: Elsevier, 1990.

3. Money J. Gay, straight, and in-between: the sexology of erotic orientation. New York: Oxford University Press, 1988.

4. The problem of ego identity. In: Erikson EH. Identity and the life cycle: psychological issues. Vol. 1. New York: International Universities Press, 1959: 101–64.

5. Troiden RR. Becoming homosexual: a model of gay identity acquisition. Psychiatry 1979;42:362–73.

6. Kinsey AC, Pomeroy WB, Martin CE. Sexual behavior in the human male. Philadelphia: W.B. Saunders, 1948.

7. Kinsey AC, Pomeroy WB, Martin CE, Gebhard PH. Sexual behavior in the human female. Philadelphia: W.B. Saunders, 1953.

8. Gebhard PH. Incidence of overt homosexuality in the United States and Western Europe: NIMH Task Force on Homosexuality: final report and background papers. Rockville, Md.: National Institute of Mental Health, 1972:22–9.

9. Billy JO, Tanfer K, Grady WR, Klepinger DH. The sexual behavior of men in the United States. Fam Plann Perspect 1993;25:52–60.

10. Fay RE, Turner CF, Klassen AD, Gagnon JH. Prevalence and patterns of same-gender sexual contact among men. Science 1989;243:338–48.

11. Seidman SN, Rieder RO. A review of sexual behavior in the United States. Am J Psychiatry 1994;151:330–41.

12. Diamond M. Homosexuality and bisexuality in different populations. Arch Sex Behav 1993;22:291–310.

13. Rotheram-Borus MJ, Gwadz M. Sexuality among youths at high risk 1993. Child Adolesc Psychiatr Clin North Am 1993;2:415–31.

14. Bell AP, Weinberg MS. Homosexualities: a study of diversity among men and women. New York: Simon & Schuster, 1978.

15. Nichols M. Lesbian relationships: implications for the study of sexuality and gender. In: McWhirter DP, Sanders SA, Reinisch JM, eds. Homosexuality/heterosexuality: concepts of sexual orientation. New York: Oxford University Press, 1990:350–64.

16. Blumstein P, Schwartz P. American couples: money, work, sex. New York: William Morrow, 1983.

17. Kanouse DE, Berry SH, Gorman EM, et al. Response to the AIDS epidemic: a survey of homosexual and bisexual men in Los Angeles County. Santa Monica, Calif.: RAND, 1991.

18. Loulon J. R1566 lesbians and the clinical applications. Women Ther 1988;7(2–3):221–34.

19. Kanouse DE, Berry SH, Gorman EM, et al. AIDS-related knowledge, attitudes, beliefs and behaviors in Los Angeles County. Santa Monica, Calif.: RAND, 1991.

20. Kelly JA, Murphy DA, Roffman RA, et al. Acquired immunodeficiency syndrome/human immunodeficiency virus risk behavior among gay men in small cities: findings of a 16-city national sample. Arch Intern Med 1992;152:2293–7.

21. Rotheram-Borus MJ, Rosario M, Meyer-Bahlburg HFL, Koopman C, Dopkins SC, Davies M. Sexual and substance use acts of gay and bisexual male adolescents in New York City. J Sex Res 1994;31:47–57.

22. Linn LS, Spiegel JS, Mathews WC, Leake B, Lien R, Brooks S. Recent sexual behaviors among homosexual men seeking primary medical care. Arch Intern Med 1989;149:2685–90.

23. Kelly JA, Kalichman SC, Kauth MR, et al. Situational factors associated with AIDS risk behavior lapses and coping strategies used by gay men who successfully avoid lapses. Am J Public Health 1991;81:1335–8.

24. Chu SY, Buehler JW, Fleming PL, Berkelman RL. Epidemiology of reported cases of AIDS in lesbians, United States 1980–89. Am J Public Health 1990;80:1380–1.

25. Handsfield HH, Schwebke J. Trends in sexually transmitted diseases in homosexually active men in King County, Washington, 1980–1990. Sex Transm Dis 1990;17:211–5.

26. Hart G. Factors associated with hepatitis B infection. Int J STD AIDS 1993;4:102–6.

27. Holly EA, Whittemore AS, Aston DA, Ahn DK, Nickoloff BJ, Kristiansen JJ. Anal cancer incidence: genital warts, anal fissure or fistula, hemorrhoids, and smoking. J Natl Cancer Inst 1989;81:1726–31.

28. Edwards A, Thin RN. Sexually transmitted diseases in lesbians. Int J STD AIDS 1990;1:178-81.

29. Weinberg GH. Society and the healthy homosexual. New York: St. Martin's Press, 1972.

30. Greenberg DF. The construction of homosexuality. Chicago: University of Chicago Press, 1988.

31. Herek GM. Stigma, prejudice, and violence against lesbians and gay men. In: Gonsiorek JC, Weinrich JD, eds. Homosexuality: research implications for public policy. Newbury Park, Calif.: Sage, 1991:60–80.

32. *Idem.* Beyond "homophobia": a social psychological perspective on attitudes toward lesbians and gay men. J Homosex 1984;10:1–21.

33. Herek GM, Berrill K, eds. Violence against lesbians and gay men: issues for research, practice and policy. J Interpersonal Violence 1990;5(3).

34. Allport GW. The nature of prejudice. Cambridge, Mass.: Addison-Wesley, 1954.

35. Herdt G, ed. Gay and lesbian youth. New York: Harrington Park Press, 1989.

36. Stein TS. Overview of new developments in understanding homosexuality. Rev Psychiatry 1993;12:9–40.

37. American Academy of Pediatrics Committee on Adolescence: homosexuality and adolescence. Pediatrics 1993;92:631–4.

38. Scheier R. For gays in medicine's closet, a haven. American Medical News. January 13, 1989:29–30.

39. Gartrell N, Kraemer H, Brodie HK. Psychiatrists' attitudes toward female homosexuality. J Nerv Ment Dis 1974;159:141–4.

40. Douglas CJ, Kalman CM, Kalman TP. Homophobia among physicians and nurses: an empirical study. Hosp Community Psychiatry 1985;36:1309–11.

41. Kelly JA, St Lawrence JS, Smith S Jr, Hood HV, Cook DJ. Medical students' attitudes toward AIDS and homosexual patients. J Med Educ 1987;62:549–56.

42. Royse D, Birge B. Homophobia and attitudes towards AIDS patients among medical, nursing, and paramedical students. Psychol Rep 1987;61:867–70.

43. Wisniewski JJ, Toomey BG. Are social workers homophobic? Social Work 1987;32:454–5.

44. Randall CE. Lesbian phobia among BSN educators: a survey. J Nurs Educ 1989;28:302–6.

45. Garnets L, Hancock KA, Cochran SD, Goodchilds J, Peplau LA. Issues in psychotherapy with lesbians and gay men: a survey of psychologists. Am Psychol 1991;46:964–72.

46. Wallick MM, Cambre KM, Townsend MH. How the topic of homosexuality is taught at U.S. medical schools. Acad Med 1992;67:601–3.

47. Stevenson MR. Promoting tolerance for homosexuality: an evaluation of intervention strategies. Sex Res 1988;25:500–11.

48. Centers for Disease Control and Prevention. HIV/AIDS Surveillance Report. December 1993.

49. AIDS and mental health–part I. The Harvard Mental Health Letter. 1994;10(7):1–4.

50. AIDS and mental health–part II. The Harvard Mental Health Letter. 1994;10(8):1–4.

51. King MB. AIDS, HIV, and mental health. Cambridge, England: Cambridge University Press, 1993.

52. Martin JL. Psychological consequences of AIDS-related bereavement among gay men. J Consult Clin Psychol 1988;56:856–62.

53. Marzuk PM, Tierney H, Tardiff K, et al. Increased risk of suicide in persons with AIDS. JAMA 1988;259:1333–7.

54. Gonsiorek JC. The empirical basis for the demise of the illness model of homosexuality. In: Gonsiorek JC, Weinrich JD, eds. Homosexuality: research implications for public policy. Newbury Park, Calif.: Sage, 1991:115–37.

55. Hooker E. The adjustment of the male overt homosexual. J Proj Tech 1957; 21:18–31.

56. Isay RA. Being homosexual: gay men and their development. New York: Farrar, Straus, Giroux, 1989.

57. Friedman RC, Downey J. Psychoanalysis, psychobiology, and homosexuality. J Am Psychoanal Assoc 1993; 41:1159–98.

58. Freund K, Langevin R, Chamberlayne R, Deosoran A, Zajac Y. The phobic theory of male homosexuality. Arch Gen Psychiatry 1974; 31:495–9.

59. Groth AN, Birnbaum HJ. Adult sexual orientation and attraction to underage persons. Arch Sex Behav 1978;7:175–81.

60. Friedman RC. Male homosexuality: a contemporary psychoanalytic perspective. New Haven, Conn.: Yale University Press, 1988.

61. Golden C. Diversity and variability in women's sexual identities. In: Boston Lesbian Psychologies Collective, eds. Lesbian psychologies: explorations and challenges. Urbana: University of Illinois Press, 1987:19–34.

62. Malyon A. Psychotherapeutic implications of internalized homophobia in gay men. J Homosexuality 1982; 17:59–69.

63. Saghir MT, Robins E. Male and female homosexuality: a comprehensive investigation. Baltimore: Williams & Wilkins, 1973.

64. Williams JBW, Rabkin JG, Remien RH, Gorman JM, Ehrhardt AA. Multidisciplinary baseline assessment of homosexual men with and without human immunodeficiency virus infection. II. Standardized clinical assessment of current and lifetime psychopathology. Arch Gen Psychiatry 1991;48:124–30.

65. Robins E. The final months: a study of the lives of 134 persons who committed suicide. New York: Oxford University Press, 1981.

66. Rich CL, Fowler RC, Young D, Blenkush M. San Diego suicide study: comparison of gay to straight males. Suicide Life Threat Behav 1986;16:448–57.

67. Hendin H. Suicide among homosexual youth. Am J Psychiatry 1992;149;1416–7.

68. Prenzlauer S, Drescher J, Winchel R. Suicide among homosexual youth. Am J Psychiatry 1992;149:1416.

69. Shaffer D. Political science. The New Yorker. May 3, 1993:116.

70. Remafedi G, Farrow JA, Deisher RW. Risk factors for attempted suicide in gay and bisexual youth. Pediatrics 1991;87:869–75.

71. Lewis CE, Saghir MT, Robins E. Drinking patterns in homosexual and heterosexual women. J Clin Psychiatry 1982;43:277–9.

72. Lohrenz LJ, Connelly JC, Coyne L, Spare KE. Alcohol problems in several midwestern homosexual communities. J Stud Alcohol 1978;39:1959–63.

73. Pillard RC. Sexual orientation and mental disorder. Psychiatr Ann 1988;18:52–6.

74. Slater BR. Essential issues in working with lesbian and gay male youths. Prof Psychol Res Pract 1988;19:226–35.

75. McWhirter DP, Mattison AM. The male couple: how relationships develop. Englewood Cliffs, N.J.: Prentice-Hall, 1984.

76. Hanley-Hackenbruck P. Working with lesbians in psychotherapy. Rev Psychiatry 1993;12:59–83.

77. Ross MW. The married homosexual man: a psychological study. London: Routledge & Kegan Paul, 1983.

78. Green GD, Bozett FW. Lesbian mothers and gay fathers. In: Gonsiorek JC, Weinrich JD, eds. Homosexuality: research implications for public policy. Newbury Park, Calif.: Sage, 1991:197–214.

79. Gottman JS. Children of gay and lesbian parents. In: Bozett FW, Sussman MB, eds. Homosexuality and family relations. New York: Harrington Park Press, 1990:177–96.

80. Patterson CJ. Children of lesbian and gay parents. Child Dev 1992;63: 1025–42.

81. Bozett FW. Children of gay fathers. In: Bozett FW, ed. Gay and lesbian parents. New York: Praeger, 1987:39–57.

82. Harvard Law Review, eds. Sexual orientation and the law. Cambridge, Mass.: Harvard University Press, 1990.

83. Kirkpatrick M, Smith C, Roy R. Lesbian mothers and their children: a comparative survey. Am J Orthopsychiatry 1981;51:545–51.

84. Golombok S, Spencer A, Rutter M. Children in lesbian and single-parent households: psychosexual and psychiatric appraisal. J Child Psychol Psychiatry 1983;24:551–72.

85. Green R, Mandel JB, Hotvedt ME, Gray J, Smith L. Lesbian mothers and their children: a comparison with solo parent heterosexual mothers and their children. Arch Sex Behav 1986;15:167–84.

86. Miller B. Gay fathers and their children. Fam Coord 1979;28:544–52.

87. Socarides CW. Homosexuality. New York: J. Aronson, 1978.

88. Bieber I, Dain HJ, Dince PR, et al. Homosexuality: a psychoanalytic study. New York: Basic Books, 1962.

89. Liss JL, Welner A. Change in homosexual orientation. Am J Psychother 1 973;27:102–4.

90. Acosta FX. Etiology and treatment of homosexuality: a review. Arch Sex Behav 1975;4:9–29.

91. Pattison EM, Pattison ML. "Ex-gays": religiously mediated change in homosexuals. Am J Psychiatry 1980;137:1553–62.

92. Haldeman DC. Sexual orientation conversion therapy for gay men and lesbians: a scientific examination. In: Gonsiorek JC, Weinrich JD, eds. Homosexuality: research implications for public policy. Newbury Park, Calif.: Sage, 1991:149–61.

93. Nicolosi J. Reparative therapy of male homosexuality. Northvale, N.J.: J. Aronson, 1991.

94. Boston Lesbian Psychologies Collective, eds. Lesbian psychologies: explorations and challenges. Urbana: University of Illinois Press, 1987.

95. Hamer DH, Hu S, Magnuson VL, Hu N, Pattatucci AM. A linkage between DNA markers on the X chromosome and male sexual orientation. Science 1993;261:321–7.

96. Bailey JM, Pillard RC. A genetic study of male sexual orientation. Arch Gen Psychiatry 1991;48:1089–96.

97. Bailey JM, Pillard RC, Neale MC, Agyei Y. Heritable factors influence sexual orientation in women. Arch Gen Psychiatry 1993;50:217–23.

98. Buhrich N, Bailey JM, Martin NG. Sexual orientation, sexual identity, and sex-dimorphic behaviors in male twins. Behav Genet 1991;21:75–96.

99. Whitam FL, Diamond M, Martin J. Homosexual orientation in twins: a report on 61 pairs and three triplet sets. Arch Sex Behav 1993;22:187–206.

100. Kallmann FJ. Heredity in health and mental disorder: principles of psychiatric genetics in the light of comparative twin studies. New York: Norton, 1953.

101. Pillard RC, Poumadere J, Carretta RA. A family study of sexual orientation. Arch Sex Behav 1982;11:511–20.

102. Pillard RC, Weinrich JD. Evidence of familial nature of male homosexuality. Arch Gen Psychiatry 1986;43:808–12.

103. King M, McDonald E. Homosexuals who are twins: a study of 46 pro-bands. Br J Psychiatry 1992;160:407–9.

104. Eckert ED, Bouchard TJ, Bohlen J, Heston LL. Homosexuality in monozygotic twins reared apart. Br J Psychiatry 1986;148:421–5.

105. Gooren L, Fliers E, Courtney K. Biological determinants of sexual orientation. Annu Rev Sex Res 1990;1:175–96.

106. Meyer-Bahlberg HFL. Psychobiologic research on homosexuality. Child Adolesc Psychiatr Clin North Am 1993;2:489–500.

107. Friedman RC, Downey J. Neurobiology and sexual orientation: current relationships. J Neuropsychiatry Clin Neurosci 1993;5:131–53.

108. Phoenix CH, Goy RW, Gerall AA, Young WC. Organizing action of prenatally administered testosterone propionate on the tissues mediating mating behavior in the female guinea pig. Endocrinology 1959;65:369–82.

109. Bell AP, Weinberg MS, Hammersmith SK. Sexual preference, its development in men and women. Bloomington: Indiana University Press, 1981.

110. Zucker KJ, Green R. Psychological and familial aspects of gender identity disorder 1993. Child Adolesc Psychiatr Clin North Am 1993;2:513–43.

111. Whitam FL, Zent M. A cross-cultural assessment of early cross-gender behavior and familial factors in male homosexuality. Arch Sex Behav 1984;13:427–39.

112. Whitam FL, Mathy RM. Childhood cross-gender behavior of homosexual females in Brazil, Peru, the Philippines, and the United States. Arch Sex Behav 1991;20:151–70.

113. Green R. Gender identity in childhood and later sexual orientation: follow-up of 78 males. Am J Psychiatry 1985;142:339–41.

114. Idem. The "sissy boy syndrome" and the development of homosexuality. New Haven, Conn.: Yale University Press, 1987.

115. Bailey JM, Zucker KJ. Childhood sex-typed behavior and sexual orientation: a conceptual analysis and quantitative review. Dev Psychol (in press).

116. Coates S. Gender identity disorder in boys: an integrative model. In: Barron JW, Eagle MN, Wolitzky DL, eds. Interface of psychoanalysis and psychology. Washington, D.C.: American Psychological Association 1992:245–65.

117. Money J, Schwartz M, Lewis VG. Adult erotosexual status and fetal hormonal masculinization and demasculinization: 46,XX congenital virilizing adrenal hyperplasia and 46,XY androgen-insensitivity syndrome compared. Psychoneuro-endocrinology 1984;9:405–14.

118. Money J, Ehrhardt AA. Man and woman, boy and girl. Baltimore: Johns Hopkins University Press, 1972.

119. Meyer-Bahlburg HFL. Gender identity development in intersex patients. In: Sexual and gender identity disorders. Child Adolesc Psychiatr Clin North Am 1993;2:501–12.

120. Swaab DF, Hofman MA. An enlarged suprachiasmatic nucleus in homosexual men. Brain Res 1990;537:141–8.

121. LeVay S. A difference in hypothalamic structure between heterosexual and homosexual men. Science 1991;253:1034–7.

122. Allen LS, Gorski RA. Sexual orientation and the size of the anterior commissure in the human brain. Proc Natl Acad Sci U S A 1992;89:7199–202.

123. Geschwind N, Galaburda AM. Cerebral lateralization: biological mechanisms, associations and pathology. I. A hypothesis and a program for research. Arch Neurol 1985;42:428–59.

124. Idem. Cerebral lateralization: biological mechanisms, associations, and pathology. II. A hypothesis and a program for research. Arch Neurol 1985;42:521–52.

125. McCormick CM, Witelson SF, Kingstone E. Left-handedness in homosexual men and women: neuroendocrine implications. Psychoneuroendocrinology 1990;15:69–76.

126. Rosenstein LD, Bigler ED. No relationship between handedness and sexual preference. Psychol Rep 1987;60:704–6.

127. Sanders G, Ross-Field L. Neuropsychological development of cognitive abilities: a new research strategy and some preliminary evidence for a sexual orientation model. Int J Neurosci 1987;36:1–16.

128. McCormick CM, Witelson SF. A cognitive profile of homosexual men compared to heterosexual men and women. Psychoneuroendocrinology 1991;16:459–73.

129. Blanchard R, Zucker KJ. Reanalysis of Bell, Weinberg, and Hammersmith's data on birth order, sibling sex ratio, and parental age in homosexual men. Am J Psychiatry 1994;151:1375–6.

130. Gorski RA. Sexual differentiation of the endocrine brain and its control. In: Motta M, ed. Brain endocrinology. 2nd ed. New York: Raven Press, 1991:71–104.

131. Ward IL, Reed J. Prenatal stress and prepubertal social rearing conditions interact to determine sexual behavior in male rats. Behav Neurosci 1985;99:301–9.

132. Ward IL. Prenatal stress feminizes and demasculinizes the behavior of males. Science 1972;175:82–4.

133. Ellis L, Peckham W, Ashley Ames M, Burke D. Sexual orientation of human offspring may be altered by severe maternal stress during pregnancy. J Sex Res 1988;25:152–7.

134. Bailey JM, Willerman L, Parks C. A test of the maternal stress theory of human male homosexuality. Arch Sex Behav 1991;20:277–93.

135. Byne W, Parsons B. Human sexual orientation: the biologic theories reappraised. Arch Gen Psychiatry 1993;50:228–39.
136. Gonsiorek JC, Weinrich JD, eds. Homosexuality: research implications for public policy. Newbury Park, Calif.: Sage, 1991.

Science, Homosexuality, and the Church
Sr. Renée Mirkes, Ph.D.

The discussion about what roles nature and nurture play in sexual orientation is a long-standing one. Those interested in identifying the etiology and causes of homosexuality pay close attention to research findings from varied disciplines: psychology, anthropology, sociology, and the medical sciences. Many took special note, then, when neurobiologist Simon LeVay recently reported that his findings support the theory that homosexuality, or at least its predisposition, is rooted in biology (Simon LeVay, "A Difference in Hypothalamic Structure Between Heterosexual and Homosexual Men," *Science,* Vol. 253, pp. 1034–7).

Generally speaking, the principal theories of the root causes of homosexuality—i.e., homosexuality is innate (biologically or genetically determined), or it is acquired as a result, for example, of a faulty childhood gender identification—are frequently associated with their respective ethical evaluations. Those who believe in the former theory, for example, usually conclude that a homosexual orientation and its sexual expression are a good or at least morally neutral sexual option. Those who hold the latter theory sometimes contend that, because homosexual orientation is a psychosexual dysfunction, its genital expression is a moral deviation. In light of these opinions, it is not surprising that, after LeVay's published report, some questioned if and how his hypothesis might impact the Church's moral teaching on homosexuality.

In this article, I would like to critique the speculation that this latest conclusion, if proved definitive, will necessitate a revision in the Church's teaching on homosexuality. To accomplish this objective, I will, first, give a synopsis of the nature and results of LeVay's research, second summarize how the Church describes the theological basis for her pastoral stance toward persons that are homosexual and, third, consider whether and how the former will affect the latter.

Le Vay's Study

At the Salk Institute for Biological Studies in San Diego, LeVay examined postmortem brain tissue from 41 subjects. Nineteen were homosexual men (all died of AIDS-related complications), 16 were presumed heterosexual men (6 died of AIDS; ten died from other causes), and 6 were presumed heterosexual women (1 died of AIDS, 5 died from other causes).

LeVay concentrated his study on the anterior hypothalamus which forms the floor and part of the wall of the third ventricle of the brain and is involved in the regulation of typical sexual behavior. In particular, he analyzed four cell groups in the anterior hypothalamus which are labeled *I*nterstitial *N*uclei of the *A*nterior *H*ypothalamus or INAH 1, 2, 3, and 4 respectively.

In prior research using male and female postmortem brain tissue, two nuclei of the anterior hypothalamus—INAH 2 and 3—were found to be twice the size in the male as in the female subjects. From this, it was conjectured that hypothalamic structure was dimorphic (two distinct forms) in accordance with the sex of the individual.

LeVay, however, had another scientific "hunch" about the meaning of the discovery of hypothalamic dimorphism.

> I tested the idea that one or both of these nuclei exhibit a size dimorphism not with sex, but with sexual orientation. Specifically, I hypothesized that inah 2 or inah 3 is large in individuals sexually oriented toward women (heterosexual men and homosexual women). Because tissue from homosexual women could not be obtained, however, only that part of the hypothesis relating to sexual orientation in men could be tested (*ibid.,* p. 1035).

The preliminary results of his investigation showed that his hunch may be right. One hypothalamic nucleus (INAH 3) was half the size in the homosexual men he examined as compared to its size in the heterosexual male subjects. The other three cell clusters (INAH 1, 2, and 4) showed no difference between the homosexual subjects and the heterosexual subjects. INAH 3 appeared, therefore, to be dimorphic not with sex but with sexual orientation. Consequently, LeVay tentatively concluded that ". . . sexual orientation in humans is amenable to study at the biological level, . . ." (*ibid.,* p. 1036).

LeVay was careful to underscore the inconclusive nature of his findings: "In particular the results do not allow one to decide if the size of INAH 3 in an individual is the cause or consequence of that individual's sexual orientation, or if the size of INAH 3 and sexual orientation covary under the influence of some third, unidentified variable" *(ibid.).*

The Church's Theological Basis for Pastoral Approach

In the *Letter to the Bishops of the Catholic Church on the Pastoral Care of Homosexual Persons* (1986), the Congregation for the Doctrine of the Faith describes not only the appropriate pastoral attitude toward homosexual persons but also elucidates the theological underpinnings for this posture.

In this document, the Church assures its readers that it recognizes and empathizes with the suffering associated with homosexuality. At the same time, however, the Church stresses that this suffering will be ". . . intensified by error and lightened by truth" (*ibid.*, #18). To teach the truth with love, then, is the motto to which anyone in the Church who ministers to homosexual persons should be loyal. But what does such a ministry include?

The first aspect of genuine pastoral care of the homosexual person is teaching the truth about the meaning of human sexuality and marriage. That entails being conversant with the following theological overview.

God created us in His image. He created us sexual beings, male or female, as complementary halves of the whole we call humanity or humanness. The fullness of humanity that is realized in the coming together of male and female is symbolic of the inner unity of God, who is the fullness of Being. That man and woman were meant to complete one another is not only naturally inscribed in the physical design of their bodies but is also Divinely affirmed in the words of the first man in the book of Genesis. "This one, at last, is bone of my bone and flesh of my flesh; . . ." (Gen. 2:23).

Human genital sexuality is a gift that is to be expressed and deepened in a specific context: the "one flesh" of marriage. Only in this context—where a man and woman permanently pledge their faithful love—can the unitive *and* procreative goods of marital love be properly fostered. It follows, then, that the union of male and female in sexual intercourse within marriage is the norm for the fulfillment of human complementariness on the genital plane.

In light of the meaning of human sexuality and marriage, the objective truth about the ethics of homosexuality can then be understood. Genital sexual relations between homosexual persons do not effect the completion of a male and a female; such relations do not take place within the permanent commitment of a heterosexual marriage, and they cannot, therefore, be open to the unitive and procreative goods that are the ends of marital sexual love. Homosexual genital behavior, even in a so-called monogamous relationship, falls outside God's design for the nature and purpose of human sexuality and its rightful expression within marriage.

With the use of reason enlightened by faith, then, the Church draws two principal ethical conclusions about homosexuality. First, the homosexual condition or orientation is *not* a sin (the person is not morally culpable for being in or having this condition). Objectively speaking, however, because the homosexual orientation is ". . . a more or less strong tendency ordered toward an intrinsic moral evil; . . ." (*ibid.*, #13), it is an objective disorder. Second, the living out of this sexual orientation in genital sexual activity is an objective moral evil (*ibid.*, #13). It follows, then, that Catholic pastors who give counsel to homosexuals, while sensitive to the impossibility of judging an individual's personal culpability, must not compromise the Church's objective moral evaluation of homosexual behavior.

Conclusion

Having reviewed LeVay's findings as well as the theological basis of the Church's pastoral ministry to homosexuals, we are ready to answer our final question: How will the former affect the latter?

From the presentation of the doctrinal core of a genuine pastoral stance toward homosexual persons given above, one can see that the Church's evaluation of homosexual orientation and homosexual activity prescinds from a consideration of the etiology of homosexuality. Whether it is acquired or innate does not change the objective moral characteristic of genital homosexual activity. Sexual relations between homosexuals are *intrinsically* disordered acts (i.e., the very nature of the act itself is a destruction or negation of the good that, in God's design, should be realized in sexual activity). An intrinsically disordered act does not become ordered, objectively speaking, because of what may be morally mitigating circumstances.

LeVay's hypothesis, even if definitively proven, does not, therefore, negate a truth of revelation regarding the Divine plan for the meaning and proper use of human sexual powers. Identifying a biological etiology of homosexual orientation will also not obviate the Church's belief following from her understanding of God's plan for human sexuality, that heterosexual orientation is normative. Yet, at the same time, the Church's sincere desire is to greet every homosexual person seeking help with the compassion and truth of Christ.

—Ethics & Medics, June 1992

Homosexuality: Reflection Questions

1. Why did Molly Stein suggest first that her cousin was hiding her real hair color?

2. Explain the final paragraph of "Science, Homosexuality, and the Church."

3. How does the Church's understanding of God's plan for human sexuality make itself evident in Church teaching about homosexuality and genital expressions of sexuality?

4. Do you believe that people choose or are born with their sexual orientation? What do scientists suggest? Are there different ways that the Church ought to minister to gays and lesbians depending on whether they are born with or choose a particular sexual orientation?

5. The Church, like the scientific world, makes a distinction between homosexual orientation and activity. What is the difference and why is it so important?

6. What recent scientific discoveries have shed light on our moral assessment of homosexuality?

7. What is the theological basis of the Church's teaching on homosexuality? Where do these theological principles come from?

8. Read verses 8 and 9 of Psalm 145. How does this understanding of God color the way we treat homosexuals in society and in the Church?

8
Life Together

Luke 10:25-37

[25]Just then a lawyer stood up to test Jesus. "Teacher," he said, "what must I do to inherit eternal life?" [26]He said to him, "What is written in the law? What do you read there?" [27]He answered, "You shall love the Lord your God with all your heart, and with all your soul, and with all your strength, and with all your mind; and your neighbor as yourself." [28]And he said to him, "You have given the right answer; do this, and you will live."

[29]But wanting to justify himself, he asked Jesus, "And who is my neighbor?" [30]Jesus replied, "A man was going down from Jerusalem to Jericho, and fell into the hands of robbers, who stripped him, beat him, and went away, leaving him half dead. [31]Now by chance a priest was going down that road; and when he saw him, he passed by on the other side. [32]So likewise a Levite, when he came to the place and saw him, passed by on the other side. [33]But a Samaritan while traveling came near him; and when he saw him, he was moved with pity. [34]He went to him and bandaged his wounds, having poured oil and wine on them. Then he put him on his own animal, brought him to an inn, and took care of him. [35]The next day he took out two denarii, gave them to the innkeeper, and said, 'Take care of him; and when I come back, I will repay you whatever more you spend.' [36]Which of these three, do you think, was a neighbor to the man who fell into the hands of the robbers?" [37]He said, "The one who showed him mercy." Jesus said to him, "Go and do likewise."

The Tradition of the Church

3. From the beginning, the tradition of the Church—is it perhaps necessary to recall it?—presents us with this privileged witness of a

constant seeking for God, of an undivided love for Christ alone, and of an absolute dedication to the growth of his kingdom. Without this concrete sign there would be a danger that the charity which animates the entire Church would grow cold, that the salvific paradox of the Gospel would be blunted, and that the "salt" of faith would lose its savor in a world undergoing secularization.

From the first centuries, the Holy Spirit has stirred up, side by side with the heroic confession of the martyrs, the wonderful strength of disciples and virgins, of hermits and anchorites. Religious life already existed in germ, and progressively it felt the growing need of developing and of taking on different forms of community or solitary life, in order to respond to the pressing invitation of Christ: "There is no one who has left house, wife, brothers, parents or children for the sake of the kingdom of God who will not be given repayment many times over in this present time, and in the world to come, eternal life."[4]

Who would venture to hold that such a calling today no longer has the same value and vigor? That the Church could do without these exceptional witnesses of the transcendence of the love of Christ? Or that the world without damage to itself could allow these lights to go out? They are lights which announce the kingdom of God with a liberty which knows no obstacles and is daily lived by thousands of sons and daughters of the Church.

[4]Lk. 18:29-30.

—Evangelica testificatio 3

Christianity and The Rise of the Nuclear Family
Robert W. Shaffern

Americans could mind some medieval lessons as they confront the problem of the breakdown of the family in an increasingly secular and relativist society. The evangelization of Europe, which took place from the third to the eleventh centuries A.D., first made possible membership in a nuclear family for all persons and classes of European society. Before their conversion to Christianity, the Romans, Germans and Irish did not even have a word equivalent to the modern English "family." The closest terms in classical Latin, Old German and Old Gaelic referred to households or clans. Whereas family denotes a husband, wife and children bound in a moral economy, households in pagan European societies varied widely.

The emperor Constantine (A.D. 312–37) ended the persecution of Christianity in the Roman Empire and established the Christian church as the most dynamic and powerful institution of late antiquity. Bishops became civil and judicial officials, as well as the pastors of their flocks. At the same time that the Christian church was being incorporated into the government of the Roman Empire, Judeo-Christian precepts concerning the family began to alter radically the structures of households in evangelized areas. In his book *Medieval Households* (1985), the late historian, David Herlihy, presented his research on the transformations of households from late antiquity into the Middle Ages (c. A.D. 300–1500). His work makes clear that Christianity regularized the household through its precepts for marriage, childrearing, sexual mores and family responsibilities, thereby making the nuclear family normative.

A Sacred Union

While pagan Europe recognized many kinds of valid marriage, Christianity permitted men and women to take only one spouse. Although the Romans were monogamous, the nations they governed recognized many different types of marriage. The Romans permitted local customs to continue throughout their empire. Pagan Ireland and Germany were polygynous, that is, men were permitted to take more than one wife, but women were permitted only one husband. Polygyny had two consequences for Irish and German society. First, since only rich men could afford more than one wife, females tended to drift into the households of the wealthy. Poor men were much less likely to find a mate. Without a stake in established society, many single males became members of wandering bands of brigands, much like the gangs of modern American inner cities. These cutthroats, who lived in the forests on the edges of settled areas, destroyed and stole property and abducted and raped women. Even among the lawful members of society, sexual mores were lax in pagan Ireland and Germany. In both societies most people traced their lineage through their female ancestors, and many people did not know their father.

The evangelization of Europe gradually replaced the diversity of the pagan household with the uniformity of the family. One ethic was enjoined upon all people, regardless of wealth, status or sex. With the gradual imposition of monogamy the number of marriageable women increased. More poor men could find mates and raise families. They were given a stake in settled society, and the numbers of wandering outlaws decreased. Christian Ireland and Germany became patrilineal in part because of the fidelity of marriage partners. The modern conception of family—consisting of parents and the children they rear—was a product of Christianity meeting the household. Words synonymous with the modern English "family" came into use.

As the turbulence of the early Middle Ages yielded to the relative calm of the central Middle Ages (c. 1000–1300), matrimony attracted the thoughtful reflection of Christendom's greatest thinkers and pastors. Since the time of St. Augustine (died 430), Christian theologians knew that Scripture itself testified to the holiness of matrimony (Eph. 5:32), although they also believed marriage inferior to the celibate religious life. Twelfth-century sacramental theologians agreed, in their interpretation of St. Paul, that matrimony was a sacrament. Pope Alexander III (1159–89), one of the most important popes of the Middle Ages, said: "While the institution of the other sacraments took place through human beings on this earth of sin and misery and on account of the variety of sins, this sacrament was instituted by the true and living God in the joys of Paradise at the beginning of time" (cited by Jaroslav Pelikan, *The Growth of Medieval Theology, 600–1300* [1980]). According to the sacramental theologian Hugh of St. Victor, marriage might be the most important sacrament because it multiplied the church's members. St. Thomas Aquinas (1224–75) taught that the foundation of marriage and family was the friendship between husband and wife. Indeed, only heretics refused to accept the sanctity of marriage.

Sacramental theologians also argued over what constituted valid marriage. Was consent or consummation or both essential for a valid marriage? If both, then Mary and Joseph were not truly married—something unthinkable to most medieval authors. The enduring tradition of Roman jurisprudence argued that the consent of the man and woman to the union constituted valid marriage. Medieval theologians and lawyers accepted their opinion, but created a new understanding of marriage that had extraordinary social implications. The bond between husband and wife affirmed in Scripture (Gen. 2:24) was closer and more important than any tie to parent, government or parish. The church declared that no one—not parents, feudal lords or even the church itself—could interfere with the right of a man and a woman to marry. When Pope Alexander III proclaimed consent as constituting valid marriage, he effected a sweeping social reform. Twelfth-century aristocratic fathers, like their Roman counterparts, wanted to maintain firm control over their children's marriages to protect or enhance patrimonies. Pope Alexander's decree meant that Christian Europe could never be a complete patriarchy and that fathers lacked arbitrary control over their wives and children. Since the consent of the couple constituted marriage, the bride and groom, not the officer of the church, ministered grace to each other. The aim of marriage was salvation, a far cry from the pagan aim of conception. Every day of their lives husband and wife mediated God's blessing to each other and to their children.

Childrearing

Marriage was, of course, ordained for childrearing. The legal traditions of Rome recognized that the purpose of marriage was to procreate and educate children properly. The purpose of the patrician Roman household was to produce sons who would defend Roman glory and serve as officials after retiring from the military. Fathers and mothers were strong presences in the lives of their children. Boys received education in Latin rhetoric, while girls were taught to administer households. But though Romans affirmed the importance of proper childrearing, a father had rights of life and death over his wife and his children. Although few fathers killed children older than infants, many practiced infanticide. The rich killed their newborns because too many offspring endangered patrimonies, whereas the poor killed newborns out of desperation. The pagan Irish and Germans likewise made use of infanticide and believed, unlike Romans, that benign neglect was also a perfectly suitable form of childraising.

Childrearing and the relationships between family members changed fundamentally during the Christianization of Europe. The Scriptures contained many precepts for the family. Like ancient and medieval Jewish families, the Christian family was an ordered whole, with mutual obligations. The Fourth Commandment ordered children to honor and respect their parents. According to St. Paul (Eph. 5:21-29), the joining of husband and wife in matrimony made of them one flesh (as in Gen. 2:24). Husbands owed to their families capable direction; to their wives they owed the deepest love, "as they love their own bodies." The husband had authority over his wife's body and she over his (1 Cor. 7:4). Fathers should train their children as befits the Lord (Eph. 6:4). The Christian family was not a patriarchal despotism, but evolved into a moral economy in which each member was called to service and grace. As early as 994, Bernard of Anjou wrote of the joy of Christian family life, describing a man who "was distinguished by a most worthy marriage and was fertile in producing children. He expended no little effort in rearing them, taking care of them above all things. For it is the natural bent of all human beings to believe that in [their families] lies the largest part of human happiness."

Secular concerns also influenced the raising of children in the Middle Ages. Families were economic units, and fathers and mothers spent much time teaching children to plow, bake, build or weave for the family's survival in a harsh world.

Sexual Mores

Sexual mores changed along with the evangelization of Europe. St. Paul held men and women to chastity before marriage, and fidelity afterward. Although the Christian Middle Ages were by no means puritanical, the more bizarre sexual practices of the pagan era diminished. The diverse households of pagan Rome, Ireland and Germany meant that many people had multiple sexual partners. The economy and society of the Roman Empire was built upon the backs of chattel slaves, whose bodies were often made to serve the sexual fancies of their masters. Pagan attitudes towards deviance were ambivalent. Incestuous marriages were common among those eager to maintain family properties. Homosexuality and pederasty had few critics in imperial Rome. Christianity, in contrast, insisted that the only licit sexual relationships were between husband and wife who intended to have children.

Of course, sexual immorality survived evangelization, as evidenced in the pages of the medieval literature. Nevertheless, the Christianization of Europe profoundly altered sexual behavior in Europe through the emergence of the family. Sources from the era of Charlemagne (c. 770–850) and his immediate successors reveal that the majority of the great king's subjects lived in nuclear families. In administrative records, the powerful landowners of the time used the *mansus* as the basic unit of record-keeping. The *mansus* was the house and land necessary to support a peasant farmer, his wife and their children. Greater uniformity in sexual practices must have accompanied the alteration and regularization of households. Christian precepts provided the much-disobeyed moral ideal.

The Christian Family

The members of Christian European families, of course, played roles suited to economic conditions and the precepts of the Scriptures. The typical medieval family consisted of a husband who had married at about the age of 30, his wife of 18 and one to three children. A surplus of marriageable women explains the difference in age between the average husband and wife. Children spent more time with their mother, and when mothers died young, widowers often married another young bride. Widowers' remarriage maintained the children's close affiliation to the mother. Fathers, older and more remote, were more likely to die when the children were still young. Widows normally did not remarry.

The structure and marriage ages of medieval families probably explain important themes in medieval devotionalism. Passionate, graphic comparisons to motherhood fill the lives of later medieval saints, and these maternal analogies were rooted in everyday family life, otherwise the saints' lives, which were intended to teach and inspire, would have fallen on deaf ears. Medieval images of the Blessed Virgin Mary, like the Mater Dolorosa and the gracious advocate of the "Salve Regina" and "Memorare," must also have originated in the medieval family. Mary was the blessed intercessor who understood and consoled the sorrows, sufferings and anxieties of men and women. On the other hand, no such devotion to St. Joseph emerged in the Middle Ages. In the 14th century especially, groups of disciples followed women visionaries, whom they called "mother." St. Catherine of Siena often referred in her letters to her "family" of followers.

The spread of Christianity in the early Middle Ages radically altered European households and promoted the stability of the family. Not diversity, but uniformity characterized the medieval Christian household. Christianity held all persons to one ethic, whether rich or poor, male or female, free or servile. The change was gradual and fitful, beginning in the fourth century and maturing around the ninth. Christian teachings altered the legal underpinnings of the household and made normative the form of social organization in which husband, wife and children were responsible to each other for survival, the fulfillment of obligations, mutual love and respect.

—America, May 7, 1994

The Rule of St. Benedict

When Benedict was a young man living in Rome, he was unimpressed by life in the big city and the apparent lack of charity in secular society as he knew it. He withdrew to a cave outside Rome where he lived as a hermit until, as his reputation for being a holy man grew, he was recruited by a group of followers who asked him to lead them in a monastic way of life. He articulated his vision, based on earlier monastic models, in a "rule" which meticulously describes a way of life that makes it possible for a community to seek God with "the help of many brethren." His rule clearly rejects individualism and promotes the common good by encouraging obedience, stability and a "monastic way of life" which includes chastity, simplicity, and humility.

Prologue

[1]Listen carefully, my son, to the master's instructions, and attend to them with the ear of your heart. This is advice from a father who loves you; welcome it, and faithfully put it into practice. [2]The labor of obedience will bring you back to him from whom you had drifted through the sloth of disobedience. [3]This message of mine is for you, then, if you are ready to give up your own will, once and for all, and armed with the strong and noble weapons of obedience to do battle for the true King, Christ the Lord.

[4]First of all, every time you begin a good work, you must pray to him most earnestly to bring it to perfection. [5]In his goodness, he has already counted us as his sons, and therefore we should never grieve him by our evil actions. [6]With his good gifts which are in us, we must obey him at all times that he may never become the angry father who disinherits his sons, [7]nor the dread lord, enraged by our sins, who punishes us forever as worthless servants for refusing to follow him to glory.

[8]Let us get up then, at long last, for the Scriptures rouse us when they say: *It is high time for us to arise from sleep* (Rom 13:11). [9]Let us open our eyes to the light that comes from God, and our ears to the voice from heaven that every day calls out this charge: [10]*If you hear his voice today, do not harden your hearts* (Ps 94[95]:8). [11]And again: *You that have ears to hear, listen to what the Spirit says to the churches* (Rev 2:7). [12]And what does he say? *Come and listen to me, sons; I will teach you the fear of the Lord* (Ps 33[34]:12). [13]*Run while you have the light* of life, *that the darkness of death may not overtake you* (John 12:35).

[14]Seeking his workman in a multitude of people, the Lord calls out to him and lifts his voice again: [15]*Is there anyone here who yearns for life and desires to see good days?* (Ps 33[34]:13). [16]If you hear this and your answer is "I do," God then directs these words to you: [17]If you desire true and eternal life, *keep your tongue free from vicious talk and your lips from all deceit; turn away from evil and do good; let peace be your quest and aim* (Ps

33[34]:14-15). [18]Once you have done this, my *eyes will be upon* you *and my ears will listen* for your *prayers; and even before you ask me, I will say* to you: *Here I am* (Isa 58:9). [19]What, dear brothers, is more delightful than this voice of the Lord calling to us? [20]See how the Lord in his love shows us the way of life. [21]Clothed then with faith and the performance of good works, let us set out on this way, with the Gospel for our guide, that we may deserve to see him *who has called* us *to his kingdom* (1 Thess 2:12).

[22]If we wish to dwell in the tent of this kingdom, we will never arrive unless we run there by doing good deeds. [23]But let us ask the Lord with the Prophet: *Who will dwell in your tent, Lord; who will find rest upon your holy mountain?* (Ps 14[15]:1). [24]After this question, brothers, let us listen well to what the Lord says in reply, for he shows us the way to his tent. [25]*One who walks without blemish,* he says, *and is just in all his dealings;* [26]*who speaks the truth from his heart and has not practiced deceit with his tongue;* [27]*who has not wronged a fellowman in any way, nor listened to slanders against his neighbor* (Ps 14[15]:2-3). [28]He has *foiled* the *evil one,* the devil, at every turn, flinging both him and his promptings far *from the sight* of his heart. While these temptations were still *young, he caught hold of them and dashed them against* Christ (Ps 14[15]:4; 136[137]:9). [29]These people *fear the Lord,* and do not become elated over their good deeds; they judge it is the Lord's power, not their own, that brings about the good in them. [30]*They praise* (Ps 14[15]:4) the Lord working in them, and say with the Prophet: *Not to us, Lord, not to us give the glory, but to your name alone* (Ps 113[115:1]:9). [31]In just this way Paul the Apostle refused to take credit for the power of his preaching. He declared: *By God's grace I am what I am* (1 Cor 15:10). [32]And again he said: *He who boasts should make his boast in the Lord* (2 Cor 10:17). [33]That is why the Lord says in the Gospel: *Whoever hears these words of mine and does them is like a wise man who built his house upon rock;* [34]*the floods came and the winds blew and beat against the house, but it did not fall: it was founded on rock* (Matt 7:24-25).

[35]With this conclusion, the Lord waits for us daily to translate into action, as we should, his holy teachings. [36]Therefore our life span has been lengthened by way of a truce, that we may amend our misdeeds. [37]As the Apostle says: *Do you not know that the patience of God is leading you to repent* (Rom 2:4)? [38]And indeed the Lord assures us in his love: *I do not wish the death of the sinner, but that he turn back to me and live* (Ezek 33:11).

[39]Brothers, now that we have asked the Lord who will dwell in his tent, we have heard the instruction for dwelling in it, but only if we

fulfill the obligations of those who live there. [40]We must, then, prepare our hearts and bodies for the battle of holy obedience to his instructions. [41]What is not possible to us by nature, let us ask the Lord to supply by the help of his grace. [42]If we wish to reach eternal life, even as we avoid the torments of hell, [43]then–while there is still time, while we are in this body and have time to accomplish all these things by the light of life–[44]we must run and do now what will profit us forever.

[45]Therefore we intend to establish a school for the Lord's service. [46]In drawing up its regulations, we hope to set down nothing harsh, nothing burdensome. [47]The good of all concerned, however, may prompt us to a little strictness in order to amend faults and to safeguard love. [48]Do not be daunted immediately by fear and run away from the road that leads to salvation. It is bound to be narrow at the outset. [49]But as we progress in this way of life and in faith, we shall run on the path of God's commandments, our hearts overflowing with the inexpressible delight of love. [50]Never swerving from his instructions, then, but faithfully observing his teaching in the monastery until death, we shall through patience share in the sufferings of Christ that we may deserve also to share in his kingdom. Amen.

Chapter 34: Distribution of Goods According to Need

[1]It is written: *Distribution was made to each one as he had need* (Acts 4:35). [2]By this we do not imply that there should be favoritism–God forbid–but rather consideration for weaknesses. [3]Whoever needs less should thank God and not be distressed, [4]but whoever needs more should feel humble because of his weakness, not self-important because of the kindness shown him. [5]In this way all the members will be at peace. [6]First and foremost, there must be no word or sign of the evil of grumbling, no manifestation of it for any reason at all. [7]If, however, anyone is caught grumbling, let him undergo more severe discipline.

The Lofty Side of Marriage
Molly K. Stein, William C. Graham

Editor's note: *Notice how the meaning and purposes of marriage are celebrated in the wedding blessing through which the reader is led in the following chapter, "The Lofty Side of Marriage" from* The Catholic Wedding Book.

Then read "The Retreat," a short story by Bobbie Ann Mason. Does Georgeann and Shelby's marriage reflect or celebrate the virtues that ought to belong to marriage?

Is Shelby's ministry, "which is not a full-time calling," a hindrance to what he and they had hoped to become? Notice that Shelby suggests that "The church isn't for just a conversation." Why is it significant that he "prepared a special sermon aimed at Hoyt Jenkins"?

Why has Georgeann "been feeling disoriented"? Shelby later asks, "What's gotten into you lately, girl?" Trace the development of Georgeann's dis-ease.

As the story concludes, Georgeann feels that she has done her duty. What is that duty?

Catholics seem to have a rather solemn view of marriage. This is reflected in the Church's use of phrases like irrevocable bond, permanent commitment, total fidelity, unbreakable oneness and holy mystery when speaking of the marriage relationship. Some may be confused about what all this really means. Beyond all the Church laws governing marriage, there ought to be an appreciation of the Church's high regard for the vocation of marriage.

If you and your beloved, or other interested parties, are looking for a short and sweet pronouncement on the Catholic theology of marriage, you need only to spend a few minutes studying the nuptial blessing. All liturgical prayers and blessings are statements about the beliefs and hopes of individuals as well as the universal Church.

What you see printed for the Church to pray is what the Church believes.

"Let us pray to the Lord for Betty and Gary . . ."

The priest begins with words so familiar that sometimes the formula fails to register, but this introduction is a significant part of the blessing. An invitation to the congregation is a reminder that marriage is not just a private event. Until this point, you might think that your feelings for each other have been a romantic secret. Now your relationship takes on a public significance that goes beyond wearing wedding rings and signing "Mr. and Mrs." in the hotel guest book. The special gift which married people enjoy becomes a sign of God's love to his people.

". . . who come to God's altar at the beginning of their married life so that they may always be united in love for each other."

Not only is your declaration of love and commitment made before Mom, Dad, Aunt Ruth, Cousin Phil and countless other members of the Gregoria and Sosser families, it is made before God. Your vows are both public and sacred. Makes you stop and think about it a little bit, doesn't it!

"Father, to reveal the plan of your love . . ."

God, who does not use the awesome power of his love lightly or without purpose, provides within marriage a means of sharing his love. As you wonder whether you really need a wedding ceremony and a marriage license to demonstrate your love commitment, it might seem as though marriage was instituted by a shrewd entrepreneur who decided to package some of this love floating around and market it to florists, dressmakers, caterers and divorce lawyers. The Christian belief is that marriage is a gift from God who is the source of all love. As Christians you have made the joint decision not only to accept this gift, but also to cherish and nurture it all the days of your lives.

". . . you made the union of husband and wife an image of the covenant between you and your people."

When God makes promises to his people, he doesn't fool around. A covenant is not merely a contract with an option to renew after three years. God, who remains faithful no matter how often his people fail him, asks you to remain faithful to each other in good times and in bad. Because married love is a sign of God's undying love, you promise permanence as well as love to one another.

"In the fulfillment of this sacrament, the marriage of a Christian man and woman is a sign of the marriage of Christ and the Church."

All sacraments are outward expressions of God's love. Marriage remains a sacrament not just on your wedding day but on every day of your married life. As Christ ministers to his people through the Church, you constantly minister to one another and become witnesses of God's love through the sacrament of matrimony.

It is especially appropriate to note that you are the ministers of the sacrament on the wedding day with the priest as a witness. After the wedding, you will minister the sacrament daily in your new vocation as husband and wife.

And what a fun and challenging ministry it can be. The fulfillment of the sacrament begins with the exchange of vows and continues as you argue over wallpaper patterns, make love while the kids are watching cartoons, plan your dream vacation, volunteer at the food shelf together, comfort and encourage each other in times of sadness, celebrate together in times of joy, and forgive each other again and again, building and strengthening your friendship day after day.

"Lord, grant that as they begin to live this sacrament they may share with each other the gifts of your love and become one in heart and mind as witnesses to your presence in their marriage."

You will not always feel the presence of God in your marriage. At times you will feel as though the First Federal Savings and Loan has more of a presence in your marriage than God does. Occasionally God will seem temporarily out of town as you struggle to live with a teething two year old, a half-remodeled kitchen or an elderly relative.

As Christian people, you come to the altar of God to ask his blessing on your marriage. You are reminded by the Church to turn constantly toward God so that his love may be reflected in your sacrament.

"Help them create a home together and give them children to be formed by the gospel and to have a place in your family."

Many people hear this line and pounce. "Aha! That's all the Church *really* cares about! Babies! Those celibate men in Rome can't wait till she starts turning out potential parishioners."

The Church recognizes that marriage has its own dignity for the partners while they are husband and wife as well as when they become mom and dad. The careful wording of this part of the blessing indicates that, though the other purposes of marriage are not to be considered less important, children are also gifts from God to parents who become co-creators with him.

God relies on the cooperative love of a man and a woman to enlarge his family. And he trusts that your vow of permanent love will ensure a stable, loving environment for your family, when it includes just the two of you and when it grows to include children.

"Give your blessings to Betty, your daughter, so that she may be a good wife and mother, caring for the home, faithful in love for her husband, generous and kind."

The nuptial blessing used to be called the bride's blessing and it ended here. Through this, the Church seemed to teach that the bride had a long hard road ahead of her and she was going to need all the help she could get.

This part of the blessing recalls the bride's baptism, and her own considerable dignity as a daughter of God. It also lists prominent examples of the virtues of the holy women whose praises are sung in the Scriptures.

"Give your blessing to Gary, your son, so that he may be a faithful husband and a good father."

Does the groom get cheated here? After petitioning for blessings on the bride, is the Church asking God a bit less for the guy standing next to her? Maybe the people writing the prayer figured it's hard enough just being a faithful husband and good father. And in twentieth-century America, they may be right. But it also seems to be taken for granted that a faithful husband will also be generous and kind and care for the home.

"Father, grant that as they come together to your table on earth, so they may one day have the joy of sharing your feast in heaven."

Sacraments give the grace and strength needed for the journey until God's people are united with him in heaven. This is one of the strongest statements of faith you can make as individuals and as a couple. The delight you find in one another is but a brief taste and promise of what waits for you at the banquet in the new and heavenly Jerusalem.

These blessings are not bestowed on you by the Church; rather the Church joins with your friends and family in asking God to grant these many blessings. And, as do all faithful Christians, ". . . **we ask this through Christ our Lord. Amen."**

The Retreat   *Bobbie Ann Mason*

Georgeann has put off packing for the annual church retreat. "There's plenty of time," she tells Shelby when he bugs her about it. "I can't do things that far ahead."

"Don't you want to go?" he asks her one evening. "You used to love to go."

"I wish they'd do something different just once. Something besides pray and yak at each other." Georgeann is basting facings on a child's choir robe, and she looks at him testily as she bites off a thread.

Shelby says, "You've been looking peaked lately. I believe you've got low blood."

"There's nothing wrong with me."

"I think you better get a checkup before we go. Call Dr. Armstrong in the morning."

When Georgeann married Shelby Pickett, her mother warned her about the disadvantages of marrying a preacher. Reformed juvenile delinquents are always the worst kind of preachers, her mother said— just like former drug addicts in their zealousness. Shelby was never that bad, though. In high school, when Georgeann first knew him, he was on probation for stealing four cases of Sun-Drop Cola and a ham from Kroger's. There was something charismatic about him even then, although he frightened her at first with his gloomy countenance—a sort of James Dean brooding—and his tendency to contradict whatever the teachers said. But she admired the way he argued so smoothly and professionally in debate class. He always had a smart answer that left his opponent speechless. He was the type of person who could get away with anything. Georgeann thought he seemed a little dangerous—he was always staring people down, as though he held a deep grudge—but when she started going out with him, at the end of her senior year, she was surprised to discover how serious he was. He had spent a month studying the life of Winston Churchill. It wasn't even a class assignment. No one she knew would have thought of doing that. When the date of the senior prom approached, Shelby said he couldn't take her because he didn't believe in dancing. Georgeann suspected that he was just embarrassed and shy. On a Friday night, when her parents were away at the movies, she put on a Kinks album and tried to get him to loosen up, to get in shape for the prom. It was then that he told her of his ambition to be a preacher. Georgeann was so moved by his sense of atonement and his commitment to the calling—he had received the call while hauling hay for an uncle—that she knew she would marry him. On the night of the prom, they went instead to the Burger King, and he showed her the literature on the seminary while she ate a Double Whopper and french fries.

The ministry is not a full-time calling, Georgeann discovered. The pay is too low. While Shelby attended seminary, he also went to night school to learn a trade, and Georgeann supported him by working at Kroger's–the same one her husband had robbed. Georgeann had wanted to go to college, but they were never able to afford for her to go.

Now they have two children, Tamara and Jason. During the week, Shelby is an electrician, working out of his van. In ten years of marriage, they have served in three different churches. Shelby dislikes the rotation system and longs for a church he can call his own. He says he wants to grow with a church, so that he knows the people and doesn't have to preach only the funerals of strangers. He wants to perform the marriages of people he knew as children. Shelby lives by many little rules, some of which come out of nowhere. For instance, for years he has rubbed baking soda onto his gums after brushing his teeth, but he cannot remember who taught him to do this, or exactly why. Shelby comes from a broken home, so he wants things to last. But the small country churches in western Kentucky are dying, as people move to town or simply lose interest in the church. The membership at the Grace United Methodist Church is seventy-five, but attendance varies between thirty and seventy. The day it snowed this past winter, only three people came. Shelby was so depressed afterward that he couldn't eat Sunday dinner. He was particularly upset because he had prepared a special sermon aimed at Hoyt Jenkins, who somebody said had begun drinking, but Hoyt did not appear. Shelby had to deliver the sermon anyway, on the evils of alcohol, to old Mr. and Mrs. Elbert Flood and Miss Addie Stone, the president of the WCTU chapter.

"Even the best people need a little reinforcement," Shelby said half-heartedly to Georgeann.

She said, "Why didn't you just save that sermon? You work yourself half to death. With only three people there, you could have just talked to them, like a conversation. You didn't have to waste a big sermon like that."

"The church isn't for just a conversation," said Shelby.

The music was interesting that snowy day. Georgeann plays the piano at church. As she played, she listened to the voices singing– Shelby booming out like Bert Parks; the weak, shaky voices of the Floods; and Miss Stone, with a surprisingly clear and pretty little voice. She sounded like a folk singer. Georgeann wanted to hear more, so she abruptly switched hymns and played "Joy to the World," which she knew the Floods would have trouble with. Miss Stone sang out, high above Shelby's voice. Later, Shelby was annoyed that Georgeann changed the program because he liked the church bulletins that she typed and mimeographed each week for the Sunday service to be an accurate record of what went on that day. Georgeann made corrections in the bulletin and filed it away in Shelby's study. She penciled in a note: "Three people showed up." She even listed their names. Writing this, Georgeann felt peculiar, as though a gear had shifted inside her.

Even then, back in the winter, Shelby had been looking forward to the retreat, talking about it like a little boy anticipating summer camp.

Georgeann has been feeling disoriented. She can't think about the packing for the retreat. She's not finished with the choir robes for Jason and Tamara, who sing in the youth choir. On the Sunday before the retreat, Georgeann realizes that it is communion Sunday and she has forgotten to buy grape juice. She has to race into town at the last minute. It is overpriced at the Kwik-Pik, but that is the only place open on Sunday. Waiting in line, she discovers that she still has hair clips in her hair. As she stands there, she watches two teenage boys— in their everyday jeans and poplin jackets—playing an electronic video game. One boy is pressing buttons, his fingers working rapidly and a look of rapture on his face. The other boy is watching and murmuring "Gah!" Georgeann holds her hand out automatically for the change when the salesgirl rings up the grape juice. She stands by the door a few minutes, watching the boys. The machine makes tom-tom sounds, and blips fly across the TV screen. When she gets to the church, she is so nervous that she sloshes the grape juice while pouring it into the tray of tiny communion glasses. Two of the glasses are missing because she broke them last month while washing them after communion service. She has forgotten to order replacements. Shelby will notice, but she will say that it doesn't matter, because there won't be that many people at church anyway.

"You spilled some," says Tamara.

"You forgot to let us have some," Jason says, taking one of the tiny glasses and holding it out. Tamara takes one of the glasses too. This is something they do every communion Sunday.

"I'm in a hurry," says Georgeann. "This isn't a tea party."

They are still holding the glasses out for her.

"Do you want one too?" Jason asks.

"No. I don't have time."

Both children look disappointed, but they drink the sip of grape juice, and Tamara takes the glasses to wash them.

"Hurry," says Georgeann.

Shelby doesn't mention the missing glasses. But over Sunday dinner, they quarrel about her going to a funeral he has to preach that afternoon. Georgeann insists that she is not going.

"Who is he?" Tamara wants to know.

Shelby says, "No one you know. Hush."

Jason says, "I'll go with you. I like to go to funerals."

"I'm not going," says Georgeann. "They give me nightmares, and I didn't even know the guy."

Shelby glares at her icily for talking like this in front of the children. He agrees to go alone and promises Jason he can go to the next one. Today the children are going to Georgeann's sister's to play with their cousins. "You don't want to disappoint Jeff and Lisa, do you?" Shelby asks Jason.

As he is getting ready to leave, Shelby asks Georgeann, "Is there something about the way I preach funerals that bothers you?"

"No. Your preaching's fine. I like the weddings. And the piano and everything. But just count me out when it comes to funerals." Georgeann suddenly bangs a skillet in the sink. "Why do I have to tell you that ten times a year?"

They quarrel infrequently, but after they do, Georgeann always does something spiteful. Today, while Shelby and the kids are away, she cleans out the henhouse. It gives her pleasure to put on her jeans and shovel manure in a cart. She wheels it to the garden, not caring who sees. People drive by and she waves. There's the preacher's wife cleaning out her henhouse on Sunday, they are probably saying. Georgeann puts down new straw in the henhouse and gathers the eggs. She sees a hen looking droopy in a corner. "Perk up," she says. "You look like you've got low blood." After she finishes with the chore, she sits down to read the Sunday papers, feeling relieved that she is alone and can relax. She gets very sleepy, but in a few minutes she has to get up and change clothes. She is getting itchy under the waistband, probably from chicken mites.

She turns the radio on and finds a country music station.

When Shelby comes in, with the children, she is asleep on the couch. They tiptoe around her and she pretends to sleep on. "Sunday is a day of rest," Shelby is saying to the children. "For everybody but preachers, that is." Shelby turns off the radio.

"Not for me," says Jason. "That's my day to play catch with Jeff."

When Georgeann gets up, Shelby gives her a hug, one of his proper Sunday embraces. She apologizes for not going with him. "How was the funeral?"

"The usual. You don't really want to know, do you?"

"No."

Georgeann plans for the retreat. She makes a doctor's appointment for Wednesday. She takes Shelby's suits to the cleaners. She visits some shut-ins she neglected to see on Sunday. She arranges with her mother to keep Tamara and Jason. Although her mother still believes Georgeann married unwisely, she now promotes the sanctity of the union. "Marriage is forever, but a preacher's marriage is longer than that," she says.

Today, Georgeann's mother sounds as though she is making excuses for Shelby. She knows very well that Georgeann is unhappy, but she says, "I never gave him much credit at first, but Lord knows he's ambitious. I'll say that for him. And practical. He knew he had to learn a trade so he could support himself in his dedication to the church."

"You make him sound like a junkie supporting a habit."

Georgeann's mother laughs uproariously. "It's the same thing! The same thing." She is a stout, good-looking woman who loves to drink at parties. She and Shelby have never had much to say to each other, and Georgeann gets very sad whenever she realizes how her mother treats her marriage like a joke. It isn't fair.

When Georgeann feeds the chickens, she notices the sick hen is unable to get up on its feet. Its comb is turning black. She picks it up and sets it in the henhouse. She puts some mash in a Crisco can and sets it in front of the chicken. It pecks indifferently at the mash. Georgeann goes to the house and finds a margarine tub and fills it with water. There is nothing to do for a sick chicken, except to let it die. Or kill it to keep disease from spreading to the others. She won't tell Shelby the chicken is sick, because Shelby will get the ax and chop its head off. Shelby isn't being cruel. He believes in the necessities of things.

Shelby will have a substitute in church next Sunday, while he is at the retreat, but he has his sermon ready for the following Sunday. On Tuesday evening, Georgeann types it for him. He writes in longhand on yellow legal pads, the way Nixon wrote his memoirs, and after ten years Georgeann has finally mastered his corkscrew handwriting.

The sermon is on sex education in the schools. When Georgeann comes to a word she doesn't know, she goes downstairs.

"There's no such word as pucelage," she says to Shelby, who is at the kitchen table, trying to fix a gun-shaped hair dryer. Parts are scattered all over the table.

"Sure there is," he says. "Pucelage means virginity."

"Why didn't you say so! Nobody will know what it means."

"But it's just the word I want."

"And what about this word in the next paragraph? Maturescent? Are you kidding?"

"Now don't start in on how I'm making fun of you because you haven't been to college," Shelby says.

Georgeann doesn't answer. She goes back to the study and continues typing. Something pinches her on the stomach. She raises her blouse and scratches a bite. She sees a tiny brown speck scurrying across her flesh. Fascinated, she catches it by moistening a fingertip. It drowns in her saliva. She puts it on a scrap of yellow legal paper and folds it up. Something to show the doctor. Maybe the doctor will let her look at it under a microscope.

The next day, Georgeann goes to the doctor, taking the speck with her. "I started getting these bites after I cleaned out the henhouse," she tells the nurse. "And I've been handling a sick chicken."

The nurse scrapes the speck onto a slide and instructs Georgeann to get undressed and put on a paper robe so that it opens in the back. Georgeann piles her clothes in a corner behind a curtain and pulls on the paper robe. As she waits, she twists and stretches a corner of the robe, but the paper is tough, like the "quicker picker-upper" paper towel she has seen in TV ads. When the doctor bursts in, Georgeann gets a whiff of strong cologne.

The doctor says, "I'm afraid we can't continue with the examination until we treat you for that critter you brought in." He looks alarmed.

"I was cleaning out the henhouse," Georgeann explains. "I figured it was a chicken mite."

"What you have is a body louse. I don't know how you got it, but we'll have to treat it completely before we can look at you further."

"Do they carry diseases?"

"This *is* a disease," the doctor says. "What I want you to do is take off that paper gown and wad it up very tightly into a ball and put it in the wastebasket. Whatever you do, don't shake it! When you get dressed, I'll tell you what to do next."

Later, after prescribing a treatment, the doctor lets her look at the louse through the microscope. It looks like a bloated tick from a dog; it is lying on its back and its legs are flung around crazily.

"I just brought it in for fun," Georgeann says. "I had no idea."

At the library, she looks up lice in a medical book. There are three kinds, and to her relief she has the kind that won't get in the hair. The book says that body lice are common only in alcoholics and indigent elderly persons who rarely change their clothes. Georgeann cannot imagine how she got lice. When she goes to the drugstore to get her prescription filled, a woman brushes close to her, and Georgeann sends out a silent message: I have lice. She is enjoying this.

"I've got lice," she announces when Shelby gets home. "I have to take a fifteen-minute hot shower and put this cream on all over, and then I have to wash all the clothes and curtains and everything—and what's more, the same goes for you and Tamara and Jason. You're incubating them, the doctor said. They're in the bed covers and the mattresses and the rugs. Everywhere." Georgeann makes creepy crawling motions with her fingers.

The pain on Shelby's face registers with her after a moment. "What about the retreat?" he asks.

"I don't know if I'll have time to get all this done first."

"This sounds fishy to me. Where would you get lice?"

Georgeann shrugs. "He asked me if I'd been to a motel room lately. I probably got them from one of those shut-ins. Old Mrs. Speed maybe. That filthy old horsehair chair of hers."

Shelby looks really depressed, but Georgeann continues brightly, "I thought sure it was chicken mites because I'd been cleaning out the henhouse. But he let me look at it in the microscope and he said it was a body louse."

"Those doctors don't know everything," Shelby says. "Why don't you call a vet? I bet that doctor you went to wouldn't know a chicken mite if it crawled up his leg."

"He said it was lice."

"I've been itching ever since you brought this up."

"Don't worry. Why don't we just get you ready for the retreat—clean clothes and hot shower—and then I'll stay here and get the rest of us fumigated?"

"You don't really want to go to the retreat, do you?"

Georgeann doesn't answer. She gets busy in the kitchen. She makes a pork roast for supper, with fried apples and mashed potatoes. For dessert, she makes Jell-O and peaches with Dream Whip. She is really hungry. While she peels potatoes, she sings a song to herself. She doesn't know the name of it, but it has a haunting melody. It is either a song her mother used to sing to her or a jingle from a TV ad.

They decide not to tell Tamara and Jason that the family has lice. Tamara was inspected for head lice once at school, but there is no reason to make a show of this, Shelby tells Georgeann. He gets the children to take long baths by telling them it's a ritual cleansing, something like baptism. That night in bed, after long showers, Georgeann and Shelby don't touch each other. Shelby lies flat with his hands behind his head, looking at the ceiling. He talks about the value of spiritual renewal. He wants Georgeann to finish washing all the clothes so that she can go to the retreat. He says, "Every person needs to stop once in a while and take a look at what's around him. Even preaching wears thin."

"Your preaching's up-to-date," says Georgeann. "You're more up-to-date than a lot of those old-timey preachers who haven't even been to seminary." Georgeann is aware that she sounds too perky.

"You know what's going to happen, don't you? This little church is falling off so bad they're probably going to close it down and reassign me to Deep Springs."

"Well, you've been expecting that for a long time, haven't you?"

"It's awful," Shelby says. "These people depend on this church. They don't want to travel all the way to Deep Springs. Besides, everybody wants their own home church." He reaches across Georgeann and turns out the light.

The next day, after Shelby finishes wiring a house, he consults with a veterinarian about chicken mites. When he comes home, he tells Georgeann that in the veterinarian's opinion, the brown speck was a chicken mite. "The vet just laughed at that doctor," Shelby says. "He said the mites would leave of their own accord. They're looking for chickens, not people."

"Should I wash all these clothes or not? I'm half finished."

"I don't itch anymore, do you?"

Shelby has brought home a can of roost paint, a chemical to kill chicken mites. Georgeann takes the roost paint to the henhouse and applies it to the roosts. It smells like fumes from a paper mill and almost makes her gag. When she finishes, she gathers eggs, and then sees that the sick hen has flopped outside again and can't get up on her feet. Georgeann carries the chicken into the henhouse and sets her down by the food. She examines the chicken's feathers. Suddenly she notices that the chicken is covered with moving specks. Georgeann backs out of the henhouse and looks at her hands in the sunlight. The specks are swarming all over her hands. She watches them head up her arms, spinning crazily, disappearing on her.

The retreat is at a lodge at Kentucky Lake. In the mornings, a hundred people eat a country ham breakfast on picnic tables, out of doors by the lake. The dew is still on the grass. Now and then a speedboat races by, drowning out conversation. Georgeann wears a badge with her name on it and BACK TO BASICS, the theme of the gathering, in Gothic lettering. After the first day, Shelby's spirit seems renewed. He talks and laughs with old acquaintances, and during social hour, he seems cheerful and relaxed. At the workshops and lectures, he takes notes like mad on his yellow legal paper, which he carries on a clipboard. He already has fifty ideas for new sermons, he tells Georgeann happily. He looks handsome in his clean suit. She has begun to see him as someone remote, like a meter reader. Georgeann thinks: He is not the same person who once stole a ham.

On the second day, she skips silent prayers after breakfast and stays in the room watching Phil Donahue. Donahue is interviewing parents of murdered children; the parents have organized to support each other in their grief. There is an organization for everything, Georgeann realizes. When Shelby comes in before the noon meal, she is asleep and the farm market report is blaring from the TV. As she wakes up, he turns off the TV. Shelby is a kind and good man, she says to herself. He still thinks she has low blood. He wants to bring her food on a tray, but Georgeann refuses.

"I'm alive," she says. "There's a workshop this afternoon I want to go to. On marriage. Do you want to go to that one?"

"No, I can't make that one," says Shelby, consulting his schedule. "I have to attend The Changing Role of the Country Pastor."

"It will probably be just women," says Georgeann. "You wouldn't enjoy it." When he looks at her oddly, she says, "I mean the one on marriage."

Shelby winks at her. "Take notes for me."

The workshop concerns Christian marriage. A woman leading the workshop describes seven kinds of intimacy, and eleven women volunteer their opinions. Seven of the women present are ministers' wives. Georgeann isn't counting herself. The women talk about marriage enhancement, a term that is used five times.

A fat woman in a pink dress says, "God made man so that he can't resist a woman's adoration. She should treat him as a priceless treasure, for man is the highest form of creation. A man is born of God—and just think, *you* get to live with him."

"That's so exciting I can hardly stand it," says a young woman, giggling, then looking around innocently with an expansive smile.

"Christians are such beautiful people," says the fat woman. "And we have such nice-looking young people. We're not dowdy at all."

"People just get that idea," someone says.

A tall woman with curly hair stands up and says, "The world has become so filled with the false, the artificial—we have gotten so phony that we think the First Lady doesn't have smelly feet. Or the Pope doesn't go to the bathroom."

"Leave the Pope out of this," says the fat woman in pink. "He can't get married." Everyone laughs.

Georgeann stands up and asks a question. "What do you do if the man you're married to—this is just a hypothetical question—say he's the cream of creation and all, and he's sweet as can be, but he turns out to be the wrong one for you? What do you do if you're just simply mismatched?"

Everyone looks at her.

Shelby stays busy with the workshops and lectures, and Georgeann wanders in and out of them, as though she is visiting someone else's dreams. She and Shelby pass each other casually on the path, hurrying along between the lodge and the conference building. They wave hello like friendly acquaintances. In bed she tells him, "Christella Simmons told me I looked like Mindy on *Mork and Mindy.* Do you think I do?"

Shelby laughs. "Don't be silly," he says. When he reaches for her, she turns away.

Georgeann walks by the lake. She watches seagulls flying over the water. It amazes her that seagulls have flown this far inland, as though they were looking for something, the source of all that water. They are above the water, flying away from her. She expects them to return, like hurled boomerangs. The sky changes as she watches, puffy clouds thinning out into threads, a jet contrail intersecting them and spreading, like something melting: an icicle. The sun pops out. Georgeann walks past a family of picnickers. The family is having an argument over who gets to use an inner tube first. The father says threateningly,

"I'm going to get me a switch!" Georgeann feels a stiffening inside her. Instead of letting go, loosening up, relaxing, she is tightening up. But this means she is growing stronger.

Georgeann goes to the basement of the lodge to buy a Coke from a machine, but she finds herself drawn to the electronic games along the wall. She puts a quarter in one of the machines, the Galaxian. She is a Galaxian, with a rocket ship something like the "Enterprise" on *Star Trek*, firing at a convoy of fleeing, multicolored aliens. When her missiles hit them, they make satisfying little bursts of color. Suddenly, as she is firing away, three of them—two red ships and one yellow ship—zoom down the screen and blow up her ship. She loses her three ships one right after the other and the game is over. Georgeann runs upstairs to the desk and gets change for a dollar. She puts another quarter in the machine and begins firing. She likes the sound of the firing and the siren wail of the diving formation. She is beginning to get the hang of it. The hardest thing is controlling the left and right movements of her rocket ship with her left hand as she tries to aim or to dodge the formation. The aliens keep returning and she keeps on firing and firing until she goes through all her quarters.

After supper, Georgeann removes her name badge and escapes to the basement again. Shelby has gone to the evening service, but she told him she had a headache. She has five dollars' worth of quarters, and she loses two of them before she can regain her control. Her game improves and she scores 3,660. The high score of the day, according to the machine, is 28,480. The situation is dangerous and thrilling, but Georgeann feels in control. She isn't running away; she is chasing the aliens. The basement is dim, and some men are playing at the other machines. One of them begins watching her game, making her nervous. When the game ends, he says, "You get eight hundred points when you get those three zonkers, but you have to get the yellow one last or it ain't worth as much."

"You must be an expert," says Georgeann, looking at him skeptically.

"You catch on after a while."

The man says he is a trucker. He wears a yellow billed cap and a denim jacket lined with fleece. He says, "You're good. Get a load of them fingers."

"I play the piano."

"Are you with them church people?"

"Unh-huh."

"You don't look like a church lady."

Georgeann plugs in another quarter. "This could be an expensive habit," she says idly. It has just occurred to her how good-looking the man is. He has curly sideburns that seem to match the fleece inside his jacket.

"I'm into Space Invaders myself," the trucker says. "See, in Galaxians you're attacking from behind. It's a kind of cowardly way to go at things."

"Well, they turn around and get you," says Georgeann. "And they never stop coming. There's always more of them."

The man takes off his cap and tugs at his hair, then puts his cap back on. "I'd ask you out for a beer, but I don't want to get in trouble with the church." He laughs. "Do you want a Coke? I'll buy you a Co-Cola."

Georgeann shakes her head no. She starts the new game. The aliens are flying in formation. She begins the chase. When the game ends—her best yet—she turns to look for the man, but he has left.

Georgeann spends most of the rest of the retreat in the basement, playing Galaxians. She doesn't see the trucker again. Eventually, Shelby finds her in the basement. She has lost track of time, and she has spent all their reserve cash. Shelby is treating her like a mental case. When she tries to explain to him how it feels to play the game, he looks at her indulgently, the way he looks at shut-ins when he takes them baskets of fruit. "You forget everything but who you are," Georgeann tells him. "Your mind leaves your body." Shelby looks depressed.

As they drive home, he says, "What can I do to make you happy?"

Georgeann doesn't answer at first. She's still blasting aliens off a screen in her mind. "I'll tell you when I can get it figured out," she says slowly. "Just let me work on it."

Shelby lets her alone. They drive home in silence. As they turn off the main highway toward the house, she says suddenly, "I was happy when I was playing that game."

"We're not children," says Shelby. "What do you want—toys?"

At home, the grass needs cutting. The brick house looks small and shabby, like something abandoned. In the mailbox, Shelby finds his reassignment letter. He has been switched to the Deep Springs church, sixty miles away. They will probably have to move. Shelby folds up the letter and puts it back in the envelope, then goes to his study. The children are not home yet, and Georgeann wanders around the house, pulling up the shades, looking for things that have changed in her absence. A short while later, she goes to Shelby's study, knocking first. One of his little rules. She says, "I can't go to Deep Springs. I'm not going with you."

Shelby stands up, blocking the light from the windows. "I don't want to move either," he says. "But it's too awful far to commute."

"You don't understand. I don't want to go at all. I want to stay here by myself so I can think straight."

"What's got into you lately, girl? Have you gone crazy?" Shelby draws the blind on the window so the sun doesn't glare in. He says, "You've got me so confused. Here I am in this big crisis and you're not standing by me."

"I don't know how."

Shelby snaps his fingers. "We can go to a counselor."

"I went to that marriage workshop and it was a lot of hooey."

Shelby's face has a pallor, Georgeann notices. He is distractedly thumbing through some papers, his notes from the conference. Georgeann realizes that Shelby is going to compose a sermon directed at her. "We're going to have to pray over this," he says quietly.

"Later," says Georgeann. "I have to go pick up the kids."

Before leaving, she goes to check on the chickens. A neighbor has been feeding them. The sick chicken is still alive, but it doesn't move from a corner under the roost. Its eyelids are half shut, and its comb is dark and crusty. The henhouse still smells of roost paint. Georgeann gathers eggs and takes them to the kitchen. Then, without stopping to reflect, she gets the ax from the shed and returns to the henhouse. She picks up the sick chicken and takes it outside to a stump behind the henhouse. She sets the chicken on the stump and examines its feathers. She doesn't see any mites on it now. Taking the hen by the feet, she lays it on its side, its head pointing away from her. She holds its body down, pressing its wings. The chicken doesn't struggle. When the ax crashes down blindly on its neck, Georgeann feels nothing, only that she has done her duty.

—Shiloh and Other Stories

When People's Concerns Meet Jesus Christ, Church Lives
John Carmody

A recent Sunday Eucharist at my local parish was so bad that it made me rethink the whole business of making a church, forming a Christian community. The young priest, traditional robes over T-shirt and green fatigues, read tonelessly a long sermon on the murder we all carry in our hearts. (Good news for the poor?)

I quit listening when he quoted his own poetry (unpublished doggerel) and turned my attention to the congregation. It was composed largely of affluent families, diverse in their summer stripes and madrases, but uniform in their stoicism. They were simply enduring, God knows how or why. My heart went out to them and my mind turned angry. They deserve much better.

It's easy to make a church and perhaps easier still to botch the job. There is a church, alive and prosperous, wherever two things come together: people's most pressing concerns and Jesus the Christ. When these two things do not come together, there is no church alive and prosperous. There is no worship worthy of the name, no imperative to preach Good News to the poor, to cure the blind and lame, to make justice roll down like a mighty torrent.

The church is not about laws, doctrines, morals or politics. These are secondary, as are rubrics, popes, priests. The church is about life: ours and God's, as focused in Jesus. It is about what terrifies us at 3 in the morning, when we are alone with death, and what delights us at 7 in the morning, when we laugh with our children and friends.

We need only be radically honest with one another about these things and bring them to Christ, to be his church. People who pray together and work together for justice, with passionate faith in Christ, are fruitful branches of his vine. People who do not are not. Practical ecclesiology is as simple, as radical, as easy and as difficult as that.

At the parish Mass that made me angry, no one said anything honest or deep to anyone else. No good news brought the priest's words aglow. The people had no chance to pour out the things swirling in their hearts. They could not weep for a lost job, a lost child, a spouse's walking out or a diagnosis of terminal cancer. There was no space, no forum, for their horror at the evils in Bosnia, South Africa, Guatemala, Los Angeles or Tulsa.

Equally, our liturgy did not invite anyone to confess doubts about God's care or anger at the sexism or racism in either the church or the local community. Finally, we did not invite any exclamations of joy. No one blessed God for the stunning clarity of the blue sky, the gentle grace of the evening breeze, the heart-stopping beauty of the children all around us—their skin more luscious than peaches.

No, at my parish, as at too many of yours, all was formal and formulaic. The astonishing claim of Christianity—that in Christ, God has saved the world definitively—never assaulted us. We got no hint of the first three chapters of Revelation, where the firstborn from the dead and Lord of all blazes like the sun of suns. Rather, all was namby-pamby, bourgeois, tame. We could mutter God's name, for the nth innocuous time, sure that nothing so boring need matter.

Ah, God: If you are boring, we have missed you. Nothing is so real as you, nothing so living. The galaxies do not stretch the width of your thumb. What are we, that you bother to keep making us? Still, by your making, every movement of our spirits toward the light, every turning from evil and ugliness, every persistence in hungering for love brings us out of ourselves, toward your limitless mystery. Then, in the beautiful, broken flesh of Jesus we can see our definition.

Then, if we eat his flesh and drink his blood, we can become deathless as he is. And then, gathering in his name, speaking the truth about what throbs in our hearts and shapes our world, we can be his proper church, his own people, real at last—human beings.

The fault is not with God. Jesus could not be better. We have the churches we have because of our stupidity. O God, incline unto our aid. O Lord, make haste to help us.

—*National Catholic Reporter,* October 1, 1993

Ethnic Snub at Child's Party Hurts 50 Years Later
Robert F. Drinan, S.J.

After a recent college lecture, a woman came up to me and identified herself as the grandchild of Rita Gill, a girl who had lived on the street where I grew up in Massachusetts. She told me Rita died last summer.

After a short chat about the enclave where I spent my childhood, I was amazed to be literally seized by a memory of Rita Gill when I was 10 years old. She invited the kids of the neighborhood to attend a birthday party for her mother. We arrived at the appointed hour and were advised to stay on the front porch because the party was a surprise. Soon it was announced that someone would give us each a card with our name on it and that we should then enter to greet Mrs. Gill.

After two of the children had received their cards and entered, one boy, Tony DiMarzio, said aloud that the name cards were being used to keep him out of the party. He exploded, saying that the Irish ones wanted nothing to do with "his kind"—using an ugly ethnic name.

My card came next, and I entered. Tony was right. He was left on the porch after all the others had received their invitations to enter. When later I saw Tony at school and in church, I thought of bringing up the incident but never did. It was awkward. I tried to think that perhaps there might be a good reason.

But the entire scene kept coming back into my memory and conscience even though it had occurred 60 years ago. I realized what I had been trying to suppress or forget: Rita and possibly her mother arranged to preclude the one Italian child from the party. Tony sensed it immediately.

The anti-Italian bias of my hometown became amazingly vivid to me after Rita's grandchild rekindled the memories. I remember the prejudice of third-generation Irish against the sons of Italian immigrants. They were seldom, if ever, invited to become altar boys. Students of Italian origin were de facto in a caste below the children of the Irish, whose parents had a more elevated position in society. There were ethnic jokes about Italians that I recall with acute embarrassment. There was seldom praise for the ambitions the Italians had for their children, their devotion to the church and the closeness of their family life.

It is easy to say that these differences were mild and inevitable. But 60 years after Rita excluded Tony from her party, I am, to my astonishment, almost "fixated" on the ethnic divisions my community and parish condoned or even caused. I have been wondering whether Tony forgot his rejection as quickly as I did. Or was it one of many rebuffs that formed his attitude to the church and the Irish that dominated the society in which he grew up?

Chatting with Rita's grandchild, I was also assured that the children at the party for Mrs. Gill had remained loyal to their roots and to their religion. They sent their youngsters to Catholic schools and often to Catholic colleges. Their marriages were stable, and their careers were normally successful.

But still, I have been wondering for days whether the bias against Italians was a byproduct of the Catholicism of that era or whether it is something that infects all American life? Clearly the ethnic and racial bias against African-Americans that has pervaded American society has a spillover affect that tends to mitigate or minimize the other ethnic differences that exist in American culture.

I am still surprised that my snapshot revisit to the world of my youth prompted so many reflections about the conduct of Rita and my own acquiescence or acceptance in ethnic prejudice. Conscience is never silent. Was it Shakespeare who said that conscience makes cowards of us all?

Rita's granddaughter reminisced about the neighbors of my childhood. She had followed their destinies and fortunes. But when I asked about the DiMarzio family, she drew a blank. This family of Italian origin is still, I thought, treated with indifference, neglect or worse.

Does Tony still remember the incident on Rita's porch? Does he feel like I do that he should have spoken out and tried to correct conduct that was designed to hurt him just because his parents came from Italy?

I offered Mass for Rita and asked God to forgive whatever sins both of us may have committed on the occasion of the 50th birthday of Rita's mother.

—National Catholic Reporter, October 21, 1994

Old Values Needed to Curb Violence   *Bishop John H. Ricard*

Violence—in our homes, our schools and streets—is destroying the lives, dignity and hopes of millions. It is paralyzing and polarizing our communities and, through our media, poisoning our children. Some teens talk of "if" they grow up, not "when," planning their funerals instead of their futures.

Beyond the violence in our streets is the violence in our hearts. Hostility, intolerance, despair and indifference are at the core of a growing culture of violence that leaves children dead on our streets.

This culture of violence begins with the individual, and we are all part of it. Look at our television screens. Look at how we drive our cars and run our political campaigns. Look at the acts that create a climate in which violence breeds and prospers. Look into the mirror.

It's all around us

Think of the all-too-common abusive language parents use toward their children. Of the expectation in football that they're going to beat up the quarterback. Of the combat video games on children's Christmas lists all across America. Of the "Die Hard" movies and all the other films full of cruelty and violence.

Rather than search for common ground and common good, this year saw a stark militarization of politics—attack ads and bitter partisan combat.

And more than ever, our society is looking to violent measures to solve problems: millions of abortions to address problem pregnancies, euthanasia and assisted suicide to cope with the burdens of illness, more executions to deal with crime.

In the face of so much violence, the Catholic bishops last month issued a statement calling for nothing less than a moral revolution. It must begin with a fundamental respect for human life, a renewed sense of right and wrong and the rejection of vengeance in the face of violence.

A society that destroys its children, abandons its old and relies on vengeance fails fundamental moral tests. How do we teach the young to curb their violence when we embrace it as a solution? Something is fundamentally wrong when children are thrown from windows, driven into lakes, killed in their homes.

Yes, people feel the fear, anger and loss that come with violent crime. But they do not believe traditional answers are adequate. We have to address simultaneously declining family life *and* increasing availability of weapons, the lure of gangs *and* the slavery of addiction, the absence of real opportunity *and* the loss of moral values.

How? People must pay a price for harming others, but we need more than new jails. We need to change hearts as well as policies. The answer is not more violence or vengeance, but a return to fundamental values: respect for life, responsibility and community, a new priority for our children's lives.

We cannot ignore the underlying cultural values that help create the environment where violence grows. Economic, social and moral forces can tear apart communities and hurt young people, not as quickly but just as surely as bullets and knives. New policies cannot substitute for a recovery of the old values of right and wrong, respect and responsibility, love and justice. "Thou shalt not kill, Thou shalt not steal" are more than words to be recited; they are imperatives for the common good.

Together we can change our culture. Family by family, neighborhood by neighborhood, we must take back our communities from the evil and fear that come with so much violence. Personal responsibility and societal responsibility must work hand in hand. To move beyond rhetoric and slogans, the bishops are encouraging participation in programs that build communities, that reach out to young adults and to children.

We must learn again the lesson of Pope Paul VI: "If you want peace, work for justice." The best antidote to violence is hope. People with a stake in society do not destroy communities. It is not only the down and out who must be held accountable, but also the rich and famous.

All Americans were moved by the Chicago child dropped to his death because he wouldn't steal. We must get beyond our fear, indifference and ideological blinders to hear his grandmother's cry at his funeral: "We hope somebody, somewhere, somehow, will do something about the conditions which are causing our children to kill each other."

It is time for all of us to respond to her plea.

—*Daily News,* December 11, 1994

Dorothy Day: A Radical Simplicity   *Jim Forest*

"Who was Brezhnev?" a Russian child of the future asks his grandfather in a contemporary Soviet joke. And he responds, "A minor politician of the Solzhenitsyn and the Sakharov period."

Perhaps the day will come when a child will ask, "Who was Billy Graham? Who was Pope Paul?" And the answer may be, "Minor religious figures of the Dorothy Day period."

Dorothy Day wouldn't approve of the joke, of course. For one thing, she has great appreciation for Pope Paul. For another, she doesn't want to be burdened with admiration. "Don't call me a saint," she fired back at one starry-eyed soul, "I don't want to be dismissed so easily."

Nor would she appreciate being torn from her context, the Catholic Worker movement. For others, that movement is incarnated in her; in her own vision it is nothing more than an awkward but necessary expression of the practical life (and the hard sayings) of Jesus. She would emphasize, without a trace of false modesty, the founding role played by a wandering scholar from France, Peter Maurin. She would talk of all those who have come into the Worker community over its forty-three long years.

And yet her friends and co-workers know, in both love and bruises, the Catholic Worker movement would be a very different thing, if it existed at all, were it not for the volcanic stubbornness of Dorothy Day.

Apart from that religious stubbornness that has become such a signature of the Catholic Worker movement, it is unlikely that contemporary Christianity would be dotted with so many occasions of hope, so many communities dedicated to the works of mercy and of peace, as many lives so closely centered on the simplicity, poverty, and vulnerability of Jesus.

To look at recent history with a biblical consciousness is to see in the Catholic Worker movement, and in Dorothy Day and others who have been its parents and guardians, one of the main vehicles of God's presence in recent history, transforming individual lives and even reviving the conscience of religious institutions. Had there been no Catholic Worker, no Christian body would be quite as respectful of the sacredness of conscience and of life.

Yet the recognition of this is rather new. If Dorothy Day is prominently featured in the latest *Who's Who* and has a full page of four-color presence in *Life's* recent special issue on women, only a few years ago she, with the Catholic Worker movement, was often viewed as a borderline heretic who rightly belonged in the prison cells she so often inhabited. Catholic theologians and bishops (but it could have been Niebuhr or Tillich) denounced the Catholic Worker pacifism—even while grudgingly admiring the Worker's houses of hospitality (which were nothing more than the Worker's witness to that absolute reverence for life which the theologians condemned).

Dorothy was viewed with intense suspicion. After all, as she herself sometimes puts it, "the bottle always smells of the liquor it once held." And Dorothy used to be a communist, if never a docile pupil of party line. She was a militantly radical secular journalist (first jailed in a feminist demonstration in front of Woodrow Wilson's White House). She was the common-law wife of an anarchist—and mother of a daughter out of wedlock. She used to drink into the small hours of the morning with Eugene O'Neill and many other Greenwich Village visionaries who were only too willing to agree with Marx that religion is the opiate of the people. "Convert" though she might be, she would never be cleansed of her absurd and dangerous notions. Why, she calls herself an "anarchist" and recommends books by Kropotkin! In a "Catholic" newspaper!

But there was, in Dorothy, no wolf in sheep's wraps. In 1927, in a conversion process brought on by her pregnancy and the birth of Tamar, she had been slowly drawn to the end of her "long loneliness," intoxicated with an ardor not only for the life taking root within herself, but for that mystery in which all life is rooted. "How can there be no God, when there are all these beautiful things?"

She became, to the scandal of most of her friends, not merely religious, not just Christian, but a Catholic—so often seen as the worst, the most reactionary, the least free, the least tolerant of all the major religious bodies. A *Catholic*.

But for Dorothy Catholicism was something altogether different from what her friends perceived. It was that immense net that had caught, not only scoundrels, but saints beyond counting. It was the church of the Mass: the persistently present Jesus waiting in bread and wine on the altar. A church of respect for those who have died, a church which, in G. K. Chesterton's words, thought of tradition as being "democracy extended through time . . . the universal suffrage of giving the vote to one's ancestors." It was a church in which there was not only the thanksgiving sacrament on the altar, but the healing sacrament of forgiveness in the confessional. It was a church insistent about the demands and discipline of faith. And it was the church of the working masses of the poor. So she saw it. Such was her experience. And she could not resist saying yes to a longing to be in it rather than at its edges.

Yet in December 1932, a freelance journalist watching a "hunger march" parading past heavily armed police into the city of Washington, she was filled with grief that, however spiritually fulfilling the church had become for her, it offered her no adequate vehicle to respond to injustice and suffering. The march she was reporting for a Catholic journal had been inspired and led by Communists, not Christians. She ached with the realization that there were so many "comfortable churchgoers" who gave "little heed to the misery of the needy and the groaning of the poor."

She went from the march route to the crypt of the National Shrine of the Immaculate Conception. It was the feast day for which the Shrine was named. "There I offered up a special prayer, a prayer which came with tears and with anguish, that some way would open for me to use what talent I possessed for my fellow workers, for the poor."

One has to watch out about prayers, particularly those of the heart. There is always the danger they will be answered.

When Dorothy returned from Washington to her New York tenement apartment, Peter Maurin was waiting for her: a rumpled, tramplike man in his fifties who spoke with a thick French accent. He came because, having read her articles, he had decided she alone could start a unique newspaper, to be the voice of a major movement. He wanted to call it *The Catholic Radical*.

Not everyone could stand Peter. He was a better talker than a listener. He had an intense vision of what needed to be done, and he pushed his

ideas with seldom a pause. But Dorothy, though not a bad talker herself, was fascinated. Peter had a plan for a movement that would help
produce a society "in which it is easier for people to be good," and the
vision struck a chord in Dorothy that has never stopped resonating.

By May 1, 1933, the first issue of the paper minted from their
friendship appeared. Its name had evolved into *The Catholic Worker*
and it was distributed first at a communist rally at Union Square.

From the first, the paper stood for certain rather definite programs.
What made the Worker different, however, from numerous publications was that the editors felt it a duty to carry out their own ideas
and not just write about them. Thus, the Catholic Worker's proposal
that every parish have a house of hospitality translated itself into the
Catholic Worker's first house of hospitality: a place of welcome and
sustenance for those who had no food or welcome.

The Catholic Worker advocated communities on the land, and
soon they had such a community. The Worker saw scant hope for a
more human society within the industrial system, whether capitalist
or Marxist in sponsorship—nor did it see cities as having much reason apart from industry. The Worker stood instead for a culture
founded in faith, agriculture and decentralism—the sort of thing
which Gandhi was already saying, half the world away, and E. F.
Schumacher and the ecology movement have said more recently.
While the urban houses of hospitality responded to devastating
needs and sufferings in practical ways, its rural communities were the
seeds of "a new society within the shell of the old."

The editors advocated, but, more significantly, they practiced "voluntary poverty," a way of life resting on the New Testament admonition, "Let the person with two coats give to the one who has none."
When some have nothing, let no one have too much. Nor let anyone
imagine that owning and controlling make life more meaningful or
secure—rather, more hemmed in by fears and less secure. They yield
more days, perhaps, but less love, less sense of dependence on God's
providence, less need for community and human caring.

But the Workers' most dangerous and alarming affirmation was of
nonviolence. They found in Jesus no closet general. He was the one
who not only ordered his disciples to "put away the sword" but who
made himself a victim of the sword—who submitted to the electric
chair of his day, and made it a passage-way to life, a sign of freedom
from bondage to those who would, in the name of law or idolatry to
flags and borders, make murderers of us.

The Catholic Worker's oft-tested pacifism was given its first trial in
the Spanish Civil War. The Worker was one of three Catholic papers
in the U.S. that refused to sanction Franco's war against the Republic.
Nor did the Worker offer its blessing to the Republican side. It published articles decrying the violence of both sides—for which it was
excommunicated from the Catholic Press Association and shorn of
the bundle orders, nearly 100,000 copies in all, which went into
parish newspaper racks.

During World War II, the Korean War, and the Indochina War, it
continued to stand for "peace without victory." Despite a controversy
within the Worker movement in the early 1940s Dorothy's conviction
prevailed that the way of Jesus had nothing to do with "just wars," or
killing of any kind. The Worker would instead continue with "the
works of mercy," a way that answered to hunger, thirst, illness, homelessness, rejection, and grief—and which would add nothing to those
forces (such as war) which create hunger, thirst, illness, homelessness,
rejection, and grief.

Amazingly, the Catholic Worker community lived its dissenting life
in a joyful spirit. "All the way to heaven is heaven," Dorothy would
say over and over, quoting from one of the saints, "because Jesus said,
'I am the way.'" In the Worker's pages one would often find a sentence
of Leon Bloy's, "Joy is the most infallible sign of the presence of God."

The Worker witness has often been marked, however, with sacri-
fices, not only of material comforts, but of freedom. No one has
counted how many in the Catholic Worker movement have gone to
prison for work against war and racism and various other injustices,
but it has been the norm rather than the exception. Dorothy herself
was arrested repeatedly for her unwillingness, in the '50s and early
'60s to join in New York City's annual war game: Citizens were required to obey a siren's wail and hurry into basements and subways—
"shelters," it was advertised, from a potential nuclear blast. (Finally,
as the number of resisters to the war ritual grew, the city gave up the
annual drill.)

The Worker's history is full of such episodes. They all offer evidence to sustain a conviction that this is a witness transcending any
particular religious tradition or non-tradition. The Worker is less a
body of doctrine than a way of life founded in compassion, a compassion so genuine—and thus so practical—that it has kept its adher-
ents in day-to-day community with those most scarred by what
Dorothy calls, in her usual plain speech, "this filthy, rotten system."

The spirit of the Worker is of love, but of a love willing to resist, and of conversation, but conversation ready for action and argument. Yet love, resistance, and action are all in the spirit of conversation—of friends sitting around a table late into the night, drinking tea or coffee and eating stale scavenged bread. Thus I often recall the words in which Dorothy ended her autobiography, *The Long Loneliness:*

> We were just sitting there talking when Peter Maurin came in.
>
> We were just sitting there talking when lines of people began to form, saying, "We need bread." We could not say, "Go, be thou filled." If there were six small loaves and a few fishes, we had to divide them. There was always bread.
>
> We were just sitting there talking and people moved in on us. Let those who can take it, take it. Some moved out and that made room for more. And somehow the walls expanded.
>
> We were just sitting there talking and someone said, "Let's all go live on a farm."
>
> It was as casual as that, I often think. It just came about. It just happened.
>
> I found myself, a barren woman, the joyful mother of children. It is not easy always to be joyful, to keep in mind the duty of delight.
>
> The most significant thing about the Catholic Worker is poverty, some say.
>
> The most significant thing is community, others say. We are not alone anymore.
>
> But the final word is love. At times it has been, in the words of Father Zossima [in *The Brothers Karamazov*], a harsh and dreadful thing, and our very faith in love has been tried through fire.
>
> We cannot love God unless we love each other, and to love we must know each other. We know Him in the breaking of the bread, and we know each other in the breaking of bread, and we are not alone anymore. Heaven is a banquet and life is a banquet, too, even with a crust, where there is companionship.
>
> We have all known the long loneliness and we have learned the only solution is love and that love comes with community.
>
> It all happened while we sat there talking, and it is still going on.
>
> —Reprinted with permission from *Sojourners,*
> 2401 15th Street N.W., Washington, D.C. 20009.

Life Together: Reflection Questions

1. When you think of a "neighbor" who or what comes to mind? Do you agree with Jesus' definition?

2. The first word in Benedict's Rule is "listen." Why do you think listening is so important in community life? What monastic values do you think are important for the entire world?

3. Did you ever think that marriage is simply a private matter, inclusive only of the husband and wife? Is it? What does the Catholic wedding blessing make evident about the theology of marriage? Why would that theology be reflected in liturgical prayer? Why do Stein and Graham suggest that "marriage remains a sacrament not just on your wedding day but on every day of your life"?

4. Comment on the marriage of Georgeann and Shelby Picket in Bobbie Ann Mason's "The Retreat." Why does Georgeann feel that she has done her duty when the ax crashes down blindly on the diseased chicken's neck?

5. What is a proper response to violence in homes and families?

6. Have you experienced ethnic divisions in your neighborhood or town? How did you respond?

7. Bishop Ricard says that hostility, intolerance, despair and indifference are forms of violence in our hearts. Do you agree or disagree?

8. Why do teenagers often feel unwilling to confide in adults?

9. The Worker movement often used Leon Bloy's comment that "Joy is the most infallible sign of the presence of God." How does this sentence embody the philosophy of the Catholic Worker Movement? Do you agree or disagree?

9
Peace and Justice

1 Corinthians 12:12-31

¹²For just as the body is one and has many members, and all the members of the body, though many, are one body, so it is with Christ. ¹³For in the one Spirit we were all baptized into one body—Jews or Greeks, slaves or free—and we were all made to drink of one Spirit.

¹⁴Indeed, the body does not consist of one member but of many. ¹⁵If the foot would say, "Because I am not a hand, I do not belong to the body," that would not make it any less a part of the body. ¹⁶And if the ear would say, "Because I am not an eye, I do not belong to the body," that would not make it any less a part of the body. ¹⁷If the whole body were an eye, where would the hearing be? If the whole body were hearing, where would the sense of smell be? ¹⁸But as it is, God arranged the members in the body, each one of them, as he chose. ¹⁹If all were a single member, where would the body be? ²⁰As it is, there are many members, yet one body. ²¹The eye cannot say to the hand, "I have no need of you," nor again the head to the feet, "I have no need of you." ²²On the contrary, the members of the body that seem to be weaker are indispensable, ²³and those members of the body that we think less honorable we clothe with greater honor, and our less respectable members are treated with greater respect; ²⁴whereas our more respectable members do not need this. But God has so arranged the body, giving the greater honor to the inferior member, ²⁵that there may be no dissension within the body, but the members may have the same care for one another. ²⁶If one member suffers, all suffer together with it; if one member is honored, all rejoice together with it.

²⁷Now you are the body of Christ and individually members of it. ²⁸And God has appointed in the church first apostles, second prophets, third teachers; then deeds of power, then gifts of healing, forms of assistance, forms of leadership,

various kinds of tongues. [29]Are all apostles? Are all prophets? Are all teachers? Do all work miracles? [30]Do all possess gifts of healing? Do all speak in tongues? Do all interpret? [31]But strive for the greater gifts. And I will show you a still more excellent way.

The Common Good

26. Because of the closer bonds of human interdependence and their spread over the whole world, we are today witnessing a widening of the role of the common good, which is the sum total of social conditions which allow people, either as groups or as individuals, to reach their fulfillment more fully and more easily. The whole human race is consequently involved with regard to the rights and obligations which result. Every group must take into account the needs and legitimate aspirations of every other group, and still more of the human family as a whole.[5]

At the same time, however, there is a growing awareness of the sublime dignity of the human person, who stands above all things and whose rights and duties are universal and inviolable. He ought, therefore, to have ready access to all that is necessary for living a genuinely human life: for example, food, clothing, housing, the right freely to choose his state of life and set up a family, the right to education, work, to his good name, to respect, to proper knowledge, the right to act according to the dictates of conscience and to safeguard his privacy, and rightful freedom even in matters of religion.

The social order and its development must constantly yield to the good of the person, since the order of things must be subordinate to the order of persons and not the other way around, as the Lord suggested when he said that the Sabbath was made for man and not man for the Sabbath.[6] The social order requires constant improvement: it must be founded in truth, built on justice, and enlivened by love: it should grow in freedom towards a more humane equilibrium.[7] If these objectives are to be attained there will first have to be a renewal of attitudes and far-reaching social changes.

The Spirit of God, who, with wondrous providence, directs the course of time and renews the face of the earth, assists at this development. The ferment of the Gospel has aroused and continues to arouse in the hearts of men an unquenchable thirst for human dignity.

[5]Cf. John XXIII, Litt. Encycl. *Mater et Magistra: AAS* 53 (1961), p. 417.
[6]Mk. 2:27.

[7]Cf. John XXIII, Litt. Encycl. *Pacem in Terris: AAS* 55(1963), p. 266.

—Gaudium et spes 26

As kingfishers catch fire, dragonflies draw flame
Gerard Manley Hopkins

As kingfishers catch fire, dragonflies draw flame;
As tumbled over rim in roundy wells
Stones ring; like each tucked string tells, each hung bell's
Bow swung finds tongue to fling out broad its name;
Each mortal thing does one thing and the same:
Deals out that being indoors each one dwells;
Selves—goes itself; *myself* it speaks and spells,
Crying *Whát I dó me: for that I came.*

Í say móre: the just man justices;
Keeps gráce: thát keeps all his goings graces;
Acts in God's eye what in God's eye he is—
Chríst—for Christ plays in ten thousand places,
Lovely in limbs, and lovely in eyes not his
To the Father through the features of men's faces.

Sheen Sham

Liberal activist Martin Sheen is getting a big kick out of his latest acting gig. In a *Murphy Brown* guest appearance to air this month on CBS, he'll play a former radical novelist from the '60s who disappeared for 25 years, only to reemerge as an ultraconservative. "Some of my lines are *very* conservative," says Sheen. "I have a little trepidation as I'm memorizing them. But having me, a known radical, saying these horrible things is where the joke is." Sheen, who has been arrested on several occasions for acting on his political beliefs, says that his character's views will never become his own. "When I was a young man, I fought very hard to maintain my liberal position. Now, as a middle-aged man, I fight very hard to *further* my liberal position. One time a guy asked me if I was a communist. I said, 'I'm far worse: I am a Catholic.'"

–Reprinted with permission from *TV Guide® Magazine* (September 4–10, 1993). Copyright © 1994 by News America Publications Inc.

Why Good Works Are So Good for You   *Laura M. Grimes*

I spent two years of my adult life in full-time social service work. The first was as a live-in minister of hospitality at a Catholic Worker house and the second as a counselor and supervisor of volunteers at a prolife, crisis pregnancy center. Those years were wonderful *and* terrible: exhausting, intense, and exhilarating. At the end of the second year I had changed and grown tremendously. Yet I had also become convinced that direct justice ministry was not my calling. I have returned to graduate school in theology while trying to incorporate my experiences into my studies. And my husband, Matt, and I now struggle to maintain a personal and financial commitment to the poor and to those who serve them more immediately.

I suspect that the frustration Matt and I face is shared by other middle-class Christians. Many of us do not feel called to full-time or permanent social-justice work. We have other gifts and vocations, financial strains, and family responsibilities. It is easy to feel a paralyzing guilt when contemplating our own relative security and the apparent hopelessness of the world's problems. And if we can fit volunteer work into our schedules, it may seem like a Band-Aid solution.

Yet scripture and tradition constantly call us to the necessity of performing the corporal and spiritual works of mercy. The challenge of the prophets and the strong words of Jesus about wealth and poverty cannot be evaded, nor can the example of countless saintly persons, from Dorcas and Stephen to Dorothy Day and Oscar Romero. They have been powerful instruments of God's compassion for those who suffer.

The special charism of the Catholic Worker movement is to bring together people of all classes in an authentic experience of community. I lived in a large wooden house that could shelter several families in addition to a few staff members. We lived in close quarters and had to share chores and work on communication. We couldn't take as many people as the larger shelter, so we were grateful that they were open as well. But the special gift we offered our guests was building real relationships with them. I developed strong friendships with some guests and special bonds with the children, who often needed extra love and attention.

The other staff members and I had to be very clear about enforcing house rules and confronting unacceptable behavior. We respected our guests enough to have high expectations of them. But we also had to be ready to accept confrontation ourselves and to admit our mistakes. I asked forgiveness of a guest more than once for a sharp remark or an unfair decision. Part of what we tried to model and to work on ourselves was healthy communication—rare in people of any income level.

I learned a lot about my own weaknesses from living at the Catholic Worker. I came face to face with my desire to control people and repeatedly had to let go of that illusion. It was a struggle to maintain a delicate balance between challenging people to healthier behavior while loving them as they were and respecting their freedom. I learned quickly how to say no, set limits, and take time for myself. My prayer and my participation in Eucharist and Reconciliation deepened for sheer survival, gave me strength for what I needed to do, and also helped me realize what was not my responsibility. Dorothy Day often spoke of this combination of diligent work and trusting God for results as an attempt to live the "little way" of St. Thérèse of Lisieux.

Like many of the former staff members, Matt and I have maintained continued involvement as part of the extended community of Holy Family house. Present and former guests and staff gather with other friends of the house. As we eat and pray together, the boundaries between us become blurred. Residents of the house enjoy the dignity of offering hospitality, and former ministers gratefully receive it.

Though I occasionally bake bread and Matt helps with repairs, our most important gift is simply our presence and friendship to those who live at the Worker house. The full-time staff members need a sympathetic ear or a lunch or coffee break out. The guests share their frustrations with unemployment and the humiliating welfare system, and we encourage them in their struggles for a better life against unfair odds.

Most of the guests are single mothers who have not had many good experiences with men. I think it is especially helpful for them to see my husband and the other men in the extended community treat women with respect and children with gentleness. This lets them know that equal, committed relationships between men and women are possible and that they deserve such relationships.

Matt and I often agree that we receive far more from our involvement in the house than we give. The clearest example is the life and death of our daughter, Rachel, who accompanied us to the house each week from the time of her conception. The community welcomed her with delight, throwing a surprise "first birthday party" when she was six days old. The house was the ideal place for the celebration after her Baptism. We were greeted each Thursday by people who competed to hold Rachel—so much that I often spent the evening without touching her except when she needed to nurse.

The children staying in the house loved to amuse her and to help us change her diapers. Rachel was received with complete love and knew the safety of many comforting arms. And since the car accident in which she was killed at 15 months, the community has continued to welcome Matt and me. They have accepted us and grieved with us week after week. Most recently, we had a beautiful prayer service to celebrate what would have been Rachel's second birthday. This generous hospitality has brought new life in the midst of tragedy and helped keep Rachel's memory alive.

There are many elements in a Christian response to the world's suffering: one is the service I've been describing; another is financial sharing with the biblical goal of tithing. We find it's important to educate ourselves about the causes of poverty and hunger and support groups that address the underlying social and political issues. Simplifying our lifestyle can keep us aware of those who lack basic necessities, as well as free our resources to be distributed more justly.

I have found prayer to be a crucial foundation for all these efforts. Deepening my experiences of God's love enables me to discern which forms of service, sharing, and lifestyle changes I am called to and to undertake them freely and peacefully. Seeking inner healing is important for ministering in a healthier way because it provides fewer temptations to control and manipulate people. Finally, faithfulness to our own vocations will naturally open us up to the needs of others. This can be a consolation when work, family responsibilities or financial constraints prevent us from being as involved in justice work as we might like.

My friend Joanne is a writer and the mother of a young daughter. Both of these demanding jobs mean that she is not extensively involved in other forms of direct service at this point in her life. But she is painfully, compassionately aware of God's poor. As she told me, "If I really love my daughter, I love all children. If I love my husband and my friends, I love all men and women, and it breaks my heart to know that they are suffering." Joanne's faithfulness to her closest neighbors has stretched her heart and made her creative and generous in her prayer for and gifts to those in need.

Direct involvement with people who are poor will vary at different times in our lives. But a certain amount is important because it keeps us aware of the reality of poverty and injustice and gives faces to the statistics. When we develop relationships with people, we are more likely to meet their needs in a loving, respectful way. It can also make overwhelming problems seem more approachable and bring us hope and perseverance in working for a transformed society. It can make us cry out to God ever more urgently to show mercy to the oppressed by changing the hearts of their oppressors.

—U.S. Catholic, November 1993

Isaiah 40:3-5

> ³A voice cries out:
> "In the wilderness prepare the way of the LORD,
>   make straight in the desert a highway for our God.
> ⁴Every valley shall be lifted up,
>   and every mountain and hill be made low;
> the uneven ground shall become level,
>   and the rough places a plain.
> ⁵Then the glory of the LORD shall be revealed,
>   and all people shall see it together,
>   for the mouth of the LORD has spoken."

Role of Christians in International Aid

88. Christians should willingly and wholeheartedly support the establishment of an international order that includes a genuine respect for legitimate freedom and friendly sentiments of brotherhood towards all men. It is all the more urgent now that the greater part of the world is in a state of such poverty that it is as if Christ himself were crying out in the mouths of these poor people to the charity of his disciples. Let us not be guilty of the scandal of having some nations, most of whose citizens bear the name of Christians, enjoying an abundance of riches, while others lack the necessities of life and are tortured by hunger, disease, and all kinds of misery. For the spirit of poverty and charity is the glory and witness of the Church of Christ.

We must praise and assist those Christians, especially those young Christians, who volunteer their services to help other men and other peoples. Indeed it is a duty for the whole people of God, under the teaching and example of the bishops, to alleviate the hardships of our times within the limits of its means, giving generously, as was the ancient custom of the Church, not merely out of what is superfluous, but also out of what is necessary.

Without being rigid and altogether uniform in the matter, methods of collection and distribution of aid should be systematically conducted in dioceses, nations, and throughout the world and in collaboration with suitable institutes.

—Gaudium et spes 88

When Fear Moves In   *Molly K. Stein*

Duluth developers have made plans to convert two abandoned grade schools into housing for low-income residents. Concerned citizens in the white, middle-class neighborhoods are predictably upset. The fact that these buildings will now accommodate families that fail to fit the standard profile has pushed us over the edge and onto the editorial page of the local paper.

To be fair, many are still angry over the closing of our schools. Developers are taking over hallways we decorated for Halloween and Winter Carnival; classrooms where our children learned to read; gymnasiums where we held square dances, and cafeterias where we served countless cups of tepid cocoa and warm Kool-Aid.

Beyond the nostalgia, however, we must admit we're having trouble turning the building over to strangers. We perceive *them* as being vastly different from *us*. Those perceived differences are giving us the excuses we need to put up barriers against people we judge harshly, based on our own assumptions.

Those barriers have not often popped up in my life, but I have had glimpses of them that make me wonder how people live with them all the time.

Recently, I was chattering away with the new driver in our family, lecturing him on the need for vigilance along a certain stretch of highway. Sure enough, a state trooper pulled up alongside of us and kept pace with us for a while.

The guy in the brown hat directed his attention to our shaggy sixteen-year-old. When he saw that a mom type was firmly planted at David's side, he pulled off into the sunset confident that God was in his heaven and all was right with I-35. David didn't notice—or care—but I suddenly felt the ache that comes with being judged solely on appearances.

The trooper did not see a mature young adult who rises at 5:30 every morning to deliver papers. He did not assume that this was a driver who always buckles up, always observes curfew and is much more conservative behind the wheel than the prim-looking 40-year-old by his side.

Simply because of his age and gender, David was classified as a potential problem. I was seen as the safe one.

Why are we immediately wary of those whose families don't resemble our own? It seems to me that even those of us who belong to the Donna Reed Society (intact marriages, adequate incomes, no waxy build-up on our kitchen floors) have close friends and relatives whose lives have taken unexpected left-hand turns. Don't we all have a sibling or a cousin or a student who has struggled with abuse or poverty or an unplanned pregnancy? If we are so proud of our Christian, middle-class values, why aren't we eager to model those same qualities for families who need them the most? Is it easier for us to extend ourselves when 16 families lose their loved ones in a plane crash than it is to pull together and offer support to two dozen families trying to live with decency and respect in our midst?

I would hope that those of us who consider ourselves Pro-life will welcome any neighbor in need with generosity and grace. It is one way to demonstrate that we do indeed care about human beings in all stages of life's journey.

—The Catholic Outlook

Peace and Justice: Reflection Questions

1. See the September 4, 1993, *TV Guide® Magazine* article in which Martin Sheen, asked if he was a Communist, answered, "I'm far worse: I'm a Catholic." What do you suppose he meant by his comment to the interviewer? In your answer, make reference to Kingdom of God theology.

2. Some contemporary thinkers feel that social injustice is a more serious problem than any sexual ones. Do you agree or disagree?

3. What does Gerard Manley Hopkins mean in saying that the just man "acts in God's eye what in God's eye he is"?

4. Are good works good for you?

5. What are some of your first hand experiences of social injustice?

6. *Gaudium et spes* says that "social order and its development must constantly yield to the good of the person" and not the other way around. In your opinion, how can this best be accomplished?

7. Listen to a video of Martin Luther King's "I Have a Dream" speech in 1963. Has the United States changed since then? If so, how? Do you see similarities between his speech and the Prophet Isaiah (40:3-5)?

10
Reproduction Issues

Psalm 139:13-16

[13]For it was you who formed my inward parts;
   you knit me together in my mother's womb.
[14]I praise you, for I am fearfully and wonderfully made.
   Wonderful are your works;
  that I know very well.
[15] My frame was not hidden from you,
  when I was being made in secret,
   intricately woven in the depths of the earth.
[16]Your eyes beheld my unformed substance.
  In your book were written
   all the days that were formed for me,
   when none of them as yet existed.

Scientific Research and Moral Criteria

2293 Basic scientific research, as well as applied research, is a significant expression of man's dominion over creation. Science and technology are precious resources when placed at the service of man and promote his integral development for the benefit of all. By themselves however they cannot disclose the meaning of existence and of human progress. Science and technology are ordered to man, from whom they take their origin and development; hence they find in the person and in his moral values both evidence of their purpose and awareness of their limits.

2294 It is an illusion to claim moral neutrality in scientific research and its applications. On the other hand, guiding principles cannot be inferred from simple technical efficiency, or from the usefulness accruing to some at the expense of others or, even worse, from prevailing ideologies. Science and technology by their very nature require unconditional respect for fundamental moral criteria. They must be at the service of the human person, of his inalienable rights, of his true and integral good, in conformity with the plan and the will of God.

—Catechism of the Catholic Church

Genesis 1:26-28

26Then God said, "Let us make humankind in our image, according to our likeness; and let them have dominion over the fish of the sea, and over the birds of the air, and over the cattle, and over all the wild animals of the earth, and over every creeping thing that creeps upon the earth."

27So God created humankind in his image,

in the image of God he created them;

male and female he created them.

28God blessed them, and God said to them, "Be fruitful and multiply, and fill the earth and subdue it; and have dominion over the fish of the sea and over the birds of the air and over every living thing that moves upon the earth."

The Regulation of Births   *Pope Paul VI*

Married Love

9. In the light of these facts the characteristic features and exigencies of married love are clearly indicated, and it is of the highest importance to evaluate them exactly.

This love is above all fully *human,* a compound of sense and spirit. It is not, then, merely a question of natural instinct or emotional drive. It is also, and above all, an act of the free will, whose dynamism ensures that not only does it endure through the joys and sorrows of daily life, but also that it grows, so that husband and wife become in a way one heart and one soul, and together attain their human fulfilment.

Then it is a love which is *total*—that very special form of personal friendship in which husband and wife generously share everything, allowing no unreasonable exceptions or thinking just of their own interests. Whoever really loves his partner loves not only for what he receives, but loves that partner for her own sake, content to be able to enrich the other with the gift of himself.

Again, married love is *faithful* and *exclusive* of all other, and this until death. This is how husband and wife understand it on the day on which, fully aware of what they were doing, they freely vowed themselves to one another in marriage. Though this fidelity of husband and wife sometimes presents difficulties, no one can assert that it is impossible, for it is always honourable and worthy of the highest esteem. The example of so many married persons down through the centuries shows not only that fidelity is conatural to marriage but also that it is the source of profound and enduring happiness.

And finally this love is *creative of life,* for it is not exhausted by the loving interchange of husband and wife, but also contrives to go beyond this to bring new life into being. "Marriage and married love are by their character ordained to the procreation and bringing up of children. Children are the outstanding gift of marriage, and contribute in the highest degree to the parents' welfare."[8]

Responsible Parenthood

10. Married love, therefore, requires of husband and wife the full awareness of their obligations in the matter of responsible parenthood, which today, rightly enough, is much insisted upon, but which, at the same time, should be rightly understood. Hence, this must be studied in the light of the various inter-related arguments which are its justification.

If first we consider it in relation to the biological processes involved, responsible parenthood is to be understood as the knowledge and observance of their specific functions. Human intelligence discovers in the faculty of procreating life, the biological laws which involve human personality.[9]

If, on the other hand, we examine the innate drives and emotions of man, responsible parenthood expresses the domination which reason and will must exert over them.

But if we then attend to relevant physical, economic, psychological and social conditions, those are considered to exercise responsible parenthood who prudently and generously decide to have a large family, or who, for serious reasons and with due respect to the moral law, choose to have no more children for the time being or even for an indeterminate period.

Responsible parenthood, moreover, in the terms in which we use the phrase, retains a further and deeper significance of paramount importance which refers to the objective moral order instituted by

God,–the order of which a right conscience is the true interpreter. As a consequence the commitment to responsible parenthood requires that husband and wife, keeping a right order of priorities, recognize their own duties towards God, themselves, their families and human society.

From this it follows that they are not free to do as they like in the service of transmitting life, on the supposition that it is lawful for them to decide independently of other considerations what is the right course to follow. On the contrary, they are bound to ensure that what they do corresponds to the will of God the Creator. The very nature of marriage and its use makes this clear, while the constant teaching of the Church affirms it.[10]

[8] *Gaudium et spes* 50.
[9] *Summa theologica* I–III, q.4, art.2.
[10] *Gaudium et spes* 50, 51.

–*Humanae vitae* 9, 10

Sex, Natural Law, and Bread Crumbs   *Robert P. Heaney, M.D.*

1994 saw the 25th anniversary of Paul VI's *Humanae vitae* and shortly thereafter, publication of John Paul II's *Veritatis splendor*. Both encyclicals relied heavily on the principles and method of natural law, a topic thrust briefly into U.S. public consciousness at the Clarence Thomas confirmation hearings (though promptly eclipsed there by other issues).

If the language of natural law is not a regular part of American public discourse, it is very much a part of our Roman Catholic self-communication, particularly in the field of moral theology. Vatican II in *Gaudium et spes,* for example, speaks of the *nature* of marriage, using that term repeatedly as it attempts its needed correction of the predominantly juridical view of marriage expressed in the 1917 Code of Canon Law.

Natural law theory was first clearly formulated by the pre-Christian stoic philosophers, and can be traced back to Plato. Its proponents held that humans possess a sufficient spark of the divine reason to be able to discern the nature of things and to judge whether concrete actions support or contradict that nature. Natural law, Cicero argued, should thus be the basis for all positive law. Natural law theory was absorbed by Christianity and given a specifically Christian turn by the scholastic philosophers. In the syllogistic approach the scholastics favored, the major premise might be, for example, "Murder is wrong," and the minor: "This action is murder." Therefore: "This action is wrong." In the practical order it was not always easy to tell whether this particular act was wrong, simply because one could not always be sure it was technically "murder." Much of the discernment process of moral theology, particularly of pastoral theology, has focused on issues relating to the minor premises of the relevant syllogisms. The major premises, basically natural law principles, were seldom if ever in question.

Few people think consciously in such syllogisms today; perhaps few ever did. I call attention to this mode of reasoning because it seems to me that much of moral theology specifically concerning sex in marriage has implicitly, at least, been operating in such a syllogistic mode. Making it explicit may help us analyze the problem we find ourselves in.

The Roman Catholic approach to sex in marriage has generally accepted the major premise that the natural purpose of intercourse is directly generative, indeed, procreative, in a theological sense. Any interference with this purpose is taken as inherently wrong. John Paul II states that we violate the *unitive meaning* of the sexual act whenever we violate the procreative meaning (emphasis mine). Within the Church we have rarely questioned that premise. Instead we have focused mainly on the minor premise, i.e., what constituted interference, what mitigating circumstances might be present, etc. I submit that that may be giving away too much before engaging the debate. Aquinas himself, in further Christianizing the corpus of natural law which he received from Bonaventure and Anselm, specifically altered the major premise of the entire system of the stoics; he asserted that human nature was oriented to God, i.e., that humans were *of their very nature* related to God. While the issue of sex in marriage is less cosmic, I nevertheless suggest that we do something similar: suspend our concentration with minor premise issues and re-examine the major premise concerning the nature and purpose of sex in human affairs.

In what I have read in the commentaries on both *Humanae vitae* and *Veritatis splendor,* I have looked in vain, even from their critics, for mention of considerations that seem evident to me, working as a biomedical scientist, but formed in the classical Roman Catholic tradition, in which I learned natural law theory from first, a Suarezian, and then a Thomistic perspective. I shall attempt to articulate here what, as a biologist, I find missing from the Roman Catholic dialog I read and hear, in the hope that doing so will contribute modestly to understanding of an issue that has divided our church as perhaps no other since the Modernist crisis of a century ago.

Natural law seems uncongenial to many today, in part, I suspect, because we are less certain that reality is knowable, or are at least more aware of the cultural and subjective elements in all knowledge, but also because those who transmit natural law to us are often high-centered on medieval notions of nature. Furthermore, anyone who has pondered the Gospels and the Pauline corpus knows that the Christian ethic transcends law, natural or otherwise. Still there is nothing wrong with natural law or natural law theory, as far as it goes, *so long as one perceives nature aright*. Therein lies what seems to me inadequate about much of the Roman Catholic pronouncement, *pro* and *con*, which I read on the topic of sexual morality.

Our reflections on what is appropriate to the nature of things and actions must arise ultimately out of observation of nature. Aquinas was quite clear that natures were to be inferred from observable phenomena, not deduced from first principles. It seems self-evident, and hardly original, to note that inferences drawn from such observations are necessarily limited by the conceptual and methodological tools we bring to the task. Hence, conclusions based ultimately on such observations must always be tentative, always subject to further nuancing and interpretation, to newer syntheses. To say that something is evil in and of itself is a strong statement, and implies a greater knowledge of the "itselfness" concerned than I suspect we have for most things in our experience. This is not to assert that there are no intrinsically evil acts, nor to assert that circumstances can make an intrinsically evil act good. Rather, I suggest something more fundamental, that our notions about the "nature" of some actions may be in error.

This is particularly crucial to John Paul II's concern to reassert moral absolutes in the prevailing climate of relativism. It is necessary to take the claims of relativism seriously if we are to find the real absolutes. Our notions of the natures of things have changed, not simply because we have lost our bearings or even because our ways of thinking have shifted, but because our observations are better. Despite the naysayers, people are hungry for absolutes—unfortunately, even specious ones. Roman Catholicism, with the papacy as a focus for unity, is the world's only potentially credible voice with which to articulate them. But moral absolutes based ultimately in faulty conceptions of nature are not inherently compelling, only authoritarian.

Much of the best of Catholic discussion of these topics since Vatican II has taken as its focus marriage, and specifically marriage as sacrament. Following *Gaudium et spes,* the ends of marriage are seen today as co-equal, and not subordinated one to the other. Yet implicit even there, and seemingly inadequately examined, is the underlying perception of the nature of sex (as distinct from marriage). I suggest that we have got the major premise about sex in marriage wrong for two reasons. First, our inferences are faulty because they are based on bad biology. Second, our analysis is excessively reductionist in character. The two are so closely related as to be almost inextricably intertwined.

Let me start with some critical contextual considerations for the interpretation of biological observations. There is a truism in biology that there are no new hormones, only new uses for old hormones. In some respects Mother Nature is profligate, in others, parsimonious. When she finds something that works, she uses it over and over in different ways. An example is the hormone we call thyroid (technically, thyroxin). In humans, as in many mammals, it regulates our basal metabolism (the "idle adjust" on our metabolic engines), and is necessary life-long. But exactly the same hormone is produced in other vertebrates as well, although sometimes with a different effect. In amphibians, for example, it appears only briefly in the life cycle, but then it is responsible for turning a tadpole into a frog. At a deep biological level it is possible to discover homologies between the two actions, but at a higher level of organization, the two seem quite distinct.

The principle of new uses for old inventions, articulated for hormones, applies more broadly. Bone is another example. Appearing half a dozen times over the course of vertebrate evolution, it served at least as many purposes—external armor, internal stiffening—but most basically it provided a buffer for the maintenance of critical levels of certain minerals in the internal environment—a place to put surplus calcium and phosphorus in times of plenty, and a reserve to draw upon in times of scarcity. For us, walking about on dry land, yet another property of bone, its mechanical stiffness and strength, dominate and seem to define for us the nature of the skeleton. A fish vertebra and an elephant vertebra are chemically, and even topologically, similar. Yet to infer the nature of bone from either, separated from its full biological context, gives at best an incomplete understanding of the matter. Other examples abound, and, in fact, the more we learn, the more universal this pattern seems to be.

I submit that sex is another case in point. In the barnyard, females are receptive only when fertile, and males are attracted to females only when they are receptive. Coupling occurs and new life is formed. Sex is clearly generative. What could be more straightforward? In the predominantly agrarian society of the Western world, the barnyard has, in fact, been the biological laboratory–the observational base–for natural law moralists. Their generalizations have been based on what they observed there. But biological reality is richer than the barnyard, and vastly more diverse, and inferences about the nature of sexual acts based on barnyard biology do not fit other biological contexts. Especially, for our purposes, do they not fit the human situation. (Countless thoughtful, committed married Christians have known that in their bones. They seem not to have had the words or the voice to say what they knew from their lived experience, at least in a way that suitably engaged dialogue with the equally sincere natural law moralists.)

When one moves beyond the barnyard into the higher social animals, and particularly the more intelligent mammals, such as dolphins and primates, one sees a far richer spectrum of sexual behaviors, including, but not limited to what a wag has termed the "scandalous behavior in the monkeyhouse." We observe males mounting males, females females, and males mounting females for non-reproductive effects–a rich variety of genital displays and pseudo-copulatory behaviors that serve not to procreate but to establish and reinforce social structures, and thus to sustain the group. The social group, of course, is necessary to sustain its individual members, and particularly its new ones. Thus these activities retain a certain generative character, even if only indirectly.

One might call this behavior pseudo-sexual, but whatever one calls it, it looks very like a new use for an old activity ("new" in the sense that the primates and the other social mammals came on the evolutionary scene more recently than did other animals). In any case, this animal behavior is inherently not directly open to the creation of new life, and to assert that it is somehow flawed for that reason would be so obviously silly as to require no comment. But that is precisely what we do assert about counterpart behaviors when we cross the primate border into human territory.

I said also that our analysis was excessively reductionist. In analyzing complex realities, it is important to choose the right level of organization. In science there are irreducible units below which the nature of a substance disappears—the atom for chemical elements, the cell for certain forms of life, the whole organism for its component tissues (e.g., bone). Each can be disaggregated further, but it then becomes something different, something less. Briefly, some things exist (have their "nature") only at a relatively high level of organization. To fragment them beyond a certain point loses something essential—in a sense, violates that nature, or at least makes it impossible to discern it accurately.

So with sex and with its role in the formation of a human being. A new human is formed not just in a single coupling of man and woman, a conjunction of sperm and egg, but in a complex web of interactions, interventions, and supports which extends over many years. The embryo that emerges from the dominantly life-supportive apparatus which follows upon conception is certainly human in important ways and deserves such protections and supports as we can give it, but it is incomplete as well as immature. The dichotomous language of essences does not serve us well as we try to think about what is here a process, just as it has not served us well in the abortion debate.

Codfish and frogs can lay eggs in the water and let events take their course. New organism-making is over for them at fertilization. All needed survival behaviors are programmed into their genes. But for all the higher mammals (even those of the barnyard), that is not true. Post-fertilization "shaping" is needed. Without it the young—and hence the species—literally cannot survive. This is yet more true of the primates, and finally of human babies which, of all higher mammals, are the most incomplete at birth—the most in need of further shaping.

The distinction between incomplete and immature is an important one. The post-conception development of a new human life is totally dependent upon positive actions taken by adults, just as is conception itself. We used to think in terms of dependence and support, but we know now there is more to it than that. It is not just learning, nor even that certain negative influences can blight the development of embryo, fetus, infant, or child. More: positive experiences are required to call forth the potential that is there. This truth has been so well established for the cuddling of infants, that it has become almost a cliché. Social scientists are fond of remarking "It takes a whole village to raise a child." That saying captures well the fact that the making of a complete human involves vastly more than the union of sperm and egg.

The scope of this human-making involves inputs well beyond psychological nurturing. Surprising as it may seem, even such seemingly basic activities and appetites as sucking, eating, and swallowing—even hunger—must be implanted. And this must all happen during critical, brief windows of opportunity in a rapidly changing biological situation. Missed, and such potentials are lost forever. (One of the sad consequences of recent medical successes in sustaining low birth weight babies is precisely the fact that many such babies never establish the ability to eat, and must be sustained through childhood as they were in the incubator, by tubes and drips. Seemingly normal in outward respects, they will not, on their own, eat enough to sustain life and grow.)

In the aggregate these human-making actions arguably contribute more to the generation of new life than did the action that led to its conception. But we need not play these components off against one another. Both are part of a continuum and both rely upon some of the same behaviors. Both occur in a community context. For agrarian societies, the social unit which sustains and reinforces these necessary, life-generating, adult behaviors is the family. (For pastoral or hunter-gatherer societies some larger social unit commonly serves the same function.) Whatever the unit, its interpersonal and social behaviors constitute the matrix which shapes the individual and renews the species. Actions which support that nuclear community support the making of new humans. I suggest that sex in marriage takes its meaning and value mainly from the relationship which it ritualizes and to which it is ordered. For the most part, it cannot be adequately analyzed out of the context of that relationship.

Humans can separate actions needed to make a whole, can choose to do one and not the other, can disaggregate this unity, as physicists can disaggregate the atom. Therein lies the moral problem: since we can choose the isolated act, how are we to judge the morality, the rightness of doing the act? What is its nature? What does it mean to violate or contradict that nature? And when we isolate the act from its proper setting, does its morality inhere in the isolated act itself, or in the choice of disaggregation, of isolating one action from the relationship which it supports?

As we ponder how we might answer these questions, it is instructive to return briefly to the barnyard—not to generalize from its biology as we have uncritically done in the past, but to reflect upon the method we apply there. We correctly note that sexual activity and attractiveness in the barnyard are confined to fertile periods, and we infer—probably correctly also—that that pattern is as it is because sexual coupling for barnyard animals at other times serves no function. But because that is true in the barnyard does not mean it is true in other contexts.

When we look at primate, and specifically at human sexual relations, the situation is manifestly quite different, with both sexes attractive and receptive at all times, without regard to biological fertility—even during pregnancy, even into senescence. What purpose could that serve? I presume that moralists must have asked that question, but, if so, their answers have not percolated into the literature readily available to educated Catholics.

It seems perverse—not to say wrong-headed—that we seem not to have drawn the obvious biological inference that this arrangement might have functional utility, or that it might tell us something about the nature of sex in human affairs. Instead we have generally considered these urges depraved, or at best something to be tolerated as the lesser of evils, a consequence of concupiscence. While the exploitation of women and of sex to sell things in our society is certainly a flagrant abuse, the fact that it succeeds conveys information about the nature of sex in human society, information we seem not adequately to have heeded.

This is not for a moment to fall into the trap of romanticizing all that occurs as "natural"—and therefore good—or to assert, as some have, that the only thing wrong with sex is the overlay of guilt imposed upon it by organized religion. Anyone who has read the Gilgamesh Epic and pondered the taming of the feral Enkidu described therein, must recognize that sex had been perceived as a powerful mystery, a force that evoked awe, respect, and taboos, long before Judaism and Christianity came onto the scene. Like any other human appetite, and perhaps more than most, it needs to be controlled both personally and socially, lest it control us.

No, my argument is that, as we draw inferences about the nature of things, we base those inferences on valid, relevant observations of nature—on sound biology studied at the right level of organization. If we can succeed in disabusing ourselves of the notion that the nature of highly adaptive behaviors is constant across all of biology (and therefore that universal principles can be inferred from observations at any point in this web), we might be able to see that, of its nature, sexual intercourse serves the enduring, committed relationship between partners, and that the openness to life inheres in the relationship and not in individual sexual acts. These acts nurture, support, even ritualize that relationship, and as such are always procreative even if only occasionally directly generative. Because it is the relationship which is the matrix in which human life is generated (not just conceived), these acts become, by that very fact, life-promoting—open to life. But they take this character from the relationship, not vice versa.

It is in this connection that the issue of natures' inhering at a higher level of organization becomes particularly relevant. The Aristotelian notion of essences seemed not to accommodate composites easily, and thus Aquinas could assert, as in the sequence for the feast of Corpus Christi, that the consecrated bread could be divided (seemingly indefinitely), and Jesus would be present whole in every particle. Few would seriously take that principle to the extremes of 40 or more years ago, simply because we understand that the substance of bread (which is the stuff, after all, of transubstantiation) inheres only at the level of the composite, something that can be divided only so far, after which we no longer have bread.

Aquinas would, I suspect, be the first to agree today. He was, after all, preeminently a realist. (How else could he have held that spontaneous generation of life took place all around him, other than on the grounds that he seemed to observe it?) He was, as we are ourselves, ultimately dependent upon conceptual models with which to interpret observations, to shape notions of the nature of things, and to draw inferences about what is right and wrong. He had to depend upon Aristotelian science. Our models, I submit, are somewhat truer to the reality (but even so, not fully exhaustive of it).

Against this background I suggest that it is a mistake to atomize the complex relationship of marriage into its component actions, just as it is to atomize bread into crumbs too small to bear the composite which we recognize as bread. We thereby both blind ourselves to the nature of bread (and marriage) and miss something important about the particles themselves, namely their relation to the composite, which is significantly more than the sum of its parts.

In the past we have asserted that any sexual coupling in marriage was licit so long as it was entered into without contraceptive intent or effect—a morality that focused on the crumbs rather than the bread, and a morality that turned a blind eye on much that was degrading in actual, lived relationships. I would assert instead that any such coupling would be licit if, instead, it promoted the union of the couple, and thereby furthered the openness to life of the union. Conversely, any acts of intercourse which express mainly dominance or subjugation, which manipulate, brutalize, or degrade the partner, would be immoral, irrespective of their mechanical "integrity," their so-called "openness to conception." This is precisely because such acts go against the nature of the *union* (rather than the *act*), and weaken its potential for making new, *whole* human beings. They are, thereby, anti-life. In this way the fundamental method of natural law morality is preserved, that is, an action is wrong if it contravenes the nature of the act. But, by shifting the level at which we discern the nature of sex in marriage, we also shift the moral judgement to a level of organization higher than the isolated act. We are right, of course, in defending the position that the union must be open to life. I suggest that it is precisely at the level of the union that the morality of the acts resides.

Although I write from the perspective of a working biomedical scientist, and come at these notions from what that work has taught me, it is gratifying to note that sacramental theologians, at least among themselves, have been exploring similar ways of thinking about these matters. Over 50 years ago, in reaction to what he considered an excessively biological approach to sex in marriage, von Hildebrand put the union of spouses first, a position condemned by the Holy Office in 1944 but effectively rehabilitated by *Gaudium et spes* at Vatican II. Rather than an *excess* of biology, I have attempted to show that our official Catholic approach has been marked instead by *bad* biology. It is important to recognize that we are not angels trapped in a prison of flesh. And, while we are more than our biology, we certainly are not less. Arguments about the "nature" of biological processes must, ultimately, be based in biology.

There is general recognition today that there is no basis for disagreement between religion and science. But neither discipline should ignore the other, for both are human endeavors, seeking ultimately to understand and come to terms with what God has wrought. Just as there was no theological need to insist, in Galileo's time, that the sun revolved around the earth, so there is no theological need today to insist upon an interpretation of sex that runs counter to biology. What seems to be involved, in both instances, is mainly a matter of authority. If, with good intent and the best information available at the time, we once said something, then we have been reluctant to change—and seem so still. We reason that confidence in our authority would thereby be undermined. One hopes that that approach is coming to an end.

Reproduction Issues: Reflection Questions

1. Why does the *Catechism of the Catholic Church* say that by themselves science and technology cannot reveal the meaning of life?

2. Is there a danger when technology evolves faster than human ability to weigh the cost and the ethics?

3. Why does or should the Church have an opinion or teaching about such matters?

4. *Humanae vitae* mentions four essential features of Christian married love. What are they? Can you think of any others?

5. *Humanae vitae* calls for responsible parenthood and says that couples need to recognize their duties toward God, themselves, their families and societies. What are these duties?

6. What evidence do Christians offer as proof that sexuality is good?

7. What does Robert Heaney suggest when he says that our theology of marriage has focused more on the crumbs than the bread?

8. What does it mean to suggest that sex is generative?

9. Heaney asserts that "our official Catholic approach has been marked" by bad biology. What does he mean?

11
Resolving Social Inequity

James 2:14-18

¹⁴What good is it, my brothers and sisters, if you say you have faith but do not have works? Can faith save you? ¹⁵If a brother or sister is naked and lacks daily food, ¹⁶and one of you says to them, "Go in peace; keep warm and eat your fill," and yet you do not supply their bodily needs, what is the good of that? ¹⁷So faith by itself, if it has no works, is dead.

¹⁸But someone will say, "You have faith and I have works." Show me your faith apart from your works, and I by my works will show you my faith.

Deeper Questionings

10. The dichotomy affecting the modern world is, in fact, a symptom of the deeper dichotomy that is in man himself. He is the meeting point of many conflicting forces. In his condition as a created being he is subject to a thousand shortcomings, but feels untrammeled in his inclinations and destined for a higher form of life. Torn by a welter of anxieties he is compelled to choose between them and repudiate some among them. Worse still, feeble and sinful as he is, he often does the very thing he hates and does not do what he wants.[1] And so he feels himself divided, and the result is a host of discords in social life. Many, it is true, fail to see the dramatic nature of this state of affairs in all its clarity for their vision is in fact blurred by materialism, or they are prevented from even thinking about it by the wretchedness of their plight. Others delude themselves that they have found peace in a world-view now fashionable. There are still others whose hopes are set on a genuine and total emancipation of mankind through human effort alone and look forward to some future earthly

paradise where all the desires of their hearts will be fulfilled. Nor is it unusual to find people who having lost faith in life extol the kind of foolhardiness which would empty life of all significance in itself and invest it with a meaning of their own devising. Nonetheless, in the face of modern developments there is a growing body of men who are asking the most fundamental of all questions or are glimpsing them with a keener insight: What is man? What is the meaning of suffering, evil, death, which have not been eliminated by all this progress? What is the purpose of these achievements, purchased at so high a price? What can man contribute to society? What can he expect from it? What happens after this earthly life is ended?

[1]Cf. Rom. 7:14ff.

−Gaudium et spes 10

This We Can Do   *Brian Wren*

1. This we can do for justice and for peace:
     we can pray,
   and work to answer prayers that other people say.
   This we can do in faith
   and see it through−
       for Jesus is alive today.

2. This we can do for justice and for peace:
     we can give
   till everyone can take life in their hands, and live.
   This we can do in love
   and see it through−
       for Jesus is alive today.

3. This we can do for justice and for peace:
     we can see
   and help our neighbors see−what is, and what could be.
   This we can do with truth
   and see it through−
       for Jesus is alive today.

4. This we can do for justice and for peace:
     we can fight
   whatever hurts and tramples down, or hides the light.

This we can do with strength
and see it through—
 for Jesus is alive today.

5. This we can do for justice and for peace:
 we can hope
 and hoping, stride along our way while others grope.
This we can do till God
makes all things new—
 for Jesus is alive today.

Rerum novarum   *Pope Leo XIII*

It would not be rash to say that during the long years of its usefulness, Leo's Encyclical has proved itself the Magna Carta on which all Christian activities in social matters are ultimately based.

         —Pope Pius XI, *Quadragesimo anno*

The following excerpts are taken from Pope Leo XIII's encyclical written over 100 years ago. His teaching marks the beginning of the church's concern with contemporary social justice issues. The church was aware of society's increasingly complex structures including socioeconomic trends which threatened the common worker. Charity seemed to be eroding as systemic greed nibbled away at the common good. This encyclical is important for several reasons: it highlights the church's right to intervene and challenge injustice; it paved the way for other significant Catholic teachings on justice issues; and finally, it reminds us that serious moral issues are not limited to sexuality and medical situations.

The true advantage of riches. 20. Most excellent and of the greatest importance is the teaching on the use to be made of wealth which philosophy discovers incompletely but the Church gives clearly and perfectly. Moreover, she does this in such a way as to influence men's conduct as well as inform their minds. The fundamental point of this teaching is that the rightful possession of riches is to be distinguished from their rightful use. As has just been established, to own goods privately is a natural right of man; and to exercise that right, particularly in society, is not only good but entirely necessary. "It is not only legitimate for a man to possess things as his own, it is even necessary for human life" (St. Thomas, *S. Theol.* II–II, Q.66, art.2). And if the question be asked, "How must possessions be used?," the Church replies without hesitation: "No man is entitled to manage things merely for himself, he must do so in the interests of all, so that he is ready to share them with others in case of necessity. This is why Paul writes to Timothy: "As for the rich of this world, charge them to be liberal and generous" (St. Thomas, *S. Theol., ibid.*). True, no one is commanded to provide aid for others out of what is required for his own needs and those of his household; or, rather, to hand over to others what he needs to provide a fitting standard for himself: "Nobody should live unbecomingly" (St. Thomas, *S. Theol.* II–II, Q.32, art.6).

22. This teaching can be summarized thus: whoever has been generously supplied by God with either corporal and external goods or those of the spirit, possesses them for this purpose–to apply them equally to his own perfection and, in his role as a steward of divine providence, to the benefit of others. "Let him who has a talent, therefore, be careful not to hide it; let him who enjoys abundance watch lest he fail in generosity to the poor; let him who possesses the skills of management be particularly careful to share them and their benefits with his neighbour" (St. Gregory the Great, *Evang. Hom.* IX, n. 7).

The innate dignity of poverty. 23. As for the poor, the Church teaches insistently that God sees no disgrace in poverty, nor cause for shame in having to work for a living. Christ our Lord confirmed this by his way of life, when for our salvation he who "was rich became poor for our sake" (2 Cor. 8:9). He chose to be seen and thought of as the son of a carpenter, despite his being the Son of God and very God himself; and having done so, made no objection to spending a large part of his life at the carpenter's trade. "Surely, this is the carpenter, the son of Mary?" (Mk. 8:3). Contemplation of this divine example makes it easier to understand that a man's worth and nobility are found in his way of life, that is to say, his virtue; that virtue is the common inheritance of mankind, within easy reach of high and low, rich and unpropertied alike; and that the reward of eternal happiness is earned only by acts of virtue and service, by whomsoever they are performed. Indeed, the will of God himself seems to give preference to people who are particularly unfortunate. Jesus Christ proclaims formally that the poor are blessed ("Happy are the poor in spirit," Mt. 5:3); most lovingly he invites all those who labour and mourn to come to him, the source of comfort ("Come to me, all you who labour and are overburdened," Mt. 11:28); with loving care he clasps closely to himself the lowly and oppressed. Knowledge of all this cannot but

lower the pride of the well-to-do and lift up the heart of the poor man
who is full of misery, turning the one to fellowship and the other to
moderation in his desires. Thus, the separation which pride tends to
create will be lessened in extent and it will not be difficult for the two
classes willingly to join themselves together in bonds of friendship.

Christian brotherhood.   24. However, if they obey Christian teaching
it will be the bond of brotherly love rather than of friendship that will
unite them. They will then feel and understand the obvious truth that
all men have the same Father, who is God the Creator; that all reach out
for the same final good, who is God himself, who alone can bring absolutely perfect happiness to both men and angels; that by the action of
Jesus Christ all alike are redeemed and re-established in the dignity of
sons of God, so that all might be bound together in fraternal love, brothers to one another as they are to Christ our Lord, "the first born among
many brothers." The same benefits of nature and gifts of divine grace
belong in common to the whole human race, without distinction, and
only those who are unworthy will be disinherited. "If we are children
we are heirs as well: heirs of God and co-heirs with Christ" (Rom. 8:17).

25. Such is the scheme of rights and duties which Christian philosophy teaches. Where this teaching flourishes will not all strife quickly
end?

The spread of Christian teaching.   26. Not content with merely pointing
out the way to set things right, the Church herself takes reform in
hand. She commits herself entirely to educating men by her teaching
and forming them by her discipline, and by the work of her bishops
and priests she seeks to spread the life-giving waters of her doctrine to
the furthest possible extent. She strives to inform minds and direct wills
so that men will allow themselves to be ruled and guided by the discipline of God's teaching. It is in this, the principal matter of importance
because on it depends all the good that is sought for, that the action of
the Church is peculiarly effective; and this because the instruments she
most uses to influence men's minds are given to her for that very purpose by Jesus Christ and derive their effectiveness from God. It is only
instruments of this kind which can touch the innermost reaches of the
heart and lead a man to put his duty first, to control his appetites, to
love God and his neighbour with his whole heart and soul and to
stamp out courageously all that stands in the way of a life of virtue.

The renewal of society.   27. In matters of this sort it is enough to
glance briefly at the pattern of antiquity. There is not the slightest
doubt about the events we bring to mind. Civil society was renewed

from its foundations by the teachings of Christianity. By virtue of this renewal the human race was lifted up to better things, called back indeed from death to life, to a life more perfect than any known before and as good as any yet to come. The first cause and final end of these benefits is Jesus Christ: as all things come from him, so all must be brought back to him. Undoubtedly, as by the light of the Gospel tidings of the great mystery of the incarnation of the Word and of the redemption of mankind were spread throughout the world, the societies of men were permeated by the life of Jesus Christ, God and man, and imbued with his faith, his teaching and his laws. If the society of mankind is to be healed, it can be done only by a recall to Christian life and teaching. If societies in decay wish to be restored, the truest starting point is a return to their origins. The perfection of all associations consists in seeking and attaining the end for which they were established, and this will be done when all social activity springs from the same cause as that which gave societies birth. It is for this reason that to fall away from the original principles is to suffer corruption and to return to them is to have wholeness restored. This is true, not only of the whole body of the state but also of that class of citizens, by far the largest, who work for their living.

The promotion of a better standard of living.   28. It must not be thought that the Church's great concern with the care of souls leads her to neglect the affairs of this earthly and mortal life. She wants expressly to see the unpropertied workers emerge from their great poverty and better their condition; and what she wants, she works for. That she calls men to virtue and forms them in its practice is no small help of itself in that direction. Complete adherence to the code of Christian morals leads directly of itself to greater prosperity. It joins men with God, the ground and fount of all good things; it restrains an excessive appetite for material possessions and a thirst for pleasure, the twin plagues which often make even the rich man unhappy: "The love of money is the root of all evils" (1 Tim. 6:10); it teaches contentment with a frugal standard of living, so that income from savings is available to meet misfortune and the vices which eat up not only small but exceedingly large fortunes and dissipate great inheritances are avoided. In addition to this, moreover, the Church takes direct action to bring prosperity to the unpropertied by founding and fostering institutions which she knows will be conducive to their escape from poverty.

30. Thus there came gradually into existence an inheritance which the Church has looked after with scrupulous care as the property of

the poor. She has always tried to collect funds to help them so as to spare them the humiliation of begging. Acting as the mother of the rich owners of the means of production and of the poor alike and drawing upon the great fount of love which she everywhere creates, the Church has founded congregations of religious and many other useful institutions which have done their work so well that there is hardly any kind of need for which help is not provided. There are many today who follow the example of the heathens of old and find fault with the Church for showing such great charity. They argue that state welfare benefits should be provided instead. But there is no human device which can take the place of this Christian charity, which thinks of nothing other than to bring help where it is needed. The Church alone possesses such virtue because its source is the heart of Jesus Christ himself. There is none other. And whoever cuts himself off from the Church wanders far from Christ.

Regard for the common good. 34. But there is another aspect to be considered which is of very great importance in this connection. The one purpose for which the state exists is common to the highest and the lowest within it. By nature, the right of the unpropertied men to citizenship is equal to that of the wealthy owners of the means of production, for they through their families are among the true and living parts which go to form the body of the state. Indeed, it can be added, in every actual state they are greatly in the majority. Since it would be utterly absurd to care for one section of citizens and neglect another, it is evident that the public authority ought to take proper care to safeguard the lives and well-being of the unpropertied class. To fail in this would be to violate justice which bids us give to every man his due. As St. Thomas has wisely said: "As a part and the whole are identical in a sense, so too in a sense that which is of the whole is also of a part" (*S. Theol.* II–II, Q.61, art.1, ad.2). Consequently, not the least nor the lightest of the duties which fall to rulers in their regard for the common good, but that which comes first of all, is to keep inviolate the justice which is called distributive by caring impartially for each and every class of citizen.

Conclusion

59. You know, venerable brethren, who are the people who must work hard to settle this very difficult question and how they must act. Everyone must gird himself for his part of the work and act with the utmost dispatch to prevent delay from making utterly irremediable

what is already so great an evil. Those who govern the state must make use of its laws and institutions; wealthy owners of the means of production and employers must be mindful of their duties; the un-propertied workers must exert themselves in legitimate ways in what is primarily their affair; and since, as we said at the beginning, religion alone is able totally to eradicate the evil, all men must be persuaded that the first thing they must do is to renew Christian morals. If that is not done even the wisest measures that can be devised to fit the case will fall short of their purpose.

59.1 As for the Church, whatever the time and circumstance her aid will never be looked for in vain. Those in whose hands lies the care of the general welfare must understand that the greater the freedom she is allowed, the more efficacious will be her action. All who are in holy orders must bring to the work their full strength of mind and body. Acting under your authority and inspired by your example, venerable brethren, they must never cease from setting before men of every class the pattern of life given to us by the Gospel. They must do all they can for the good of the people, particularly by way of strenuous efforts to nourish in themselves and to inspire in others the practice of charity, mistress and queen of all the virtues. For indeed it is from a great outpouring of charity that the desired results are principally to be looked for. It is of Christian charity that we speak, the virtue which sums up the whole Gospel law. It is this which makes a man ever and entirely ready to sacrifice himself for the good of others. It is this which is man's most effective antidote against worldly pride and immoderate love of self. It is of this that the Apostle Paul spoke in these words expressing its function and divine likeness: "Love is always patient and kind; it is never jealous; love is never boastful or conceited; it is never rude or selfish; it does not take offence, and is not resentful. Love takes no pleasure in other people's sins but delights in the truth; it is always ready to excuse, to trust, to hope, and to endure whatever comes" (1 Cor. 13:4-7).

60. As a pledge of God's mercies and a sign of our good-will towards each and every one of you, venerable brethren, and to your clergy and people, we lovingly bestow upon you the apostolic benediction in the Lord.

61. Given at St. Peter's, Rome, the 15th day of May 1891, in the fourteenth year of our pontificate.

Centesimus annus   **Pope John Paul II**

On the 100th anniversary of Leo XIII's groundbreaking encyclical Rerum
novarum, *John Paul II reminds the church of its duty to be vigilant and untir-
ing regarding the rights of workers. In fact, John Paul claims that the encyclical
is valuable specifically because it reminds us that the church's social teaching is a
"valid instrument of evangelization." In other words, by being concerned with all
social justice issues, we actually bear the good news of Jesus Christ to the world.*

Man Is in the Way of the Church

53. Faced with the poverty of the working class, Pope Leo XIII
wrote: "We approach this subject with confidence and in the exercise
of the rights which manifestly pertain to us. . . . By keeping silence
we would seem to neglect the duty incumbent on us."[107] During the
last 100 years the church has repeatedly expressed her thinking,
while closely following the continuing development of the social
question. She has certainly not done this in order to recover former
privileges or to impose her own vision. Her sole purpose has been
care and responsibility for man, who has been entrusted to her by
Christ himself: for this man, who, as the Second Vatican Council recalls, is the only creature on earth which God willed for its own sake,
and for which God has his plan, that is, a share in eternal salvation.
We are not dealing here with man in the "abstract," but with the real,
"concrete," "historical" man. We are dealing with each individual,
since each one is included in the mystery of redemption and through
this mystery Christ has united himself with each one forever.[108] It follows that the church cannot abandon man and that "this man is the
primary route that the church must travel in fulfilling her mission . . .
the way traced out by Christ himself, the way that leads invariably
through the mystery of the incarnation and the redemption."[109]

53.1. This, and this alone, is the principle which inspires the
church's social doctrine. The church has gradually developed that
doctrine in a systematic way, above all in the century that has followed the date we are commemorating, precisely because the horizon
of the church's whole wealth of doctrine is man in his concrete reality as sinful and righteous.

54. Today, the church's social doctrine focuses especially on man
as he is involved in a complex network of relationships within modern societies. The human sciences and philosophy are helpful for in-
terpreting man's central place within society and for enabling him to

understand himself better as a "social being." However, man's true identity is only fully revealed to him through faith, and it is precisely from faith that the church's social teaching begins. While drawing upon all the contributions made by the sciences and philosophy, her social teaching is aimed at helping man on the path of salvation.

54.1. The encyclical *Rerum novarum* can be read as a valid contribution to socioeconomic analysis at the end of the 19th century, but its specific value derives from the fact that it is a document of the magisterium and is fully a part of the church's evangelizing mission, together with many other documents of this nature. Thus the church's social teaching is itself a valid instrument of evangelization. As such, it proclaims God and his mystery of salvation in Christ to every human being and for that very reason reveals man to himself. In this light, and only in this light, does it concern itself with everything else: the human rights of the individual and in particular of the "working class," the family and education, the duties of the state, the ordering of national and international society, economic life, culture, war and peace and respect for life from the moment of conception until death.

57. As far as the church is concerned, the social message of the Gospel must not be considered a theory, but above all else a basis and a motivation for action. Inspired by this message, some of the first Christians distributed their goods to the poor, bearing witness to the fact that despite different social origins it was possible for people to live together in peace and harmony. Through the power of the Gospel, down the centuries monks tilled the land, men and women religious founded hospitals and shelters for the poor, confraternities as well as individual men and women of all states of life devoted themselves to the needy and to those on the margins of society, convinced as they were that Christ's words "as you did it to one of the least of these my brethren, you did it to me" (Mt. 25:40) were not intended to remain a pious wish, but were meant to become a concrete life commitment. Today more than ever, the church is aware that her social message will gain credibility more immediately from the witness of actions than as a result of its internal logic and consistency. This awareness is also a source of her preferential option for the poor, which is never exclusive or discriminatory toward other groups. This option is not limited to material poverty, since it is well known that there are many other forms of poverty, especially in modern society—not only economic, but cultural and spiritual poverty as well. The church's

love for the poor, which is essential for her and a part of her constant tradition, impels her to give attention to a world in which poverty is threatening to assume massive proportions in spite of technological and economic progress. In the countries of the West, different forms of poverty are being experienced by groups which live on the margins of society, by the elderly and the sick, by the victims of consumerism and even more immediately by so many refugees and migrants. In the developing countries, tragic crises loom on the horizon unless internationally coordinated measures are taken before it is too late.

58. Love for others, and in the first place love for the poor, in whom the church sees Christ himself, is made concrete in the promotion of justice. Justice will never be fully attained unless people see in the poor person, who is asking for help in order to survive, not an annoyance or a burden, but an opportunity for showing kindness and a chance for greater enrichment. Only such an awareness can give the courage needed to face the risk and the change involved in every authentic attempt to come to the aid of another. It is not merely a matter of "giving from one's surplus," but of helping entire peoples which are presently excluded or marginalized to enter into the sphere of economic and human development. For this to happen, it is not enough to draw on the surplus goods which in fact our world abundantly produces; it requires above all a change of lifestyles, of models of production and consumption, and of the established structures of power which today govern societies. Nor is it a matter of eliminating instruments of social organization which have proved useful, but rather of orienting them according to an adequate notion of the common good in relation to the whole human family. Today we are facing the so-called "globalization" of the economy, a phenomenon which is not to be dismissed, since it can create unusual opportunities for greater prosperity. There is a growing feeling, however, that this increasing internationalization of the economy ought to be accompanied by effective international agencies which will oversee and direct the economy to the common good, something that an individual state, even if it were the most powerful on earth, would not be in a position to do. In order to achieve this result, it is necessary that there be increased coordination among the more powerful countries and that in international agencies the interests of the whole human family be equally represented. It is also necessary that in evaluating the consequences of their decisions, these agencies always give sufficient consideration to peoples and countries which have little weight

in the international market, but which are burdened by the most acute and desperate needs and are thus more dependent on support for their development. Much remains to be done in this area.

61. At the beginning of industrialized society, it was "a yoke little better than that of slavery itself" which led my predecessor to speak out in defense of man. Over the past 100 years the church has remained faithful to this duty. Indeed, she intervened in the turbulent period of class struggle after World War I in order to defend man from economic exploitation and from the tyranny of the totalitarian systems. After World War II, she put the dignity of the person at the center of her social messages, insisting that material goods were meant for all and that the social order ought to be free of oppression and based on a spirit of cooperation and solidarity. The church has constantly repeated that the person and society need not only material goods, but spiritual and religious values as well. Furthermore, as she has become more aware of the fact that too many people live, not in the prosperity of the Western world, but in the poverty of the developing countries amid conditions which are still "a yoke little better than that of slavery itself," she has felt and continues to feel obliged to denounce this fact with absolute clarity and frankness, although she knows that her call will not always win favor with everyone.

61.1. One hundred years after the publication of *Rerum novarum,* the church finds herself still facing "new things" and new challenges. The centenary celebration should therefore confirm the commitment of all people of good will and of believers in particular.

62. The present encyclical has looked at the past, but above all it is directed to the future. Like *Rerum novarum,* it comes almost at the threshold of a new century, and its intention, with God's help, is to prepare for that moment.

62.1. In every age the true and perennial "newness of things" comes from the infinite power of God, who says: "Behold, I make all things new" (Rv. 21:5). These words refer to the fulfillment of history, when Christ "delivers the kingdom to God the Father . . . that God may be everything to everyone" (1 Cor. 15:24, 28). But the Christian well knows that the newness which we await in its fullness at the Lord's second coming has been present since the creation of the world, and in a special way since the time when God became man in Jesus Christ and brought about a "new creation" with him and through him (2 Cor. 5:17; Gal. 6:15).

The Horrors of Our Century   *Brian Wren*

The Fruit of the Tree

1. The horrors of our century
        have iced the wells of grief.
   We greet each new atrocity
        in frozen disbelief;
   yet all the evil energies
        that haunt the human race
    come not from alien galaxies,
        but from our inner space:
            and Auschwitz and Hiroshima
            intrude on every prayer
            with shades that whisper, "Where is God?
            If only God were there!"

2. By torture, war and poverty,
        by flame and firing squad,
   for freedom and democracy,
        or in the name of god,
   God's image finds a thousand ways
        to torment and to kill,
   and asks how love could justify
        its terrible freewill:
            for Vietnam and South Africa
            will drive us back to prayer,
            as victims clamor, "Where is God?
            If only God were there!"

3. Yet if, made like some android race,
        though warm with flesh and blood,
   our happy self, with smiling face,
        was programmed to be good,
   and had no freedom, seeing wrong,
        to choose it, or say no,
   our praise would be a puppet-song,
        and love an empty show:
            Pol Pot and Stalin are the cost
            of every willing prayer
            that chooses justice, love and trust,
            and hopes that God is there.

4. And God is not an analyst,
   observing gain and loss,
but loves us to the uttermost,
   and suffers on a cross:
for love comes not like Heads of State,
   in power and glamour known,
but as a loser, desolate,
   in anguish, and alone:
      Golgotha and the Empty Tomb
      enlighten every prayer
      when faith discovers: "There is God,
      and all of God is there!"

5. The fruits of knowledge, plucked and prized,
   have scattered wide their seed:
we are as gods, with open eyes,
   for shame or glory freed,
and share, as midwives to our God,
   the pain of giving birth
to faith's fulfilment, mercy's child:
   new heavens and new earth.
      Come blow, you winds of Pentecost!
      Let all the churches dare
      to struggle, suffer, die with God,
      and show that God is there!

Christianity and the Social Crisis   *Walter Rauschenbusch*

The Social Gospel is one of the most significant theological movements (1865–1920) ever to develop in United States history. The Social Gospelers saw the Christian message of salvation applying to the structures of society no less than to individuals. God, already present in the world, would work out the divine will through humankind and human institutions. The Social Gospel leaders led a crusade to advance the Reign of God by combating evil in an urban and industrial society.

Walter Rauschenbusch, a German Baptist pastor in the Hell's Kitchen neighborhood of New York City at the turn of the century, was one of the movement's best spokesmen. His sense of social consciousness and mission stemmed from reading the Gospel of Jesus as the inspired solution to social problems.[1]

[1]See *Half Finished Heaven: The Social Gospel in American Literature* by William C. Graham (Lanham, Maryland: University Press of America, 1995).

Introduction

Western civilization is passing through a social revolution unparalleled in history for scope and power. Its coming was inevitable. The religious, political, and intellectual revolutions of the past five centuries, which together created the modern world, necessarily had to culminate in an economic and social revolution such as is now upon us.

By universal consent, this social crisis is the overshadowing problem of our generation. The industrial and commercial life of the advanced nations are in the throes of it. In politics all issues and methods are undergoing upheaval and re-alignment as the social movement advances. In the world of thought all the young and serious minds are absorbed in the solution of the social problems. Even literature and art point like compass-needles to this magnetic pole of all our thought.

The social revolution has been slow in reaching our country. We have been exempt, not because we had solved the problems, but because we had not yet confronted them. We have now arrived, and all the characteristic conditions of American life will henceforth combine to make the social struggle here more intense than anywhere else. The vastness and the free sweep of our concentrated wealth on the one side, the independence, intelligence, moral vigor, and political power of the common people on the other side, promise a long-drawn grapple of contesting forces which may well make the heart of every American patriot sink within him.

It is realized by friend and foe that religion can play, and must play, a momentous part in this irrepressible conflict.

The Church, the organized expression of the religious life of the past, is one of the most potent institutions and forces in Western civilization. Its favor and moral influence are wooed by all parties. It cannot help throwing its immense weight on one side or the other. If it tries not to act, it thereby acts; and in any case its choice will be decisive for its own future.

Apart from the organized Church, the religious spirit is a factor of incalculable power in the making of history. In the idealistic spirits that lead and in the masses that follow, the religious spirit always intensifies thought, enlarges hope, unfetters daring, evokes the willingness to sacrifice, and gives coherence in the fight. Under the warm breath of religious faith, all social institutions become plastic. The religious spirit removes mountains and tramples on impossibilities. Unless the economic and intellectual factors are strongly reinforced by religious enthusiasm, the whole social movement may prove abortive, and the New Era may die before it comes to birth.

It follows that the relation between Christianity and the social crisis is one of the most pressing questions for all intelligent men who realize the power of religion, and most of all for the religious leaders of the people who give direction to the forces of religion.

The question has, in fact, been discussed frequently and earnestly, but it is plain to any thoughtful observer that the common mind of the Christian Church in America has not begun to arrive at any solid convictions or any permanent basis of action. The conscience of Christendom is halting and groping, perplexed by contradicting voices, still poorly informed on essential questions, justly reluctant to part with the treasured maxims of the past, and yet conscious of the imperious call of the future.

This book is to serve as a contribution to this discussion. Its first chapters are historical, for nothing is more needed than a true comprehension of past history if we are to forecast the future correctly and act wisely in the present. I have tried to set forth the religious development of the prophets of Israel, the life and teachings of Jesus, and the dominant tendencies of primitive Christianity, in order to ascertain what was the original and fundamental purpose of the great Christian movement in history. Every discussion of the question which appeals to history has to cover this ground, but usually only detached fragments of the material are handled at all, and often without insight adequate to give their true meaning even to these fragments. I am in hopes that these chapters will contribute some facts and points of view that have not yet become common property.

The outcome of these first historical chapters is that the essential purpose of Christianity was to transform human society into the kingdom of God by regenerating all human relations and reconstituting them in accordance with the will of God. The fourth chapter raises the question why the Christian Church has never undertaken to carry out this fundamental purpose of its existence. I have never met with any previous attempt to give a satisfactory historical explanation of this failure, and I regard this chapter as one of the most important in the book.

The fifth chapter sets forth the conditions which constitute the present social crisis and which imperatively demand of Christianity that contribution of moral and religious power which it was destined to furnish.

The sixth chapter points out that the Church, as such, has a stake in the social movement. The Church owns property, needs income, employs men, works on human material, and banks on its moral prestige. Its present efficiency and future standing are bound up for weal or woe with the social welfare of the people and with the outcome of the present struggle.

The last chapter suggests what contributions Christianity can make and in what main directions the religious spirit should exert its force.

In covering so vast a field of history and in touching on such a multitude of questions, error and incompleteness are certain, and the writer can claim only that he has tried to do honest work. Moreover, it is impossible to handle questions so vital to the economic, the social, and the moral standing of great and antagonistic classes of men, without jarring precious interests and convictions, and without giving men the choice between the bitterness of social repentance and the bitterness of moral resentment. I can frankly affirm that I have written with malice toward none and with charity for all. Even where I judge men to have done wrong, I find it easy to sympathize with them in the temptations which made the wrong almost inevitable, and in the points of view in which they entrench themselves to save their self-respect. I have tried—so far as erring human judgment permits—to lift the issues out of the plane of personal selfishness and hate, and to put them where the white light of the just and pitying spirit of Jesus can play upon them. If I have failed in that effort, it is my sin. If others in reading fail to respond in the same spirit, it is their sin. In a few years all our restless and angry hearts will be quiet in death, but those who come after us will live in the world which our sins have blighted or which our love of right has redeemed. Let us do our thinking on these great questions, not with our eyes fixed on our bank account, but with a wise outlook on the fields of the future and with the consciousness that the spirit of the Eternal is seeking to distil from our lives some essence of righteousness before they pass away.

I have written this book to discharge a debt. For eleven years I was pastor among the working people on the West Side of New York City. I shared their life as well as I then knew, and used up the early strength of my life in their service. In recent years my work has been turned into other channels, but I have never ceased to feel that I owe help to the plain people who were my friends. If this book in some far-off way helps to ease the pressure that bears them down and increases the forces that bear them up, I shall meet the Master of my life with better confidence.

–Originally published in 1907 by The Macmillan Company

Resolving Social Inequity: Reflection Questions

1. If you could bring about one change to make the world a better place, what would it be?

2. Have you had any first-hand experience of social injustice?

3. Relate Pope Leo XIII to Walter Rauschenbusch, and both to James 1:9-27; 2:1-26. Is what is required different today from the year 90 or 1900?

4. Why is the landlord's response in the following *Et Cetera* item humorous? What is his moral obligation? How does it differ from his legal obligation?

Et Cetera

Is This Consequentialism?

New York has had an early cold snap, and it's been cold in here. Our official complainer called this to the attention of the building management. The management representative held that under the law he didn't have to order up some heat till October 15. On the other hand, he added, "We have a moral obligation to provide heat for tenants when it's cold outside. Otherwise, they'll leave."

–*Commonweal,* October 21, 1994

12
Responsible Sexuality

Song of Solomon 3:1-4

Upon my bed at night
  I sought him whom my soul loves;
I sought him, but found him not;
  I called him, but he gave no answer.
²"I will rise now and go about the city,
  in the streets and in the squares;
I will seek him whom my soul loves."
  I sought him, but found him not.
³The sentinels found me,
  as they went about in the city.
"Have you seen him whom my soul loves?"
⁴Scarcely had I passed them,
  when I found him whom my soul loves.
I held him, and would not let him go
  until I brought him into my mother's house,
  and into the chamber of her that conceived me.

On Sexual Ethics

4. Consequently, it is wrong to assert as many do today that neither human nature nor revealed law provide any absolute and unchangeable norms as a guide for individual actions, that all they offer is the general law of charity and respect for the human person. Proponents of this view allege in its support that the norms of the natural law, as they are called, and the precepts of sacred scripture are to be seen rather as patterns of behaviour found in particular cultures at given moments of history.

Since revelation and, in its own sphere, philosophy have to do with the deepest needs of mankind, they inevitably at the same time reveal the unchangeable laws inscribed in man's nature and which are identical in all rational beings.

The Church was founded by Christ as "the pillar and bulwark of the truth."[6] It preserves without ceasing and transmits without error the truths of the moral order. It interprets authentically both revealed positive law and "the principles of the moral order which spring from human nature itself"[7] and which relate to man's full development and sanctification. Throughout its history the Church has always held a certain number of precepts of the natural law to be absolute and unchangeable and in its eyes to disobey them is to go against the teaching and spirit of the gospel.

5. Since sexual ethics have to do with certain fundamental values of human and Christian life, this general teaching applies equally to sexual ethics. There are principles and norms in sexual ethics which the Church has always proclaimed as part of her teaching and has never had any doubt about it, however much the opinions and mores of the world opposed them. These principles and norms in no way owe their origin to a particular culture, but rather to knowledge of the divine law and of human nature. They do not therefore cease to oblige or become doubtful because cultural changes take place.

These are the principles on which the Second Council of the Vatican based its suggestions and directives for the establishment and the organization of a social order in which due account would be taken of the equal dignity of men and women, while respecting the difference between them.[8]

In speaking of "man's sexuality and the faculty of reproduction," the Council noted that they "wondrously surpassed the endowments of lower forms of life."[9] It then dealt one by one with the principles and rules which relate to human sexuality in marriage and which are based on the specific purpose of sexuality.

With regard to the matter in hand, the Council declares that when assessing the propriety of conjugal acts, determining if they accord with true human dignity, "it is not enough to take only the good intention and the evaluation of motives into account. Objective criteria must be used, criteria based on the nature of the human person and of human action, criteria which respect the total meaning of mutual self-giving and human procreation in the context of true love."[10]

This last quotation summarizes the Council's teaching on the finality of the sexual act and on the principal criterion of its morality:

when the finality of the act is respected the moral goodness of the act is ensured. This teaching is explained in greater detail in the same Constitution.[11]

This same principle, which the Church derives from divine revelation and from its authentic interpretation of the natural law, is at the core of its traditional teaching that only in legitimate marriage does the use of the sexual faculty find its true meaning and its probity.[12]

[6]1 Tim 3:15.

[7]*Dignitatis humanae,* 14: *AAS* 58 (1966), p. 940; cf. Pius XI, Encyclical Letter *Casti connubii,* December 31, 1930: *AAS* 22 (1930), pp. 579–580; Pius XII, Allocution of November 2, 1954; *AAS* 46 (1954), pp. 671–672; John XXIII, Encyclical Letter *Mater et magistra,* May 15, 1961: *AAS* 53 (1961), p. 457; Paul VI, Encyclical Letter *Humanae vitae,* 4, July 25, 1968: *AAS* 60 (1968), p. 483.

[8]Cf. Second Vatican Ecumenical Council, Declaration *Gravissimum educationis,* 1, 8: *AAS* 58 (1966), pp. 729–730; 734–736. *Gaudium et spes,* 29, 60, 67: *AAS* 58 (1966), pp. 1048–1049, 1080–1081, 1088–1089.

[9]*Gaudium et spes,* 51: *AAS* 58 (1966), p. 1072.

[10]*Ibid.;* cf. also 49: *loc cit.,* pp. 1069–1070.

[11]*Ibid.,* 49, 50: *loc cit.,* pp. 1069–1072.

[12]The present Declaration does not go into further detail regarding the norms of sexual life within marriage; these norms have been clearly taught in the Encyclical Letters *Casti connubii* and *Humanae vitae.*

—*Declaration on Certain Questions Concerning Sexual Ethics* 4, 5

Chastity as Shared Strength: An Open Letter to Students
Mary Patricia Barth Fourqurean, David N. Fourqurean

At this university we rightly celebrate diversity in many different areas, though we seem to offer less diversity when it comes to the area of sexuality. But there is also an invisible, though substantial, minority of students who have freely chosen either to remain chaste or to reclaim their chastity. If you are part of this minority, I assure you that more of your peers than you realize have chosen this option and have done so for a variety of reasons: out of faith commitments, or after positive experiences with chaste friendships (with both sexes) or after negative experiences of genital sexuality, often induced by alcohol. But their choice remains silent because they tend to be less vocal than their sexually active peers. They remain silent because they sometimes feel less "with it," and they do not want to appear judgmental. They also believe that chastity is a purely private matter. I hope this letter stimulates them to start student-led groups to discuss chastity and sexuality and to increase the visible range of sexual options on campus.

To write about chastity is to walk into a minefield, and I wish I could invent a better word. To many, "chastity" implies repression or simply the inability to get a date. But I believe that avoiding the word avoids its substance, and I affirm the substance for several reasons. *Positively,* chastity increases our own sincerity by assuring us that we will not say more with our bodies than we mean in our hearts. It also increases our confidence in the sincerity of others by assuring us (in deed, not word) that our friend seeks more from us than what is skin-deep. Chastity also creates an opportunity for us not to repress but to redirect our sexual energies—for example, in athletics and in community service. I know many college students who have found great joy in athletic accomplishments and in selfless community service, especially when such training and giving are pursued with others. *Negatively,* chastity protects us physically from sexually transmitted diseases (S.T.D.'s) and AIDS (it is not "safe sex" but "safest sex"). It protects us emotionally by assuring us that we will not be used merely for someone else's pleasure or power.

In my 11 years in campus ministry at Holy Cross, Duke and Georgetown, I have seen the secret anguish of many students who have been used or abused, and although the fact of this anguish is reported in student newspapers, its extent is not. The hidden experience of these students matters, for they feel deceived by our culture's promises of instant gratification. They have come to suspect that gratification and fulfillment may be two different realities.

What do I mean by "chastity" and "sexuality"? Chastity means passionate love for God, others and ourselves, a three-fold love expressed in three different ways. In marriage, chastity does not mean sexlessness but faithfulness, i.e., a *permanent, genital* commitment to our spouse, out of this three-fold love, that is both exclusive and sensual. In celibacy (including both heterosexual and homosexual celibates), chastity means a *permanent, non-genital* commitment to God and therefore to the world, out of this three-fold love. It frees religious women and men from the exclusive bond of marriage in order to be freer (not purer) to serve God and to be more inclusive in befriending others. In singleness, chastity means a *temporary, non-genital* commitment to this three-fold love of God, others and ourselves. Many have found this liberating because they are finally freed from having to play sexual games. I tend to image chastity as a *disciplined* warmth, not as ice.

"Sexuality" is far more than sexual intercourse. It is an emotional, spiritual and physical fire permeating our whole life that is as beautiful as it is dangerous. On the one hand it is the means by which married couples unite themselves to each other and bring new life into the world. But on the other hand, as I have seen so often among college students, it is also the destructive means by which many lives are sundered and wasted. To make matters more complex, in an age of S.T.D.'s and AIDS, the sexual act that was meant to be a giver of life is now a taker of life, for both homosexuals and heterosexuals.

Our sexual world has changed drastically. The sexual revolution's message of "liberation" in the 1960's and 70's falls on deaf ears in the 90's. For fighting sexual repression before the sexual revolution is not the same thing as fighting sexual chaos after it. Professor Lisa Sowle Cahill of Boston College asks us in "Can We Get Real About Sex?" (*Commonweal*, 9/14/90), to realize this difference: "Each generation has its own questions. Those of us who were teen-agers before Vatican II still carry on a struggle of 'liberation' from a negative and restrictive picture of sexual dangers. But most young adults today face a different battle: to carve out some sense of sexual direction in a peer and media culture which presents sex as a sophisticated recreational activity for which the only moral criterion is mutual consent."

I have met many undergraduate and graduate students over the years who are actively but silently pursuing chastity. I will never forget an encounter I had recently with a bright, athletic and attractive student named Steve, who confided in me that he decided to maintain his chastity until he marries, at which time he assured me laughingly that he will "go wild"! Steve's appreciation for the goodness of sexuality is strong, but he is courageously waiting for its fullest expression in marriage. His peers would be surprised at his determination to be chaste, because they know he loves to party. Steve asked a colleague of mine, a Catholic priest at another university, this heartfelt question: "Why is it, Father, that those of us struggling to be chaste on a campus like this have *never* heard you encourage us to be chaste?" Taken aback, the priest explained that he didn't want the students to think that the Catholic Church had a prudish view of sexuality, for "God made sexuality good." Notice: a celibate priest who practiced but never preached chastity, and a student of the 1990's wanting him to preach it.

Steve's appreciation of chastity is not unique. I have seen Protestant students pack a university auditorium to hear a married Protestant tell them encouragingly that chastity before marriage makes sexuality within marriage all the more wonderful. At a recent retreat I asked the students to give me their reactions to "chastity," and I was surprised at how positive they were. Chastity for most in this group raised after the sexual revolution was "underrated," "disciplined," "patient," "selfless," "pure" and a "gift of God." Of course, a few others said that chastity was "unrealistic," "irrelevant," even "abnormal."

But to those of you who have chosen in private to maintain your virginity or to reclaim your chastity, I have found that such a personal choice made alone does not endure over the years without encouragement or respect from others. What Aristotle said about bravery is also true for chastity: "The brave are found where bravery is honored." What Martin Buber said is equally true, that we are who we are in our relationships. Our private choices may work for a while, but they tend to break down when we are separated from supportive friends for long periods. For chastity is challenged by almost everything we see outside ourselves in the American media, and it is also challenged by almost everything we feel inside ourselves in our yearnings for intimacy and passion.

Students rise to challenges when challenged well and consistently. At Georgetown many of you give your time and talents to D.C.'s hungry, homeless and illiterate, and you participate in the Jesuit Volunteer Corps, the Peace Corps, Teach for America, Habitat for Humanity and the Nicaragua Program. On spring break, as the media focus only on those students partying at the beach, they tend to ignore those of you who spend your break in Appalachia serving the poor or on the five-day silent retreat. My objection is not to those students who go to the beach but to the media that render the other students invisible. At other times throughout the year I see Catholic students attending the Agape retreat, Protestant students attending the Wellspring and Koinonia retreats, and Jewish students attending the Ahavah retreat. In all of this I see you seeking a deeper relationship with God and others.

It is interesting to me how many college students admire Mother Teresa and Dorothy Day. Malcolm Muggeridge's conversations with Mother Teresa in *Something Beautiful for God* exhibit the power of this attraction. He repeatedly inquired if she were not asking too much of her "educated, middle-class or upper-class" Missionaries of Charity. After all, she asks them to make not only the standard three vows of poverty, chastity and obedience, but a fourth, "free-hearted service to the poorest of the poor":

MALCOLM: Did many find it too much, Mother?

TERESA: Very few, very, very few have left. We can count them on our fingers. It's the most extraordinary thing that so many of our Sisters have been so faithful right from the very first.

MALCOLM: Although it was such a severe test, they found fulfillment in it?

TERESA: It was a challenge for them. They wanted to give everything, and they wanted the hardest. We have to live this life, this hard life, to be able to continue the work among the people [as] . . . the means of expressing our love for God . . . .

MALCOLM: That is asking a lot, isn't it?

TERESA: That is what they want to give. They want to give to God everything.

Of course, the cultural situation of students at this university is radically different from that of a Calcutta slum. But the idea of challenging "educated, middle-class and upper-class" young adults, only to have many embrace the challenge, is very much alive. For after speaking with many students about this, I am surprised how they admitted, positively, that they yearn for challenges, and, negatively, how they do not want to settle for less sexually. A senior woman explained it to me this way:

Chastity has been an enormous challenge during my college years. I have failed at it because I couldn't answer the question, "Why shouldn't I have sex?" I gave in because I figured, since I didn't have a solid answer, I must be wrong. And I still sometimes feel that if I remain chaste, other people must feel like I'm looking down on them. I want to be able to celebrate my chastity without feeling like I'm pressuring anyone else.

Dealing with expectations is probably the hardest. I'm considered "repressed." I read stuff all the time that claims that virginity is unnatural, abnormal or that it makes you a slave to a false idea. I know that many women consider it almost anti-women's rights.

And yet I don't feel like I'm clinging to old traditions for the sake of security. It's because when I have sex I don't want to say "Yeah, I guess there's nothing wrong with it." I want to say "YES!" passionately with my whole being. Maybe this sounds idealistic, but that's how I feel. Waiting isn't always fun but that doesn't mean I shouldn't wait. For I don't want to settle. I want the best. And I know that, when I'm most happy and most filled-up on life, that's when I realize that it's worth the wait!

A senior man shared a similar comment with me:

I think we desire to be deeply challenged and to go for our deepest desires for intimacy, but we end up "settling" for sex.

Not every model of sexuality is challenging. A model common since the 1960's and 1970's has been liberation from repression, as if we were pressure-cookers ready to burst, needing release above all else before we can feel healthy. This model asks too little of us. I'm more drawn to the athletic model of discipline striving for excellence. If the liberation model is basically an *opening,* the athletic model is basically an *aiming.* You would never tell a crew member, "Relax and free yourself from your oppressive training!" As a successful athlete, she understands that her freedom and joy come only from her discipline and hard work. She would not want you to divorce the two. In the film "Chariots of Fire" the Scottish runner's spiritual joy comes from within his athletic training: "When I run, I feel God's pleasure."

Many people today think that our physical desires are just too strong. But I wonder if the deeper issue is not whether our spiritual desires are just too weak. C. S. Lewis preached a sermon to college students at Oxford, to this effect, encouraging them not to "settle" but to strive for far more: "Indeed, if we consider the unblushing promises of reward and the staggering nature of the rewards promised in the Gospels, it would seem that our Lord finds our desires, not too strong, but too weak. We are half-hearted creatures, fooling about with drink and sex and ambition when infinite joy is offered us, like an ignorant child who wants to go on making mud pies in a slum because he cannot imagine what is meant by the offer of a holiday at the sea. We are far too easily pleased."

If older adults are "far too easily pleased," a substantial minority of younger adults in college are not. Many prize what athletes accomplish physically, and what Mother Teresa accomplishes spiritually, and understand how much hard work both types of accomplishment require.

I have been helped in my understanding of chastity by John Francis Kavanaugh, S.J., in his *Following Christ in a Consumer Society: The Spirituality of Cultural Resistance:* "Chastity both in the marital and celibate form stands as a rare testimonial to human integrity, to the symbolic and actual importance of being embodied selves, to the preeminence of personhood and covenantal life. In a hedonistic culture, moreover, chastity is a most effective concrete critique [and] . . . a living refutation of the reduction of persons to either machines or animals, to progeny or to pleasure."

What Father Kavanaugh calls "human integrity" can certainly flourish without genital expressions of sexuality, but it cannot flourish without human expressions of intimacy. I know this distinction between sex and intimacy from my own previous experience in religious life, for I saw many religious women and men living rich emotional lives without romantic or genital attachments—involving passionate love of God and deep friendships with both sexes, but without sex. Students in the 1990's can understand this too, especially after they experience how rich intimacy and friendships can be without sexual intercourse and how barren sexual intercourse can be without intimacy. Others have told me that they know sex exists without intimacy and have come to wonder if intimacy exists without sex.

But I know that intimacy or *friendship without sex* exists at this university, although I also know it is not easy to find and that it is a challenge to keep. We do not need to create it but to encourage it, and for three reasons: 1) to lessen the pressure on you to find a romantic partner during college and to explode the myth that college is your last chance to find a mate; 2) to learn that genital relationships are not the only means for the intimacy we desire, and 3) to recognize that such relationships are not the means toward anything positive if intimacy and friendship are not there already (think of date-rape or loveless marriages).

Friendship without sex demands patience, forgiveness and trust, for it takes time to learn how to communicate and to connect inwardly when it is so easy to connect outwardly instead. But the difficulties are well worth it if we are ever to move beyond the surface in order to enjoy the hard-won intimacy earned by real friends. So in terms of chastity let me encourage you not to mistake the means for the end. During college, genital expression can easily become genital exploitation, for these years are so filled with options and transitions that even the most sincere romantic commitments are frequently broken.

I recall a senior who shared her frustration with me that although she often needs nothing more than a reassuring hug, she knows that it is too easily interpreted as an invitation to "jump into bed." The reality is that without chastity we no longer know how to be affectionate without its implying something sexual. Then when hugs lead to foreplay, we don't know how to say "No" with a conviction stemming from high self-esteem.

In conclusion, a renewed emphasis on chastity has nothing to do with returning to negative views of sexuality. For I am in favor not of *recovering* chastity the way it was, but of *redeeming* it from the negative associations it had in the past by *rethinking* it in positive ways for the future—chastity as an empowering strength. That is, as a virtue, understood neither heroically nor privately but socially, an interpersonal power that 1) is supported by others and 2) frees the self *for* a trusting relationship with God and others, and *from* the mixed signals of sexual games.

Those students who helped me write this letter unanimously desired to create student-led groups that would discuss the issues addressed by it. If Buber is right that the "I" needs a "Thou" to be a better "I," then we need the help of like-minded peers if we are to seek in earnest more than the "drink and sex and ambition" C. S. Lewis writes of. What is freely chosen will remain freely chosen only when those maintaining their chastity are no longer embarrassed by it, and when those reclaiming their chastity find the support they need from like-minded friends. Can we begin to create such support at this university, not so much to compete with those who choose other sexual options but to support those of us who choose this one?

—America, November 6, 1993

St. John's and the Sexual Dilemma

Three male students were expelled from St. John's University in New York City some years ago after a difficult court case. The situation was clearly a dilemma for officials and students at the largest Roman Catholic University in the United States.

The *New York Times* reported on October 10, 1991, that the Rev. Donald Harrington, president of the University, heeded the recommendation of a disciplinary committee which included faculty members and students. They found that each of the three students, who had been acquitted in a court of law, were nonetheless guilty of "conduct adversely affecting his suitability as a member of the academic community of St. John's."

The three had been acquitted in court of sodomy and other criminal charges related to a reported attack on a female student. A spokesman for the University said that the court verdict involved "different standards" from those related to "the code of behavior that governs students to students and students to teachers."

The three who were expelled were members of the St. John's lacrosse team in early 1990. At a party in a house near the campus, the men allegedly forced a 21-year-old female student to engage in oral sex, later taking advantage of her when she passed out after consuming liquor that one of them pressured her to drink.

Two of the men argued that the woman had consented to engaging in whatever sexual activity took place, and later decided to say that she had been attacked. Jurors found that her testimony was filled with what they determined were lies and inconsistencies.

After their indictment but prior to their expulsion, the three had been suspended from the University. Two of them were seniors, and one a junior. After the expulsion, one of their lawyers suggested that Father Harrington incorrectly assumed that the defendants had been found guilty by the jury. The lawyer added, according to the *New York Times*, that "A university should stand for more than just going with the mood of the crowd."

The woman involved dropped out of the University after the incident.

Declaration on Certain Questions Concerning Sexual Ethics
Pope John Paul II

1. According to contemporary scientific research, the human person is so profoundly affected by sexuality that it must be considered as one of the factors which give to each individual's life the principal traits that distinguish it. In fact it is from sex that the human person receives the characteristics which, on the biological, psychological and spiritual levels, make that person a man or a woman, and thereby largely condition his or her progress towards maturity and insertion into society. Hence sexual matters, as is obvious to everyone, today constitute a theme frequently and openly dealt with in books, reviews, magazines and other means of social communication.

In the present period, the corruption of morals has increased, and one of the most serious indications of this corruption is the unbridled exaltation of sex. Moreover, through the means of social communication and through public entertainment this corruption has reached the point of invading the field of education and of infecting the general mentality.

In this context certain educators, teachers and moralists have been able to contribute to a better understanding and integration into life of the values proper to each of the sexes; on the other hand there are those who have put forward concepts and modes of behavior which are contrary to the true moral exigencies of the human person. Some members of the latter group have even gone so far as to favor a licentious hedonism.

As a result, in the course of a few years, teachings, moral criteria and modes of living hitherto faithfully preserved have been very much unsettled, even among Christians. There are many people today who, being confronted with so many widespread opinions opposed to the teaching which they received from the Church, have come to wonder what they must still hold as true.

2. The Church cannot remain indifferent to this confusion of minds and relaxation of morals. It is a question, in fact, of a matter which is of the utmost importance both for the personal lives of Christians and for the social life of our time.[1]

The Bishops are daily led to note the growing difficulties experienced by the faithful in obtaining knowledge of wholesome moral teaching, especially in sexual matters, and of the growing difficulties experienced by pastors in expounding this teaching effectively. The Bishops know that by their pastoral charge they are called upon to meet the needs of their faithful in this very serious matter, and important documents dealing with it have already been published by some of them or by Episcopal Conferences. Nevertheless, since the erroneous opinions and resulting deviations are continuing to spread everywhere, the Sacred Congregation for the Doctrine of the Faith, by virtue of its function in the universal Church[2] and by a mandate of the Supreme Pontiff, has judged it necessary to publish the present Declaration.

3. The people of our time are more and more convinced that the human person's dignity and vocation demand that they should discover, by the light of their own intelligence, the values innate in their nature, that they should ceaselessly develop these values and realize them in their lives, in order to achieve an ever greater development.

In moral matters man cannot make value judgments according to his personal whim: "In the depths of his conscience, man detects a law which he does not impose on himself, but which holds him to obedience. . . . For man has in his heart a law written by God. To obey it is the very dignity of man; according to it he will be judged."[3]

Moreover, through his revelation God has made known to us Christians his plan of salvation, and he has held up to us Christ, the Saviour and Sanctifier, in his teaching and example, as the supreme and immutable Law of life: "I am the light of the world; anyone who follows me will not be walking in the dark, he will have the light of life."[4]

Therefore there can be no true promotion of man's dignity unless the essential order of his nature is respected. Of course, in the history of civilization many of the concrete conditions and needs of human life have changed and will continue to change. But all evolution of morals and every type of life must be kept within the limits imposed by the immutable principles based upon every human person's constitutive elements and essential relations–elements and relations which transcend historical contingency.

These fundamental principles, which can be grasped by reason, are contained in "the divine law–eternal, objective and universal–whereby God orders, directs and governs the entire universe and all the ways of the human community, by a plan conceived in wisdom and love. Man has been made by God to participate in this law, with the result that, under the gentle disposition of divine Providence, he can come to perceive ever increasingly the unchanging truth."[5] This divine law is accessible to our minds.

4. Hence, those many people are in error who today assert that one can find neither in human nature nor in the revealed law any absolute and immutable norm to serve for particular actions other than the one which expresses itself in the general law of charity and respect for human dignity. As a proof of their assertion they put forward the view that so-called norms of the natural law or precepts of Sacred Scripture are to be regarded only as given expressions of a form of particular culture at a certain moment of history.

But in fact, divine Revelation and, in its own proper order, philosophical wisdom, emphasize the authentic exigencies of human nature. They thereby necessarily manifest the existence of immutable laws inscribed in the constitutive elements of human nature and which are revealed to be identical in all beings endowed with reason.

Furthermore, Christ instituted his Church as "the pillar and bulwark of truth."[6] With the Holy Spirit's assistance, she ceaselessly preserves and transmits without error the truths of the moral order, and she authentically interprets not only the revealed positive law but "also . . . those principles of the moral order which have their origin in human nature itself"[7] and which concern man's full development and sanctification. Now in fact the Church throughout her history has always considered a certain number of precepts of the natural law as having an absolute and immutable value, and in their transgression she has seen a contradiction of the teaching and spirit of the Gospel.

5. Since sexual ethics concern certain fundamental values of human and Christian life, this general teaching equally applies to sexual ethics. In this domain there exist principles and norms which the Church has always unhesitatingly transmitted as part of her teaching, however much the opinions and morals of the world may have been opposed to them. These principles and norms in no way owe their origin to a certain type of culture, but rather to knowledge of the divine law and of human nature. They therefore cannot be considered as having become out of date or doubtful under the pretext that a new cultural situation has arisen.

It is these principles which inspired the exhortations and directives given by the Second Vatican Council for an education and an organization of social life taking account of the equal dignity of man and woman while respecting their difference.[8]

Speaking of "the sexual nature of man and the human faculty of procreation," the Council noted that they "wonderfully exceed the dispositions of lower forms of life."[9] It then took particular care to expound the principles and criteria which concern human sexuality in marriage, and which are based upon the finality of the specific function of sexuality.

In this regard the Council declares that the moral goodness of the acts proper to conjugal life, acts which are ordered according to true human dignity, "does not depend solely on sincere intentions or on an evaluation of motives. It must be determined by objective standards. These, based on the nature of the human person and his acts, preserve the full sense of mutual self-giving and human procreation in the context of true love."[10]

These final words briefly sum up the Council's teaching—more fully expounded in an earlier part of the same Constitution[11]—on the finality of the sexual act and on the principal criterion of its morality: it is respect for its finality that ensures the moral goodness of this act.

This same principle, which the Church holds from divine Revelation and from her authentic interpretation of the natural law, is also the basis of her traditional doctrine, which states that the use of the sexual function has its true meaning and moral rectitude only in true marriage.[12]

6. It is not the purpose of the present Declaration to deal with all the abuses of the sexual faculty, nor with all the elements involved in the practice of chastity. Its object is rather to repeat the Church's doctrine on certain particular points, in view of the urgent need to oppose serious errors and widespread aberrant modes of behavior.

7. Today there are many who vindicate the right to sexual union before marriage, at least in those cases where a firm intention to marry and an affection which is already in some way conjugal in the psychology of the subjects require this completion, which they judge to be connatural. This is especially the case when the celebration of the marriage is impeded by circumstances or when this intimate relationship seems necessary in order for love to be preserved.

This opinion is contrary to Christian doctrine, which states that every genital act must be within the framework of marriage. However firm the intention of those who practice such premature sexual relations may be, the fact remains that these relations cannot ensure, in sincerity and fidelity, the interpersonal relationship between a man and a woman, nor especially can they protect this relationship from whims and caprices. Now it is a stable union that Jesus willed, and he restored its original requirement, beginning with the sexual difference. "Have you not read that the creator from the beginning made them male and female and that he said: This is why a man must leave father and mother, and cling to his wife, and the two become one body? They are no longer two, therefore, but one body. So then, what God has united, man must not divide."[13] Saint Paul will be even more explicit when he shows that if unmarried people or widows cannot live chastely they have no other alternative than the stable union of marriage: ". . . it is better to marry than to be aflame with passion."[14] Through marriage, in fact, the love of married people is taken up into that love which Christ irrevocably has for the Church,[15] while dissolute sexual union[16] defiles the temple of the Holy Spirit which the Christian has become. Sexual union therefore is only legitimate if a definitive community of life has been established between the man and the woman.

This is what the Church has always understood and taught,[17] and she finds a profound agreement with her doctrine in men's reflection and in the lessons of history.

Experience teaches us that love must find its safeguard in the stability of marriage, if sexual intercourse is truly to respond to the requirements of its own finality and to those of human dignity. These requirements call for a conjugal contract sanctioned and guaranteed by society—a contract which establishes a state of life of capital importance both for the exclusive union of the man and the woman and for the good of their family and of the human community. Most often, in fact, premarital relations exclude the possibility of children. What is represented to be conjugal love is not able, as it absolutely should be, to develop into paternal and maternal love. Or, if it does happen to do so, this will be to the detriment of the children, who will be deprived of the stable environment in which they ought to develop in order to find in it the way and the means of their insertion into society as a whole.

The consent given by people who wish to be united in marriage must therefore be manifested externally and in a manner which makes it valid in the eyes of society. As far as the faithful are concerned, their consent to the setting up of a community of conjugal life must be expressed according to the laws of the Church. It is a consent which makes their marriage a Sacrament of Christ.

8. At the present time there are those who, basing themselves on observations in the psychological order, have begun to judge indulgently, and even to excuse completely, homosexual relations between certain people. This they do in opposition to the constant teaching of the Magisterium and to the moral sense of the Christian people.

A distinction is drawn, and it seems with some reason, between homosexuals whose tendency comes from a false education, from a lack of normal sexual development, from habit, from bad example, or from other similar causes, and is transitory or at least not incurable; and homosexuals who are definitively such because of some kind of innate instinct or a pathological constitution judged to be incurable.

In regard to this second category of subjects, some people conclude that their tendency is so natural that it justifies in their case homosexual relations within a sincere communion of life and love analogous to marriage, in so far as such homosexuals feel incapable of enduring a solitary life.

In the pastoral field, these homosexuals must certainly be treated with understanding and sustained in the hope of overcoming their personal difficulties and their inability to fit into society. Their culpability will be judged with prudence. But no pastoral method can be employed which would give moral justification to these acts on the grounds that they would be consonant with the condition of such people. For according to the objective moral order, homosexual relations are acts which lack an essential and indispensable finality. In Sacred Scripture they are condemned as a serious depravity and even presented as the sad consequence of rejecting God.[18] This judgment of Scripture does not of course permit us to conclude that all those who suffer from this anomaly are personally responsible for it, but it does attest to the fact that homosexual acts are intrinsically disordered and can in no case be approved.

9. The traditional Catholic doctrine that masturbation constitutes a grave moral disorder is often called into doubt or expressly denied today. It is said that psychology and sociology show that it is a normal phenomenon of sexual development, especially among the young. It is stated that there is real and serious fault only in the measure that the subject deliberately indulges in solitary pleasure closed in on self ("ipsation"), because in this case the act would indeed be radically opposed to the loving communion between persons of different sex which some hold is what is principally sought in the use of the sexual faculty.

This opinion is contradictory to the teaching and pastoral practice of the Catholic Church. Whatever the force of certain arguments of a biological and philosophical nature, which have sometimes been used by theologians, in fact both the Magisterium of the Church—in the course of a constant tradition—and the moral sense of the faithful have declared without hesitation that masturbation is an intrinsically and seriously disordered act.[19] The main reason is that, whatever the motive for acting in this way, the deliberate use of the sexual faculty outside normal conjugal relations essentially contradicts the finality of the faculty. For it lacks the sexual relationship called for by the moral order, namely the relationship which realizes "the full sense of mutual self-giving and human procreation in the context of true love."[20] All deliberate exercise of sexuality must be reserved to this regular relationship. Even if it cannot be proved that Scripture condemns this sin by name, the tradition of the Church has rightly understood it to be condemned in the New Testament when the latter speaks of "impurity," "unchasteness" and other vices contrary to chastity and continence.

Sociological surveys are able to show the frequency of this disorder according to the places, populations or circumstances studied. In this way facts are discovered, but facts do not constitute a criterion for judging the moral value of human acts.[21] The frequency of the phenomenon in question is certainly to be linked with man's innate weakness following original sin; but it is also to be linked with the loss of a sense of God, with the corruption of morals engendered by the commercialization of vice, with the unrestrained licentiousness of so many public entertainments and publications, as well as with the neglect of modesty, which is the guardian of chastity.

On the subject of masturbation modern psychology provides much valid and useful information for formulating a more equitable judgment on moral responsibility and for orienting pastoral action. Psychology helps one to see how the immaturity of adolescence (which can sometimes persist after that age), psychological imbalance or habit can influence behavior, diminishing the deliberate character of the act and bringing about a situation whereby subjectively there may not always be serious fault. But in general, the absence of serious responsibility must not be presumed; this would be to misunderstand people's moral capacity.

In the pastoral ministry, in order to form an adequate judgment in concrete cases, the habitual behavior of people will be considered in its totality, not only with regard to the individual's practice of charity and of justice but also with regard to the individual's care in observing the particular precepts of chastity. In particular, one will have to examine whether the individual is using the necessary means, both natural and supernatural, which Christian asceticism from its long experience recommends for overcoming the passions and progressing in virtue.

10. The observance of the moral law in the field of sexuality and the practice of chastity have been considerably endangered, especially among less fervent Christians, by the current tendency to minimize as far as possible, when not denying outright, the reality of grave sin, at least in people's actual lives.

There are those who go as far as to affirm that mortal sin, which causes separation from God, only exists in the formal refusal directly opposed to God's call, or in that selfishness which completely and deliberately closes itself to the love of neighbor. They say that it is only then that there comes into play the fundamental option, that is to say the decision which totally commits the person and which is necessary if mortal sin is to exist; by this option the person, from the depths of the personality, takes up or ratifies a fundamental attitude towards God or people. On the contrary, so-called "peripheral" actions (which, it is said, usually do not involve decisive choice), do not go so far as to change the fundamental option, the less so since they often come, as is observed, from habit. Thus such actions can weaken the fundamental option, but not to such a degree as to change it completely. Now according to these authors, a change of the fundamental option towards God less easily comes about in the field of sexual activity, where a person generally does not transgress the moral order in a fully deliberate and responsible manner but rather under the influence of passion, weakness, immaturity, sometimes even through the illusion of thus showing love for someone else. To these causes there is often added the pressure of the social environment.

In reality, it is precisely the fundamental option which in the last resort defines a person's moral disposition. But it can be completely changed by particular acts, especially when, as often happens, these have been prepared for by previous more superficial acts. Whatever the case, it is wrong to say that particular acts are not enough to constitute mortal sin.

According to the Church's teaching, mortal sin, which is opposed to God, does not consist only in formal and direct resistance to the commandment of charity. It is equally to be found in this opposition to authentic love which is included in every deliberate transgression, in serious matter, of each of the moral laws.

Christ himself has indicated the double commandment of love as the basis of the moral life. But on this commandment depends "the whole Law, and the Prophets also."[22] It therefore includes the other particular precepts. In fact, to the young man who asked, ". . . what good deed must I do to possess eternal life?" Jesus replied: ". . . if you wish to enter into life, keep the commandments. . . . You must not kill. You must not commit adultery. You must not steal. You must not bring false witness. Honor your father and mother, and: you must love your neighbor as yourself."[23]

A person therefore sins mortally not only when his action comes from direct contempt for love of God and neighbor, but also when he consciously and freely, for whatever reason, chooses something which is seriously disordered. For in this choice, as has been said above, there is already included contempt for the divine commandment: the person turns himself away from God and loses charity. Now according to Christian tradition and the Church's teaching, and as right reason also recognizes, the moral order of sexuality involves such high values of human life that every direct violation of this order is objectively serious.[24]

It is true that in sins of the sexual order, in view of their kind and their causes, it more easily happens that free consent is not fully given; this is a fact which calls for caution in all judgment as to the subject's responsibility. In this matter it is particularly opportune to recall the following words of Scripture: "Man looks at appearances but God looks at the heart."[25] However, although prudence is recommended in judging the subjective seriousness of a particular sinful act, it in no way follows that one can hold the view that in the sexual field mortal sins are not committed.

Pastors of souls must therefore exercise patience and goodness; but they are not allowed to render God's commandments null, nor to reduce unreasonably people's responsibility. "To diminish in no way the saving teaching of Christ constitutes an eminent form of charity for souls. But this must ever be accompanied by patience and goodness, such as the Lord himself gave example of in dealing with people. Having come not to condemn but to save, he was indeed intransigent with evil, but merciful towards individuals."[26]

11. As has been said above, the purpose of this Declaration is to draw the attention of the faithful in present-day circumstances to certain errors and modes of behavior which they must guard against. The virtue of chastity, however, is in no way confined solely to avoiding the faults already listed. It is aimed at attaining higher and more positive goals. It is a virtue which concerns the whole personality, as regards both interior and outward behavior.

Individuals should be endowed with this virtue according to their state in life: for some it will mean virginity or celibacy consecrated to God, which is an eminent way of giving oneself more easily to God alone with an undivided heart.[27] For others it will take the form determined by the moral law, according to whether they are married or single. But whatever the state of life, chastity is not simply an external state; it must make a person's heart pure in accordance with Christ's words: "You have learned how it was said: You must not commit adultery. But I say this to you: if a man looks at a woman lustfully, he has already committed adultery with her in his heart."[28]

Chastity is included in that continence which Saint Paul numbers among the gifts of the Holy Spirit, while he condemns sensuality as a vice particularly unworthy of the Christian and one which precludes entry into the kingdom of heaven.[29] "What God wants is for all to be holy. He wants you to keep away from fornication, and each one of you to know how to use the body that belongs to him in a way that is holy and honorable, not giving way to selfish lust like the pagans who do not know God. He wants nobody at all ever to sin by taking advantage of a brother in these matters. . . . We have been called by God to be holy, not to be immoral. In other words, anyone who objects is not objecting to a human authority, but to God, who gives you his Holy Spirit."[30] "Among you there must not be even a mention of fornication or impurity in any of its forms, or promiscuity: this would hardly become the saints! For you can be quite certain that nobody who actually indulges in fornication or impurity or promiscuity—which is worshipping a false god—can inherit anything of the kingdom of God. Do not let anyone deceive you with empty arguments: it is for this loose living that God's anger comes down on those who rebel against him. Make sure that you are not included with them. You were darkness once, but now you are light in the Lord; be like children of light, for the effects of the light are seen in complete goodness and right living and truth."[31]

In addition, the Apostle points out the specifically Christian motive for practicing chastity when he condemns the sin of fornication not only in the measure that this action is injurious to one's neighbor or to the social order but because the fornicator offends against Christ who has redeemed him with his blood and of whom he is a member, and against the Holy Spirit of whom he is the temple. "You know, surely, that your bodies are members making up the body of Christ. . . . All the other sins are committed outside the body; but to fornicate is to sin against your own body. Your body, you know, is the temple of the Holy Spirit, who is in you since you received him from God. You are not your own property; you have been bought and paid for. That is why you should use your body for the glory of God."[32]

The more the faithful appreciate the value of chastity and its necessary role in their lives as men and women, the better they will understand, by a kind of spiritual instinct, its moral requirements and counsels. In the same way they will know better how to accept and carry out, in a spirit of docility to the Church's teaching, what an upright conscience dictates in concrete cases.

12. The Apostle Saint Paul describes in vivid terms the painful interior conflict of the person enslaved to sin: the conflict between "the law of his mind" and the "law of sin which dwells in his members" and which holds him captive.[33] But man can achieve liberation from his "body doomed to death" through the grace of Jesus Christ.[34] This grace is enjoyed by those who have been justified by it and whom "the law of the spirit of life in Christ Jesus has set free from the law of sin and death."[35] It is for this reason that the Apostle adjures them: "That is why you must not let sin reign in your mortal bodies or command your obedience to bodily passions."[36]

This liberation, which fits one to serve God in newness of life, does not however suppress the concupiscence deriving from original sin, nor the promptings to evil in this world, which is "in the power of the evil one."[37] This is why the Apostle exhorts the faithful to overcome temptations by the power of God[38] and to "stand against the wiles of the devil"[39] by faith, watchful prayer[40] and an austerity of life that brings the body into subjection to the Spirit.[41]

Living the Christian life by following in the footsteps of Christ requires that everyone should "deny himself and take up his cross daily,"[42] sustained by the hope of reward, for "if we have died with him, we shall also reign with him."[43]

In accordance with these pressing exhortations, the faithful of the present time, and indeed today more than ever, must use the means which have always been recommended by the Church for living a chaste life. These means are: discipline of the senses and the mind, watchfulness and prudence in avoiding occasions of sin, the observance of modesty, moderation in recreation, wholesome pursuits, assiduous prayer and frequent reception of the Sacraments of Penance and the Eucharist. Young people especially should earnestly foster devotion to the Immaculate Mother of God, and take as examples the lives of the Saints and other faithful people, especially young ones, who excelled in the practice of chastity.

It is important in particular that everyone should have a high esteem for the virtue of chastity, its beauty and its power of attraction. This virtue increases the human person's dignity and enables him to love truly, disinterestedly, unselfishly and with respect for others.

13. It is up to the Bishops to instruct the faithful in the moral teaching concerning sexual morality, however great may be the difficulties in carrying out this work in the face of ideas and practices generally prevailing today. This traditional doctrine must be studied more deeply. It must be handed on in a way capable of properly enlightening the consciences of those confronted with new situations and it must be enriched with a discernment of all the elements that can truthfully and usefully be brought forward about the meaning and value of human sexuality. But the principles and norms of moral living reaffirmed in this Declaration must be faithfully held and taught. It will especially be necessary to bring the faithful to understand that the Church holds these principles not as old and inviolable superstitions, nor out of some Manichaean prejudice, as is often alleged, but rather because she knows with certainty that they are in complete harmony with the divine order of creation and with the spirit of Christ, and therefore also with human dignity.

It is likewise the Bishops' mission to see that a sound doctrine enlightened by faith and directed by the Magisterium of the Church is taught in Faculties of Theology and in Seminaries. Bishops must also ensure that confessors enlighten people's consciences and that catechetical instruction is given in perfect fidelity to Catholic doctrine.

It rests with Bishops, the priests and their collaborators to alert the faithful against the erroneous opinions often expressed in books, reviews and public meetings.

Parents, in the first place, and also teachers of the young must endeavor to lead their children and their pupils, by way of a complete education, to the psychological, emotional and moral maturity befitting their age. They will therefore prudently give them information suited to their age; and they will assiduously form their wills in accordance with Christian morals, not only by advice but above all by the example of their own lives, relying on God's help, which they will obtain in prayer. They will likewise protect the young from the many dangers of which they are quite unaware.

Artists, writers and all those who use the means of social communication should exercise their profession in accordance with their Christian faith and with a clear awareness of the enormous influence which they can have. They should remember that "the primacy of the objective moral order must be regarded as absolute by all,"[44] and that it is wrong for them to give priority above it to any so-called aesthetic purpose, or to material advantage or to success. Whether it be a question of artistic or literary works, public entertainment or providing information, each individual in his or her own domain must show tact, discretion, moderation and a true sense of values. In this way, far from adding to the growing permissiveness of behavior, each individual will contribute towards controlling it and even towards making the moral climate of society more wholesome.

All lay people, for their part, by virtue of their rights and duties in the work of the apostolate, should endeavor to act in the same way.

Finally, it is necessary to remind everyone of the words of the Second Vatican Council: "This Holy Synod likewise affirms that children and young people have a right to be encouraged to weigh moral values with an upright conscience, and to embrace them by personal choice, to know and love God more adequately. Hence, it earnestly entreats all who exercise government over people or preside over the work of education to see that youth is never deprived of this sacred right."[45]

At the audience granted on November 7, 1975 to the undersigned Prefect of the Sacred Congregation for the Doctrine of the Faith, the Sovereign Pontiff by divine providence Pope Paul VI approved this Declaration "On certain questions concerning sexual ethics," confirmed it and ordered its publication.

Given in Rome, at the Sacred Congregation for the Doctrine of the Faith, on December 29, 1975.

FRANJO Card. ŠEPER, Prefect

Notes

[1]Cf. Second Vatican Ecumenical Council, Constitution on the Church in the Modern World *Gaudium et spes,* 47: *AAS* 58 (1966), p. 1067.

[2]Cf. Apostolic Constitution *Regimini ecclesiae universae,* 29 (August 15, 1967): *AAS* 59 (1967), p. 897.

[3]*Gaudium et spes,* 16: *AAS* 58 (1966), p. 1037.

[4]Jn 8:12.

[5]Second Vatican Ecumenical Council, Declaration *Dignitatis humanae,* 3: *AAS* 58 (1966), p. 931.

[6]1 Tim 3:15.

[7]*Dignitatis humanae,* 14: *AAS* 58 (1966), p. 940; cf. Pius XI, Encyclical Letter *Casti connubii,* December 31, 1930: *AAS* 22 (1930), pp. 579–580; Pius XII, Allocution of November 2, 1954: *AAS* 46 (1954), pp. 671–672; John XXIII, Encyclical Letter *Mater et magistra,* May 15, 1961: *AAS* 53 (1961), p. 457; Paul VI, Encyclical Letter *Humanae vitae,* 4, July 25, 1968: *AAS* 60 (1968), p. 483.

[8]Cf. Second Vatican Ecumenical Council, Declaration *Gravissimum educationis,* 1, 8: *AAS* 58 (1966), pp. 729–730; 734–736. *Gaudium et spes,* 29, 60, 67: *AAS* 58 (1966), pp. 1048–1049, 1080–1081, 1088–1089.

[9]*Gaudium et spes,* 51: *AAS* 58 (1966), p. 1072.

[10]*Ibid.;* cf. also 49: *loc. cit.,* pp. 1069–1070.

[11]*Ibid.,* 49, 50: *loc. cit.,* pp. 1069–1072.

[12]The present Declaration does not go into further detail regarding the norms of sexual life within marriage; these norms have been clearly taught in the Encyclical Letters *Casti connubii* and *Humanae vitae.*

[13]Cf. Mt 19:4-6.

[14]1 Cor 7:9.

[15]Cf. Eph 5:25-32.

[16]Sexual intercourse outside marriage is formally condemned: 1 Cor 5:1; 6:9; 7:2; 10:8; Eph 5:5; 1 Tim 1:10; Heb 13:4; and with explicit reasons: 1 Cor 6:12-20.

[17]Cf. Innocent IV, Letter *Sub catholica professione,* March 6, 1254, *DS* 835; Pius II, *Propos. damn. in Ep. Cum sicut accepimus,* November 14, 1459, *DS* 1367; Decrees of the Holy Office, September 24, 1665, *DS* 2045; March 2, 1679, *DS* 2148. Pius XI, Encyclical Letter *Casti connubii,* December 31, 1930: *AAS* 22 (1930) pp. 558–559.

[18]Rom 1:24-27: "That is why God left them to their filthy enjoyments and the practices with which they dishonor their own bodies, since they have given up divine truth for a lie and have worshipped and served creatures instead of the creator, who is blessed for ever. Amen! That is why God has abandoned them to degrading passions: why their women have turned from natural intercourse to unnatural practices and why their menfolk have given up natural intercourse to be consumed with passion for each other, men doing shameless things with men and getting an appropriate reward for their perversion." See also what Saint Paul says of *masculorum concubitores* in 1 Cor 6:10; 1 Tim 1:10.

[19]Cf. Leo IX, Letter *Ad splendidum nitentis,* in the year 1054: *DS* 687–688, Decree of the Holy Office, March 2, 1679: *DS* 2149; Pius XII, *Allocutio,* October 8, 1953: *AAS* 45 (1953), pp. 677–678; May 19, 1956: *AAS* 48 (1956), pp. 472–473.

[20]*Gaudium et spes,* 51: *AAS* 58 (1966), p. 1072.

[21] ". . . if sociological surveys are useful for better discovering the thought patterns of the people of a particular place, the anxieties and needs of those to whom we proclaim the word of God, and also the opposition made to it by modern reasoning through the widespread notion that outside science there exists no legitimate form of knowledge, still the conclusions drawn from such surveys could not of themselves constitute a determining criterion of truth," Paul VI, Apostolic Exhortation *Quinque iam anni,* December 8, 1970, *AAS* 63 (1971), p. 102.

[22]Mt 22:38, 40.

[23]Mt 19:16-19.

[24]Cf. notes 17 and 19 above: Decree of the Holy Office, March 18, 1666, *DS* 2060; Paul VI, Encyclical Letter *Humanae vitae,* 13, 14: *AAS* 60 (1968), pp. 489–496.

[25]1 Sam 16:7.

[26]Paul VI, Encyclical Letter *Humanae vitae,* 29: *AAS* 60 (1968), p. 501.

[27]Cf. 1 Cor 7:7, 34; Council of Trent, Session XXIV, can. 10: *DS* 1810; Second Vatican Council, Constitution *Lumen gentium,* 42, 43, 44: *AAS* 57 (1965), pp. 47–51; Synod of Bishops, *De sacerdotio ministeriali,* part II, 4, b: *AAS* 63 (1971), pp. 915–916.

[28]Mt 5:28.

[29]Cf. Gal 5:19-23; 1 Cor 6:9-11.

[30]1 Thess 4:3-8; cf. Col 3:5-7; 1 Tim 1:10.

[31]Eph 5:3-8; cf. 4:18-19.

[32]1 Cor 6:15, 18-20.

[33]Cf. Rom 7:23.

[34]Cf. Rom 7:24-25.

[35]Cf. Rom 8:2.

[36]Rom 6:12.

[37]1 Jn 5:19.

[38]Cf. 1 Cor 10:13.

[39]Eph 6:11.

[40]Cf. Eph 6:16, 18.

[41]Cf. 1 Cor 9:27.

[42]Lk 9:23.

[43]2 Tim 2:11-12.

[44]Second Vatican Ecumenical Council, Decree *Inter mirifica,* 6: *AAS* 56 (1964), p. 147.

[45]*Gravissimum educationis,* 1: *AAS* 58 (1966), p. 730.

Can We Get Real about Sex?   *Lisa Sowle Cahill*

During my years as college professor (since 1976), lecturer, writer, and mother I have learned that the task of trying to make sense of Catholic teaching on sexuality has to be geared to different audiences with different life experiences. Each generation has its own questions. Those of us who were teen-agers before Vatican II still carry on a struggle of "liberation" from a negative and restrictive picture of sexual dangers. But most younger adults and virtually all teens today face a different battle: to carve out some sense of sexual direction in a peer and media culture which presents sex as a sophisticated recreational activity for which the only moral criterion is mutual consent. I have finally learned that my invitations to appreciate the goodness and pervasiveness of sexuality sound not only redundant but even naive to audiences hungry for a solid answer to shallow or cynical versions of precisely that same message.

Currents of ethical and theological thought within the church manifest similar differences in perspective. Controversies over sexual morality are shaped by at least four constituencies, having different and perhaps incompatible agendas. Though this is to simplify, we may think of them as the traditionalists, the revisionists, the skeptics, and the alienated. These groups represent different responses to the exciting but tumultuous changes which beset the church as well as the culture in the 1960s. The traditionalists put conformity to magisterial teaching high on the list of Catholic identity markers. They stand behind the idea that Vatican positions on matters like premarital sex, birth control, abortion, homosexuality, and divorce can brook no "dissent." Holding a united front on these questions is perceived as essential to the continued strength of church authority. Traditionalists try to connect past teaching with the modern world by arguing that those who *experience* sexual intimacy and honestly examine it will agree that the relationship is a form of "mutual self-gift" (in a phrase of John Paul II), which intrinsically requires heterosexuality, commitment, permanency, exclusivity, and procreation.

A second group, the "revisionists," mostly grew to maturity before Vatican II, and remember vividly the revitalization the council brought. These Catholics, some parents of adolescents and young adults, see the church as their religio-cultural home, even as "mother" and "teacher," but they disagree that sexual and marital experience necessarily confirm all current church teaching. At least since the sixties, they have had serious doubts about whether the positions on contraception and divorce can really hold water. They continue to struggle within the church to find room and a voice for moderate reformulations of—and possibly a few exceptions to—the Catholic view that sex belongs in indissoluble marriage and leads to parenthood.

A third group might be called the "skeptics." Many, but not all, of them are younger adults who are less willing to take church credibility for granted. They tend to look on in disbelief as the church of their parents promotes teachings on sex which appear oblivious to the realities of human relationships, at least in the U.S. They observe the same phenomena as do the "revisionists"—the widespread acceptance of contraception, "living together," homosexuality, abortion; the threats of AIDS and marital breakdown. But although the skeptics still consider themselves "Catholic," they differ from the "revisionists." They openly assert that church teaching on sex as formulated primarily by celibate male clergy should be declared irrelevant to modern needs. Ready to relegate the traditionalists to the lunatic fringe, they smile at the earnest and rather dogged reinterpretive efforts of the revisionists, wondering when they will realize the impossibility of making headway toward change within present structures.

The fourth group, the "alienated," no longer feel any special tie to the Catholic church or any necessity to justify, struggle with, or refute its teachings. Roman Catholicism is not a resource to which they turn (at least not consciously) for guidance on sex or any other issue. Church sexual teachings, when considered at all, are written off as obsolete, oppressive and outrageous. Even though "alienated" Catholics are in a sense no longer a "constituency" for church teaching, it is significant that that teaching evokes so negative a response in a group whose size is far from negligible.

This author would be best identified as a member of constituency two attempting to convince constituency three that there is something worthwhile about sex still to be mined in Catholic teaching—though I would have to concur in the quite legitimate impression that its practical value is not always easy to discover.

The Catholic tradition on sexuality has always defined its moral parameters in terms of *marriage*. More than a union of two individuals, marriage is set in the context of *family,* and especially of *procreation.* Augustine and Aquinas saw procreation in marriage as the only reason fully justifying sexual intercourse, and saw both procreation and marriage as especially important insofar as they contribute to the species, the society, and the kinship network or extended family. Although companionship and friendship of spouses were ideals, premodern authors, like the society around them, were unable to recognize the later ideal of "interpersonal union" both because they lacked our sense of the importance of individuals, and because women were considered inferior and subordinate to their male partners. Procreation as the primary purpose of sex was maintained as late as 1930 (in Pius XI's encyclical *Casti connubii*). A breakthrough occurred in Vatican II's *Gaudium et spes* (1965) and in the encyclical *Humanae vitae* (1968), when love and procreation were ranked equally as the purposes of marriage. This shift raising love to a level with procreation represented the influence of philosophical "personalism," and the emergent awareness of women's equality. Yet official church teaching continues to tie respect for these values very much to the physical act of sexual intercourse, not to the overall or long-range relationship of the couple. Today it teaches that both purposes must be present in "each and every act." That is, every act must be part of a permanently committed, heterosexual, love relationship; and every single act must be procreative, *in the sense that* the outcome of procreation must not be artificially prevented.

Contemporary experience and thought raise challenges to this specific presentation of the teaching that should not be underestimated. "Sexuality" is now recognized as a basic dimension of the personality, and covers far more than genital acts designed for reproduction. The affective and interpersonal dimensions of sex, along with the occasions it offers for intimacy and reciprocal pleasure, have become far more important. The wrongness and harm of defining all or most nonprocreative sexual pleasure as "sinful" is evident. The feminist movement has sharply critiqued the distorted forms with which patriarchy has shaped both marriage and family, and has begun to reshape sexuality with a new appreciation of women's experiences of sex, spousehood, and motherhood. Delayed marriage for many young adults who pursue educational and vocational goals also means a longer period of sexual maturity and potential relationships before marriage. The responsibility of the marriageable to choose their own partners rather than relying on parental negotiations or social and religious similarity, along with the high incidence of divorce, has led to premarital sex and "trial marriages," which many see as prudent exploratory arrangements. And there are many single adult Catholics who may not have the opportunity or desire for marriage, but who yearn for intimacy and sexual expression, for which they may find occasions outside marriage. Many lesbian and gay persons see their sexuality as a gift to be valued both for personal identity and in relationships. They call for church support of their efforts to live as faithful Christians and to gain protection of their civil rights. All of these considerations pose challenges to church teaching which, it must be admitted, the church has not adequately met. They also raise questions which I cannot pursue here, though I have advocated modifications (a group-two goal!) of church teaching on many of these points. Indeed, it sometimes seems that both "conservatives" and "liberals" (terms that in practice refer to the traditionalists and the revisionists, since neither the skeptics nor the alienated see the relevant intra-ecclesial debates as worth the investment) become unduly distracted from more fundamental issues by battles over the morality of sexual acts: premarital, contraceptive, homosexual, etc. If we could transcend the limits of such discussions, we might recover the essential message about sexuality which Roman Catholicism transmits.

What is that message? What is a credible, convincing, and helpful expression of Christian sexual values today? I think that message pertains to three dimensions of sexuality: 1) sex as a physical drive for pleasure; 2) sex as intimacy or love; 3) sex as procreative. It is the value of the third that is the most necessary and the most difficult to communicate to today's young adults.

Sex as a physical drive. In the past, there has been in Christianity (in Augustine, for instance) a deep suspicion of sexual drives or sexual desire. This suspicion was no doubt based on sex's undeniable tendency to break social and moral restraints, and to seek fulfillment in self-centered, manipulative, and even violent ways. Today this attitude might be revised into the recognition that the sexual drive has real limits as a guide to sexual relationships. The dominant "cultural message"—that sex is natural, enjoyable, good, and even recreational—has an obvious legitimacy in itself, and exponents of a Catholic Christian approach to sexuality should not appear grudging in their acceptance of the "joy of sex." But the message is incomplete and inadequate. Using sexual acts and relationships as an outlet for our physical drives or as a means of access to physical enjoyment is not *bad,* but it is *limited.* Media images aside, I doubt that many people really disagree with this point, however much some may be tempted to rationalize indiscriminate sexual behavior. Physical desire and enjoyment taken alone as motives for sex make sex unfulfilling, lonely, and perhaps ultimately boring. Although women seem to understand better than men that sexual intimacy naturally entails psychological intimacy, I doubt this difference is innate. Rather it is a matter of women being socialized or socially encouraged to take intimacy more seriously. Intimacy adds to the fulfillment of both men's and women's sexuality. This leads to sex's second dimension.

Sex as love. Seeing sex as an expression of love seems to verge on the romantic, yet it is not all that foreign to most of our experiences and personal goals. Our culture is prone to cynicism about the trustworthiness of human relationships. But sexual intimacy can express and augment psychological intimacy, affection, reciprocal understanding and encouragement, partnership, companionship, compassion, and even commitment. One Catholic Christian value of sexuality is permanence: the love relationship established sexually between a woman and a man should be long-term and not transient. Sex with little or no commitment shortchanges sex's potential for intimacy. Unlike other animal species, humans have a deep capacity for friendship and interpersonal reciprocity, which, when expressed sexually, constitutes the most intense of human relationships. The appropriate moral context for complete sexual union is a commensurate level of interpersonal commitment. Unequal commitment between partners leads to manipulation, disappointment, and pain. Sex without commitment is unfaithful to the human potential of sexuality.

The psychological and personal aspects of sexual union are complemented by the relation of the sexual couple to the family and society. Our sexuality is not simply an individualistic capacity but binds us with others in families, that is, in some of the most rewarding and most demanding of human relationships. A man and woman bring to their union links with and commitments to other persons, including their respective families and friends and, eventually, the children their union may produce. Although not all sexual couples give birth to children, the procreative potential of sex is always a part of that relationship. The prospect of pregnancy and parenthood is not always intentional and dominant in the relationship, but it is nonetheless a latent and morally important possibility. Obviously a faithful commitment between parents is the best context for the nurture of children.

Like many group-two Catholics, I have often considered the common practice of "living together" with some misgivings along with the feeling that there might be in it something to be learned about the nature of sexual commitment. Some of my intuitions came together upon hearing a Ugandan bishop observe that, in his culture, marriage was a *progressive* reality, which did not come into being in an instant during a single ceremony, but which developed through a process of negotiation, visiting, and gift-giving among bride, groom, and their families. Although at some time during the process the couple might have sexual relations and even bear children, there was actually no one "point" before which a marriage did not exist and after which it did. Perhaps many couples in our culture are making a similar statement about their growing trust in and love for each other. However, the shortcoming of "progressive marriage" as we see it in the U.S. is the isolation of the unmarried sexual couple from the social support and accountability that accompanies formal marriage. In Uganda, the whole family has an investment in the growing relationship and expects the couple to make it work, persuading, admonishing, and supporting them as need be. This system also has clear understandings about how children will be cared for within the families if the couple subsequently parts. In other words, the African form of gradual marriage carries with it at every stage an increasing level of personal, familial, and social weight and responsibility. One thinks also of ancient Israelite betrothal and marriage, reflected in Matthew's and Luke's stories of the premarital pregnancy of Mary. The sexual relations permitted before marriage occurred in a context of religiously and socially specified conditions. Though the provisional sexual relationships common in our culture may represent a valid insight about the development of commitment, they still lack the social forms which would make them accountable to the genuine personal and communal significances of sex. One of these is parenthood, which leads us to the next point.

Sex as procreation. In modern Western cultures, the value of procreative sex may be harder to "sell" than pleasurable sex and loving sex. We are in an era in which procreation has been reduced to an incidental meaning of sex, usually to be avoided, and certainly to be accepted only if freely chosen. The deep associations and mutual reinforcements of sex, love, and parenthood are missing—partly because the church's teaching authority itself has narrowed their reciprocity to an experientially unintelligible focus on reproductive genital acts taken as separate events. But it is the unity of sex, love, and parenthood in this broader sense that is probably the major message Roman Catholicism has to offer today's young adults, who more easily see that sex expresses love than that sexual love leads to permanent commitment, parenthood, and family.

A better expression of this link, one we should aim to attain, lies in contemporary thought's repudiation of dualism, and its insistence that the body and the spirit or psyche form an integrated reality, not two uneasily aligned "components." We no longer tolerate a sexual ethics that sees the body as "bad," and to be repressed, while only our spiritual side is "holy." But a nondualistic view of sex requires that we premise a sexual morality on the goodness of sexual acts and sexual pleasure. It also requires that we look at these acts and their reproductive potential as an integrated whole or process. This is not to say that it is always wrong to interfere with conception as an outcome; but that moral analysis starts with a presumption in favor of the conduciveness of sex to shared parenthood. In other words, physical satisfaction or pleasure, interpersonal intimacy, and parenthood are not three separate "variables," *or possible* meanings of sex which we are morally free to combine or omit in different ways. Sex and love as fully *embodied* realities have an intrinsic moral connection to procreativity and to the shared creation and nurturing of new lives and new loves.

A more flexible and experientially adequate way to express this unity is not in terms of acts, but of *relationships.* Certain basic human relationships come together through our sexuality and link us not only to our partners but to the wider community, through the social relationships of marriage and family. These basic relationships are the woman-man and the parent-child relationships. Spousehood and parenthood are linked in the long-term commitment of the couple, sexually expressed. Both are not only intersubjective, but also embodied relationships. *Spousehood* is embodied through the shared material conditions of economic and domestic life, and through sexuality, which can give rise to a shared physical relation to the child. *Parenthood* is embodied through the shared material conditions of family life, again through the genetic link, and through the fact that the physical relation of spousehood is that which gives rise to parenthood.

To recapitulate, the Catholic tradition yields a set of moral attitudes toward sexuality, even before the point of dealing with concrete moral dilemmas or moral norms and prohibitions. The tradition can encourage respect and appreciation for sexuality as mutual physical pleasure, as intimacy, and as parenthood (or at least receptivity to it). These three relationships come together in the ongoing relationship of a couple. In all its dimensions, sex is both a psychospiritual experience and an embodied one, and both aspects contribute to its moral character.

Having said this, however, one also realizes that human circumstances sometimes arise in which not all three values (sex itself, commitment or love, and parenthood) can be realized simultaneously. In their sexual lives, as elsewhere, human beings are often confronted with moral conflicts, in which no choice is free of ambiguity. Of the three values, it is certainly love which is the *sine qua non,* the primary value in the triad. Since personhood is the most distinctive quality of the human being, it is the most personal aspect of sexuality which is *most* morally important. In unusual or difficult circumstances, the other two (sexual intercourse and procreation) can be subordinated to the love relationship of the couple as long as they are still given significant practical recognition. For example, in the use of contraception, procreation is temporarily set aside, but it still can be realized in the total relationship of the couple. In some infertility therapies, sex itself is set aside as the means to conception, but certainly the relationship of the couple which is both loving and procreative is otherwise given sexual expression. On the other hand, couples who are absolutely intolerant of the prospect of parenthood, perhaps resorting even to abortion as a means of birth control, do not give adequate moral recognition to the relation of sex, love, and procreation. Similarly, couples so desperate to conceive that they are willing to set aside the unity of their spousal-sexual-parental bond by using donor sperm or a surrogate mother to create a reproductive union between one spouse and a third party are also less than faithful to the values which sexuality represents. Although marriages as human realities sometimes fail, a tragedy that church teaching on "indissolubility" may not have met satisfactorily, the asset of the tradition is that it holds up an ideal of permanency. The meaning of "love" in the sexual triad goes far beyond romantic affections. It means a commitment to build a mutually satisfying sexual relationship, to mutual respect, to understanding and support. It entails persistence, repentance, and forgiveness. However justified divorce may sometimes be, the very high incidence of divorce seems to be due to cultural forgetfulness that the commitment to marital partnership requires both ongoing personal dedication and strong social supports.

Since at least the 1960s, interpersonal values have moved to center stage in the Catholic picture of sex, just as more attention has been paid to the experience of actual sexual relationships. At the same time, the inclusion of love and commitment as central along with parenthood has been sidetracked by acrimonious exchanges over contraception and other issues. Such debates have drained energies from the real task of reappropriating the essentials of Catholic teaching for the next generation. What our culture most needs to hear is an effective critique of individualist, materialist, and transient sexual relationships—not lists of specific transgressions which are "against church teaching." The Catholic "message" is that the interdependence of sex's pleasurable, intimate, and parental aspects can anchor our sexuality in some of the most enduring and rewarding human relationships. That message will be heard only if it is addressed honestly to the real sexual experiences of young adult Catholics, and only if the messengers can listen to and even learn from their audience's response.

—Commonweal, September 14, 1990

Responsible Sexuality: Reflection Questions

1. Name some specific ways in which you see society at odds with the teaching of the Church on sexual ethics.

2. Pope Paul VI referred to a growing attitude in society which he called "a contraceptive mentality." Do you see any evidence that he was correct?

3. Analyze and comment on what Mary Patricia Barth Fourqurean has to say in "Chastity as Shared Strength: An Open Letter to Students," *America,* November 6, 1993, 10–15. Be sure to review her thesis, comment on her major points, compare or contrast what she says with certain moral principles and with biblical references.

4. Why was the "St. John's Sex Case" a dilemma?

5. Lisa Sowle Cahill suggests that the inclusion of love and commitment is central along with parenthood in sexual relationships, but that this reality has often been sidetracked by acrimonious exchanges over contraception and other issues. These debates, she writes, drain energies from what ought to be the real task. Explain. What do you think?

6. What does the newspaper advertisement reproduced here suggest about some contemporary attitudes regarding sexuality?

13
Reverence for the Earth

Psalm 24

¹The earth is the LORD's and all that is in it,
   the world, and those who live in it;
²for he has founded it on the seas,
   and established it on the rivers.

³Who shall ascend the hill of the LORD?
   And who shall stand in his holy place?
⁴Those who have clean hands and pure hearts,
   who do not lift up their souls to what is false,
   and do not swear deceitfully.
⁵They will receive blessing from the LORD,
   and vindication from the God of their salvation.
⁶Such is the company of those who seek him,
   who seek the face of the God of Jacob.   *Selah*

⁷Lift up your heads, O gates!
   and be lifted up, O ancient doors!
   that the King of glory may come in.
⁸Who is the King of glory?
   The LORD, strong and mighty,
   the LORD, mighty in battle.
⁹Lift up your heads, O gates!
   and be lifted up, O ancient doors!
   that the King of glory may come in.
¹⁰Who is this King of glory?
   The LORD of hosts,
   he is the King of glory.

Respect for the Integrity of Creation

2415 The seventh commandment enjoins respect for the integrity of creation. Animals, like plants and inanimate beings, are by nature destined for the common good of past, present, and future humanity.[194] Use of the mineral, vegetable, and animal resources of the universe cannot be divorced from respect for moral imperatives. Man's dominion over inanimate and other living beings granted by the Creator is not absolute; it is limited by concern for the quality of life of his neighbor, including generations to come; it requires a religious respect for the integrity of creation.[195]

[194]Cf. *Gen* 1:28-31.
[195]Cf. CA 37–38.

—Catechism of the Catholic Church

Pied Beauty   *Gerard Manley Hopkins*

Glory be to God for dappled things—
    For skies of couple-colour as a brinded cow;
        For rose-moles all in stipple upon trout that swim;
Fresh-firecoal chestnut-falls; finches' wings;
    Landscape plotted and pieced—fold, fallow, and plough;
        And áll trádes, their gear and tackle and trim.

All things counter, original, spare, strange;
    Whatever is fickle, freckled (who knows how?)
        With swift, slow; sweet, sour; adazzle, dim;
He fathers-forth whose beauty is past change:
                Praise him.

Reverence for the Earth as a Religious Concern? *Rose Zuzworsky*

Most Catholics, if asked, would probably agree that a *religious person* should go to church, receive the sacraments, and love (or at least like) their neighbors. These *shoulds* are not, of course, limited to Catholics; they are, in fact, shared by all Christian denominations. In the last few decades, however, the question has been raised as to whether another *should* needs to be a part of the way people define themselves as religious persons. This newer *should* goes by different descriptions: concern for the environment, reverence for the earth, concern for creation, or ecological awareness. While the words are different, they share in common the belief that concern for how the earth is faring at the hands of humankind should be part of a religious person's response to his or her faith.

How has this come about? Can it really be legitimately claimed that reverence for the earth (or any of the other ways of expressing this) is actually a concern of the Churches and of religion? Isn't *religion* about things more directly related to God and to *holy things?*

The Opening Salvo

Back in 1967, historian Lynn White dropped a bombshell which helped stir the religious community in facing these very questions. In his article, "The Historical Roots of Our Environmental Crisis," White claimed, among other things, that Christianity bears a large portion of the blame for the disregard of the natural world at the hands of humanity. To explain his thesis, White raised the question, "What did Christianity tell people about their relations with the environment?" Answering this question from his own point of view, he claimed that Christianity's creation story in Genesis is at the root of our ecological problems. First, according to White, Adam's naming (at God's command) of all the "wild animals" and all the "birds of heaven" (Gen 2:19) established humanity's domination over the rest of creation. In this way, human beings are understood to be the center of the created world, with everything else in physical creation existing to serve humanity's needs. Secondly, and confirming this central position of human beings, is Genesis' depiction of humanity as made in God's image (Gen 1:26-27). Therefore, although human beings' bodies are made of the clay of the earth (Gen 2:7), they are more than just part of nature, they are the only creatures also made in the image of their creator. As the center of the created world, and as made in God's image, humanity shares in God's transcendence of nature. It is this *top heavy* relationship of human domination over the rest of creation—with the understanding that all other creatures and all of nature are there simply to be used as desired—which Lynn White faulted at Christianity's expense.

The pagan religions which Christianity replaced, White also noted, had put great stock in the *guardian spirits* which inhabited every tree, every stream, and every hill. By replacing this more personal relationship between humans and the rest of creation—this pagan *animism*—with a different relationship between human beings and the natural world, White claimed that "Christianity made it possible to exploit nature in a mode of indifference to the feelings of natural objects."

Over the years, theologians and scholars of many religious stripes have responded to White's harsh critique of Christianity's role in the on-going ecological crisis. While noting the article's usefulness in understanding concern for the natural world as a religious issue, most of those critiquing White's thesis have concluded that it was superficial in its analysis of Genesis and in its interpretation of the relationship between Christianity and the degradation of the natural world.

The Response of the Roman Catholic Church

In recent decades, Catholic theologians and scholars, as well as the bishops of the United States, and the Pope himself, have begun to address this concern for the natural world of creation. This is not to say that each of them was responding explicitly to White's article; nevertheless, they have each lent their theological expertise to a fuller understanding of how Christians, and Catholic Christians in particular, are to respond to the religious implications of the on-going ecological crisis. In doing so, they have given a deeper theological meaning to the Genesis creation story, as well as to a fuller understanding of what being made in God's image means in the relationship between human beings and the rest of God's creation.

In the Catholic Church, one of the major ways of getting this understanding across to people has been through papal encyclicals and the pastoral letters of the bishops of this country. These encyclicals and letters are part of the Church's tradition of speaking out on issues of social concern. And, at least since the 1970s, concern for the natural world has increasingly become a part of the social issues addressed within this tradition, which seeks to reach Catholics and all people of good will. Again, while it is unlikely that this attention to environmental concerns was directly related to Lynn White's personal castigation of Christianity, the fact remains that *religion* and *reverence for the earth* have been joined as an issue of concern for those who speak on behalf of the Catholic Church.

The Pope Responds

Pope John Paul II has addressed the condition of the environment beginning with his first encyclical *The Redeemer of Humanity* in 1979. In this encyclical the pope began to give a fuller understanding of Genesis' description of the relationship of humans to other creatures and to the earth. Here the interpretation of Genesis 1:28 as meaning that all creation is ordered to meet human needs is tempered with the understanding that "it was the creator's will that humans should communicate with nature as an intelligent 'master' and 'guardian' and not as a heedless 'exploiter' and 'destroyer'."

In his 1987 encyclical *On Social Concern,* John Paul II referred to that same Genesis passage again, claiming that "the dominion" given to humanity by the Creator "is not an absolute power nor can one speak of a freedom to 'use and misuse' or to dispose of things as one pleases." There are moral issues to consider here, since "from the beginning" God has put limits on human use of the things of the earth, as "expressed symbolically" by the admonition that the "fruit of the tree was not to be eaten" (Gen 2:16-17). This same moral imperative applies now, the pope implied, as we consider humanity's use and abuse of the air, waters, and soil which sustain all life. John Paul II addressed other aspects of the environmental crisis in *On Social Concern*. He recognized the rightness of *ecological concern*–which he described as "a greater realization of the limits of available resources, and of the need to respect the integrity and the cycles of nature." He also talked about "consumerism" and the fact that we have become a throw away society with very wasteful habits.

In what seems to be a direct response to Lynn White's basic criticism of Christianity, the pope claimed that human beings are to develop a greater awareness that "one cannot use with impunity the different categories of being, whether living or inanimate–animals, plants, the natural elements–simply as one wishes." Instead, one must take into consideration "the nature of each being and of its mutual connection in an ordered system, which is precisely the 'cosmos.'" The pope went on to say that since natural resources are limited, and some indeed are not "renewable," humanity is not to use these resources with "absolute dominion," but to pay due attention to the needs of generations to come.

Showing the deep-seatedness of this ecological concern, John Paul II addressed this issue again in 1989 by devoting an entire message to this topic. In "The Ecological Crisis: A Common Responsibility" the pope made an explicit point of addressing those in the Catholic Church, reminding them of "their serious obligation to care for all of creation." In the pope's view, the commitment of believers to a healthy environment for everyone, he said, stems directly from their belief in God the Creator. All of creation is to be respected because *all* of creation is called upon to praise God (Ps 148:96).

The American Bishops Respond

The pope speaks for the universal Church, and to Catholics (as well as others) all over the world. Bishops, on the other hand, speak as the highest teaching authority of their own dioceses. The bishops of the United States, both as individual bishops and as a group working together as an episcopal conference, have also spoken out on reverence for the earth as a religious concern.

In a 1991 pastoral letter to American Catholics (and meant as well for all concerned people of the country) the bishops outlined the relationship, as they saw it, between religious faith and reverence for the earth. Their letter, "Renewing the Earth: An Invitation to Reflection and Action on Environment in Light of Catholic Social Teaching," is a densely-packed and exceedingly rewarding work. While so much could be said about this letter, we will be limited here to what the bishops added to the understanding of Genesis in relation to reverence for the earth. We will also briefly touch upon how the bishops understand Catholic sacraments to call for reverence for the earth.

First, in their letter the American bishops build on John Paul II's fuller understanding of the relationship between humanity and the rest of God's creation as depicted in the Genesis creation accounts. They remind us that in Genesis "God looked at everything he had made and he found it very good" (Gen 1:31). Men and women as made in the image of God means, they explained, that they bear a "unique responsibility" under God, to safeguard the created world and even to "enhance" that world through their creative efforts. Safeguarding creation means "living responsibly" within creation, and not living as though we humans were outside of creation. In what is becoming a more common way of examining the fullness of Genesis' meaning in relation to the environment, the bishops also spoke of the covenant God made with Noah after the flood. This *lasting covenant* was made with Noah's descendants, and with *"every living creature"* (Gen 9:9-11). Because all creatures are part of this on-going covenental relationship with God, all creatures are shown to be meaningful to God. We are not, therefore, to use created things "capriciously."

For the American bishops, reverence for the earth is also based upon the importance of the sacraments in the life of the Church. The sacramental life of the Church depends on created goods: water, oil, bread, and wine. The message implicit in the bishops' reference to the material elements which are made holy in Catholic sacraments is clear: how can we despoil the very elements—the water, the soil, and the grapes and wheat which are the fruits of the earth—through which we celebrate the sacraments? This alone, it would seem, calls believers to reverence the earth. Has that call been heard, and if so, will it be answered?

Signs of Hope

It is important, of course, that theologians, bishops, and the pope speak out on the religious dimensions of concern for the earth. It is just as important that the *people in the pews*—as well as those in their offices, homes, and schools—come to understand this connection. For it is, of course, in the hands and hearts of *just plain folks* that this reverence for the earth must take root if the natural world of creation is to be healed.

It is heartening, then, that reverence for the earth as a religious issue has moved from the *hierarchy* of the Church to the *grassroots* level of the people. This is evidenced by the number of books being written to engage the attention of students (from grade schools to universities), parish groups such as liturgy committees, and catechists who are entrusted with passing on the faith to others. The communications media has also been called into service by different religious groups. The United States Catholic Conference, for one, has recently produced several videos explaining the theological background for the Church's concern for the fate of the natural world. More importantly, in pulpits, classrooms, parish halls—wherever religious instruction is done—these resources are increasingly being used. In all cases, a deeper understanding of the Genesis creation accounts, as well as the importance of the Church's sacramental life (as based on the goods of the earth which are made holy through sacramental action), are central to the discussion.

Clearly, if reverence for the earth is to become part and parcel of what it means to be a *religious person* these efforts must continue. Pointing the way, at the conclusion of "Renewing the Earth," the bishops of the United States called on every group—scientists, theologians, parents, teachers and educators, ethicists, and business leaders—to "explore, deepen and advance" the relationship between religious faith and the health of the environment. Aided by the Holy Spirit, each of these groups—spanning the breadth of humanity—holds the responsibility for stemming the tide of destruction against God's creation:

> Guided by the Spirit of God, the future of the earth lies in human hands . . . Even as humanity's mistakes are at the root of earth's travail today, human talents and invention can and must assist in its rebirth and contribute to human development. . .

It would seem, then, that the issue is now not *whether* reverence for the earth is a religious issue; it is, rather, a question of determining *how* Christian believers might demonstrate reverence for the earth in effective and enduring ways.

Reverence for the Earth: Reflection Questions

1. Do you think the Church should teach that it is a sin NOT to recycle?

2. What do you consider to be the worst offense of the human race against creation?

3. What of the vision of the earth in Psalm 24? Is it a modern or out-of-date understanding of the earth and all creation?

4. How does Gerard Manley Hopkins assist you in understanding the relationship of humanity to creator?

5. Explain your understanding of how Jesus' command to love our neighbors might have a bearing on caring for the natural world of God's creation.

6. If we are to reverence the earth, how far do you think human "domination" of non-human creation—animals, marine life, birds, as well as the atmosphere, trees, bodies of water, and the earth itself—should go?

7. If, as the American bishops claim, parents, teachers, and scientists are to be involved in furthering attention to concern for the earth, what is the Church's own particular role in this endeavor? Does it differ essentially from other groups' roles?

8. What would you add to this discussion which might convince people that reverence for the earth is a religious issue?

9. In your own life and in your own situation, how do you show your respect for God's creation?

10. Have you ever considered that all of creation is meaningful to God, and not just the human creation? How does Genesis' account of God's covenant with Noah as including all creation bear on your response?

14
Right to Life

Deuteronomy 30:19-20

¹⁹I call heaven and earth to witness against you today that I have set before you life and death, blessings and curses. Choose life so that you and your descendants may live, ²⁰loving the LORD your God, obeying him, and holding fast to him; for that means life to you and length of days, so that you may live in the land that the LORD swore to give to your ancestors, to Abraham, to Isaac, and to Jacob.

First Right of a Person

11. The first right of the human person is his life. He has other goods and some are more precious, but this one is fundamental—the condition of all the others. It does not belong to society, nor does it belong to public authority in any form to recognize this right for some and not for others: all discrimination is evil, whether it be founded on race, sex, colour or religion. It is not recognition by another that constitutes this right. This right is antecedent to its recognition; it demands recognition and it is strictly unjust to refuse it.

12. Any discrimination based on the various stages of life is no more justified than any other discrimination. The right to life remains complete in an old person, even one greatly weakened, it is not lost by one who is incurably sick. The right to life is no less to be respected in the small infant just born than in the mature person. In reality, respect for human life is called for from the time that the process of generation begins. From the time that the ovum is fertilized, a life is begun which is neither that of the father nor of the mother; it is rather the life of a new human being with his own growth. It would never be made human if it were not human already.

—Declaration on Procured Abortions 11, 12

Giving Up the Gift: One Woman's Abortion Decision
Madeleine Gray

Until I crashed against my limitations, I seemed to be the perfect Catholic mother. I was known as an active parishioner and eucharistic minister who had borne three children despite a serious chronic illness. I cherished them as signs of grace and kept these lively children at the center of my life. Though I often felt drained, I welcomed the possibility of a fourth child some day.

When I actually became pregnant again, an astonishingly intense depression, along with further deterioration of my health, led to an abortion. Nearly three years later, I am still appalled by what I have done. I still mourn my baby and my former idea of who I was. My grief is compounded by my estrangement from my church.

I do not wish to grieve silently any longer, partly because I realize that I have many co-mourners. It is horrifying to realize that a million-and-a-half uniquely painful stories are played out each year in the United States. But the real women behind the statistics rarely tell their stories. In the abortion debate, this public battle about the most personal of matters, the voices left unheard, the stories lost among the placards and drowned out by simplistic slogans are those of the very women who have felt desperate enough to seek abortion.

If we are Catholic, we are afraid of being shamed and hurt even more than we already are. We fear we would be accused of being selfish and thoughtless. Wounded as we are, we remain silent, alone, unreconciled.

I am intensely aware of the precious gift a baby is. I have Crohn's disease, which causes chronic inflammation and ulceration of the digestive tract. The illness flares without pattern or warning, sometimes leaving me gravely ill, feverish, and weak. During each of my pregnancies I had to take potent steroid medications to restore my health and prayed that my baby would be all right.

I bled early during my first pregnancy, and my doctor dimly hinted that the fetus might no longer be alive and ordered an ultrasound examination. At eight weeks' gestation we were amazed to see a lima bean-sized creature exuberantly flipping through the amniotic fluid, her little heart rapidly beating. She is now a tall, talented, and especially kind nine-year-old.

From the day I brought home my third baby, my middle child had a rough time, obviously feeling displaced too early. I began to feel buried under the chaos of our lives, as well as financial hardship and the precarious state of my health. With three children I was at my limit, but, because of my health problems, birth control pills were not an option for me. My husband and I could not bring ourselves to choose sterilization, so we were left with less reliable methods of contraception.

For nearly three years now I have lived with the ghost of a child. Over and over again I speculate how the story might have been written otherwise, about what might have brought this child to light. I replay in my mind the sequence of events.

December 1990—I am shocked to find out I am pregnant for the fourth time. In a romantic moment during a "safe" time of the month we had let our better judgment lapse. It was human failure, pure and simple.

I am even more shocked by my reaction. I fall into a deep depression. It is so hard to face reality that I literally spend days in bed under a heap of blankets, coming out from under them only when absolutely necessary. Life was such a precarious balance already. How can we handle a fourth child?

I have the awful feeling that I am losing my three children. They are still so young—ages six, three, and one. They need a mother who is fully present, happy, and relaxed. I do not have the energy and spirit to raise four young children. The option of abortion enters my mind. The thought horrifies me, but I feel backed into a corner.

My physician tells me that if I carry on with the pregnancy I will have to discontinue one of my medications. It has taken me years of gradually increasing doses of this medicine to overcome an allergy to it, and, so far, it has saved me from major surgery.

My husband worries about my getting very sick and not being there for him or the children. He has visions of himself as a single father of four children. Thinking over the state of my health, he feels sure that I need to end this pregnancy.

December 25, 1990—At Midnight Mass I pray as fervently as I can. I know that if anything can convert me, this magical liturgy, the celebration of the unlikely infant, should do it. Could we make room in our crowded lives, could I make room in my diseased and aging body for this infant?

Being Catholic, I feel alienated from my church when I most need it. At a time when I am very vulnerable, I cannot take the risk of seeking help from anyone who would condemn me simply for considering abortion or who might not keep my experience confidential. So I avoid any counselor with a pro-life bias. With the help of a women's health center, I find a counselor who will express no point of view. But the counseling seems superficial. Since I am obviously not happy to be pregnant, she concludes—too easily—that I must want an abortion.

I take my plight directly to God through prayer. I receive the answer that, having borne three children already, I know the gift of a baby. But I can give back the gift if the burden is too great, and it will be taken back into the universe. The greatest punishment I will receive is that which I am already suffering—the knowledge that I will never know this child.

This child, already built to outlast me, will never see the light of day, never be loved by its sisters and brother, will never learn or marry or have children, never grow old.

My husband makes an appointment for me at a "women's clinic" in a large city a hundred miles away. I tell the counselor there that I will only terminate this pregnancy if I can do it very early, before the baby takes form, before there is a heartbeat. But I am informed that they will not do abortions before eight weeks of pregnancy; otherwise it cannot be done properly.

I am in the most hellish situation I can imagine. I carry the pregnancy for three weeks more so the embryo can grow large enough to be destroyed.

During those weeks I develop an odd relationship with this incipient baby. Even though an abortion is scheduled, I cannot imagine drinking alcohol during Christmas and New Year's festivities while I am pregnant.

January 7, 1991—My child's last night. I cry as I try to drift off to sleep. I say good-bye to the little creature and tell the child I love it. I dream that I go out to a field and release the being. I see it flutter out of me and into the sky like a butterfly.

January 8, 1991—It's a cold, dark, two-hour ride before dawn to the clinic. I remember last night's dream, which was my true good-by. Now I steel myself for hard reality. No butterflies and meadows now. This being will be vacuumed through a tube and put out with the trash.

I'm amazed at how full the waiting room is. And it's like this every day. I am surprised at how casual it all is. We could be waiting for teeth cleaning. Women and their companions are reading magazines; a couple of teen-age girls smirk and kid around.

I am run through a succession of steps in this efficient system: blood test, viewing of a video, a quick physical exam, a perfunctory chat with a counselor who sends us to the financial officer. They want payment in advance, which we pay with MasterCard, which seems obscene. I am offered and gratefully accept a Valium.

Because of the medications I take for my illness, I am given a cortisone shot and told to wait in the recovery room for a half hour while it takes effect. I watch one woman after another come out of the procedure rooms in street clothes, shoes in hand. It all looks reassuringly routine. But even in my relaxed Valium-induced state unbidden thoughts pop into my head, voices which shout, "You can still change your mind! Run for it!"

But I suppress those voices. I cannot get through this with doubts. And I know that if I bolt, I'll be talked back into returning. It would only be worse.

The nurse finally calls for me. She instructs me to talk so that it won't hurt so much. She asks about our two-hour drive there. How were the roads? I chatter my way through the four-minute procedure, blabbering frantically about the weather and the condition of the interstate, as I try to ward off the intense sensations.

I am relieved to be back in the recovery room. The nurses are very kind. They flit about taking orders for tea, coffee, and toast from each of us. They chat with one of the women, who says she'll be right back at work tonight on the graveyard shift. Their mundane, matter-of-fact manner is comforting, and I am grateful to these nurses, who seem to know just what we need.

My chair happens to face the hall by the procedure rooms. The nurse periodically walks out of one of them with the glass receptacles used in the procedure. I see them as hard lifeless wombs into which we have delivered our children.

The recovery room is lined with recliner chairs all around the walls. Unlike the waiting room, this one is silent. I know that I will forever see the pained faces of that quiet circle of women.

After my half-hour of recovery, I gratefully escape. I cry in the parking lot, and then we go to lunch.

Back at home, I sleep well for the first time in several weeks. Then I fall into a period of despair. I stop seeing friends. I have told none of them what I've done and now feel that I live in a different universe from those good mothers. I have a few really bad nights where I consider, with enough vividness to frighten me, the idea of jumping off a bridge into the river.

When I am not in despair, I feel nothing. The easy eradication of an incipient person makes my own life, as well as my children's, seem fragile and meaningless. We could so easily not be here, have never existed. One piece of the mind of God has evaporated and become lost in the universe.

August 19, 1991–My due date. I have a private burial ceremony in the back yard for the child whose name is known by no one but me. Under a lilac bush I bury the only concrete evidence that this being existed–the blue-tipped plastic stick, indicating a positive result, from my home pregnancy test. I lay a withered carnation on the ground.

I know that I have passed by any greatness of spirit. Had I been Mary, Jesus would never have been born.

I remain depressed through autumn and winter.

April 1992–I see an article in our diocesan newspaper about postabortion counseling. A toll-free number is listed for those in need of help. It takes me a week to work up the nerve to call. A kind-sounding woman refers me to a diocesan office. Since I cannot summon the confidence to phone them, I write a letter asking who in my city could help me.

I immediately receive a reply, a wonderfully warm letter from a nun, along with some brochures written by someone who obviously understands exactly how I feel. Names are provided of three priests in my area with training in Project Rachel, the church's postabortion counseling program.

Despite the promise of reconciliation which is offered in the brochure, I feel too fragile to contact any of these priests. I need my church too much to risk being hurt more deeply than I already am.

July 1992–I contact a minister of the United Church of Christ, whose name was also given me by Project Rachel. She invites me to her home on a sunny summer afternoon. There, over coffee at her dining room table, she listens to my story. I cry lots, telling her that I don't know how I'll get beyond the pain. She brings me a box of Kleenex and recounts the story of Jacob, how he wrestled with the angel and received his new name, Israel, but walked with a limp the rest of his life.

She tells me I am not alone, that she had counseled a militant pro-lifer who, when her own teen-age daughter became pregnant, obtained an abortion for her.

Though I am grateful for this accepting woman, this minister who shares coffee and Kleenex, I remain troubled by the fact that I am actually excommunicated from the church. According to church law, I am digging myself in a continually deeper hole toward hell by continuing to participate in the Eucharist. But without God, without my community, I would die spiritually.

I think of the many Catholic women like me who must be suffering alone and cannot summon the courage to reconcile within the church.

Autumn 1992—My family and I spend this season living in a college community far from home, in the countryside. In this pastoral setting, in this leave of absence from home and routine, strong bonds are forged among our group of new friends. My depression begins to lift. I realize I am smiling and laughing more than I have in years.

I walk miles each day. One sunny afternoon on a country walk under the wide October sky, I can palpably feel redemption.

Two months later, at the end of my last day at that place, as the red sun touches the winter landscape like an eye shutting peacefully on a season of grace, I feel God's hand touch the top of my head.

I return home knowing that God forgave me long ago. I begin to forgive myself. But I crave the kind of reconciliation that we as flesh and blood creatures most understand, to be touched and forgiven by another human being. That is what I need to be set free.

I have begun talking to a counselor. She happens to be an active Catholic, but she does not know of any priest in my city whom she would trust to listen to me with compassion. If, indeed, there are Catholic clergy who are approachable, they are well hidden.

I do not ask the church to change its position on abortion. I am not trying to justify my action or exonerate myself. But I do ask the church for a more open invitation to counseling and reconciliation, as well as reassurance to women that they will not be shamed or condemned. Had I not feared harsh judgment, I might have sought a counselor who might have helped me to see how I could bear this baby.

I also ask for understanding. My choice was not simple: it was not made out of disregard for life but because of the desire to protect my family. No one loved that incipient child more than I did.

I ask for the type of compassion and friendship that Jesus offered Mary Magdalene.

                                              —*Commonweal*, February 25, 1994

Inconvenient Human   *Meg Abbey*

In an op-ed piece about Santa Claus in The New York Times on Dec. 12, Russell Baker wrote: ". . . in just simply having arrived here in this amazing wonder called life, you have been the beneficiary of miracles far more improbable than it would take to get Santa Claus through that metal pipe and out of our wood-burning stove."

On the same day, the Rev. Alfred R. Gutherie, separated from Russell Baker only by the newspaper's crease, wrote a letter to the Times commenting on whether anti-abortion protesters have a right to identify themselves with the civil rights protesters of the 1960's. "I have gone to jail for my nonviolent breaking of an unjust law that permits elimination of inconvenient humans," he wrote.

In 1946 I was a fetus and the most inconvenient of humans. When I was conceived, my biological mother, Elizabeth, was 44 and believed that she was post-menopausal. She was the poor mother of three teen-age daughters she supported by working in a factory. Her oldest daughter, now the C.E.O. of a large Catholic hospital, was preparing to enter the convent when her mother became pregnant.

Years earlier Elizabeth had left her husband, an alcoholic who had the disquieting habit of coming home drunk and flipping lighted matches around, because she was afraid that he would harm their children or herself.

Shortly after she left her husband, she was "befriended," in the words of the Catholic Charities file on my adoption, by one Leo Wright, my biological father. He loved her passionately—still does half a century later—and helped raise her children. It was 1940, they were Catholic, and marriage, or even open cohabitation, was out of the question. Her family was hostile toward her for leaving her husband even though, again according to Catholic Charities, his alcoholism was so advanced that he did not even recognize his children.

When I was growing up Catholic and middle-class in the 1960's, an unwed pregnancy was the ultimate disgrace. A young woman who gave birth less than nine months after her marriage was considered a tramp. A married woman who lived ("shacked up") with anyone but her husband, regardless of any problems in her marriage, was a social outcast. How much more shocking and unacceptable the extramarital pregnancy of a middle-aged mother of three must have seemed 20 years earlier!

Elizabeth's pregnancy had to be a secret. Her mother and brothers could not know, and her daughters could suspect nothing. She left her job and went into hiding. The girls were farmed out to neighbors. She suffered what was diagnosed as a heart attack, but, given her robust good health now at the age of 90+, it seems likely that it was not a heart attack, but a severe anxiety attack.

While she was in hiding, her mother died. She has told me that the worst part of the ordeal was having to miss her mother's funeral. She is still saddened by the memory of sneaking into the side door of the funeral home to say good-bye.

When I was born, Elizabeth had already made arrangements with Catholic Charities to put me up for adoption. I imagine that she was embarrassed about this too, because my official file states that she told Catholic Charities she was undecided about surrendering me and would think about it and come back.

Elizabeth recently told me that Catholic Charities insisted she could not see me after I was born but that a night nurse, believing it cruel she should never see her child, led her to the nursery. Her memory is of a fair baby with a halo of light hair.

After my birth, Elizabeth rounded up her other daughters, found a better job and resumed her life. She was haunted, however, by the secret she carried. Some 10 years after my birth she had a nervous breakdown. She was institutionalized and given shock treatments. Her psychiatrist told her that she had to tell someone her secret. She told her daughter the nun, but many years later, when I met her, she had completely forgotten that she had once told this daughter. As a result of the shock treatments she has only limited memory of her daughters' childhoods.

Elizabeth, at 90, is an irrepressible, irresistible shoo-in for the role of Mrs. Claus. She sparkles. There is no other word. The younger of my sons has always been a mystery to us. A learning-disabled child who has known nothing but failure and humiliation in school, he is unfailingly cheerful, has dozens of friends all over the continent, instantly charms everyone he meets and instinctively knows how to joke his parents out of the darkest mood. "Where on earth did this kid come from?" we often asked. Meeting Elizabeth, I knew.

It is hard for me to hear the story of my birth. Elizabeth and Leo, now her husband and a man uncannily like my sensitive, kind, introspective, older son, suffered so much. And yet . . . .

When I was a young teen-ager, I was repulsed by the anti-abortionists in New York's Port Authority who sat at card tables displaying bottled fetuses. Since reading, at the age of 12 or so, a diary-article of an unborn baby looking forward to seeing the world and meeting her mother—a baby who was never born—I had not liked the idea of abortion, but I wasn't crazy about the card-table people either.

When I was in college, the Vietnam War was in full swing, and it seemed to me that the most vocal anti-abortionists were virulent hawks. I could not reconcile their passion for unborn babies with what I saw as their indifference toward the lives of the American soldiers of my generation and Vietnamese of all ages.

Now in the age of the great abortion clinic clashes between pro-lifers and pro-choicers, I feel drawn toward the pro-choicers. They are liberal and feminist—like me. Visible pro-choicers include the likes of Surgeon General Joycelyn Elders, who speaks passionately of the right of every child to be planned and wanted. Pro-choicers speak for poor women whose lives have been stunted by unwanted pregnancies. They tell stories of desperate women dying in attempts to end pregnancies that threaten to enrage their families and sidetrack their lives. The opposition, the Rev. Gutherie and his ilk excepted, appear strident and seem to attract fundamentalists, fanatics, people intolerant of differences and the occasional gun-toting thug. I have nothing in common with these people. And yet . . . .

Every time I hear intelligent, socially concerned, feminist people proclaim that no one should have to bear an unwanted fetus, I feel a stab. I am that fetus. Every time I read an editorial in a newspaper I respect urging that the tissue of aborted fetuses be used in medical research, I feel ambivalent. Of course I want seriously ill people to have every chance to survive. But what about those fetuses? They too are me. When I read about Norma McCorvey, a.k.a. Jane Roe of Roe v. Wade fame, and the lawyers who advised her to seek judicial permission to abort her child rather than give her up for adoption, I feel indignant on behalf of baby McCorvey, although, thanks to the glacial pace of the courts, she was in no real danger. She and I, and the products of every other unplanned, unwanted, wildly inconvenient pregnancy, are unique, non-recurring humans. We are not our mothers and, in fact, may be nothing like our mothers.

Do I, and does every *in utero* nuisance like me, have less right to a stretch on earth than any other class of inconvenient human—demanding infants, bullying bosses, abusive spouses, dependent invalids, feeble old people? Yes, I admit that we are parasites, but so, to a large extent, are babes in cradles and post-ops in intensive care.

On the other hand, would I have wanted to see Elizabeth jailed, had she decided to have an abortion? I am a parent. I empathize with the agony she must have suffered at dropping out of her children's lives for months with no explanation. Had I been on an imaginary committee convened to decide whether, given all the pain caused by Elizabeth's pregnancy, she should be allowed to abort her fetus, how could I have voted "no"?

The answer may lie in a sense of perspective. On my birthday, a year or two after I had met Elizabeth, I was driving home from work along a hilly, sun-dappled summer road. I saw a man out walking his dog and was filled with a feeling of camaraderie. "Hey," I wanted to shout, "I'm alive too. I'm cruising along on top of the ground. I'm here to feel the delicious sensation of moving from sun to shade on a hot summer afternoon."

I visit Elizabeth and Leo once in a while and see them surrounded by their well-adjusted, successful daughters, women now in their 60's, and the 11 grandchildren and 20, soon to be 21, great-grandchildren, who write, call, visit and name children after them. They are survivors, retired from satisfying careers, enjoying their quiet routine, and radiant in their love for one another and for their family.

My real dad, who along with my now deceased real mother adopted me when I was an infant, is now 92 and ailing. He often says that my sister, also adopted, and I are all that he has. He is a person of unsurpassed integrity and generosity who has taken superb care of us all our lives. Now it is our great pleasure to take care of him. Because he adopted us, he has advocates to save him from the over-zealous social workers who want him in the nursing home he fears above all things. He has grandchildren with whom to play scrabble and share holidays, sons-in-law to tend his property, push his wheel-chair along the beach and try to beat him at poker, and daughters to take him to museums and on the long car rides he loves.

As a prime candidate for the abortionist's scalpel, my view of abortion is different. My perspective is longer. Yes, an unwanted pregnancy is horribly disruptive, but the disruption does not have to last forever. And how I hate the thought that I, or any of my fellow inconvenient fetuses, should miss our one chance to sample the improbable miracle of life.

—*America,* March 12, 1994

Right to Life: Reflection Questions

1. Where does the right to life come from? Can one give up that right? Can it be taken away?

2. When the right to life conflicts with a woman's right over her body, where and why does the discussion often break down into heated argument?

3. What does Madelin Gray ask for? What did you think about her dilemma? How did her article make you feel?

4. Compare Madelin Gray's story to Meg Abbey's. Who was the inconvenient human? Why? What did you think about that dilemma? How did her article make you feel?

15
Substance Abuse

1 Corinthians 3:16-18

[16]Do you not know that you are God's temple and that God's Spirit dwells in you? [17]If anyone destroys God's temple, God will destroy that person. For God's temple is holy, and you are that temple.

[18]Do not deceive yourselves. If you think that you are wise in this age, you should become fools so that you may become wise.

Matthew 18:5-6

[5]Whoever welcomes one such child in my name welcomes me.

[6]"If any of you put a stumbling block before one of these little ones who believe in me, it would be better for you if a great millstone were fastened around your neck and you were drowned in the depth of the sea.

Respect for Health

2288 Life and physical health are precious gifts entrusted to us by God. We must take reasonable care of them, taking into account the needs of others and the common good.

Concern for the health of its citizens requires that society help in the attainment of living conditions that allow them to grow and reach maturity: food and clothing, housing, health care, basic education, employment, and social assistance.

2289 If morality requires respect for the life of the body, it does not make it an absolute value. It rejects a neo-pagan notion that tends to promote the *cult of the body,* to sacrifice everything for it's sake, to idolize physical perfection and success at sports. By its selective preference of the strong over the weak, such a conception can lead to the perversion of human relationships.

2290 The virtue of temperance disposes us to *avoid every kind of excess:* the abuse of food, alcohol, tobacco, or medicine. Those incur grave guilt who, by drunkenness or a love of speed, endanger their own and others' safety on the road, at sea, or in the air.

2291 The *use of drugs* inflicts very grave damage on human health and life. Their use, except on strictly therapeutic grounds, is a grave offense. Clandestine production of and trafficking in drugs are scandalous practices. They constitute direct co-operation in evil, since they encourage people to practices gravely contrary to the moral law.

—Catechism of the Catholic Church

Something More about Alcohol   *Roman Paur, O.S.B.*

I am wondering what new information can be provided about alcohol that would catch the eye. Some years ago I wrote that alcohol is as much a part of our tradition as Johnnie Bread. The St. John's Community has enjoyed alcohol, probably without interruption, since its beginning. Beer was undoubtedly one of the "staples" that the mostly German monks unpacked while moving in 1866 to the first stone building in the vicinity of St. Raphael Hall, as it also must have been when they first settled in Stearns County from Pennsylvania ten years earlier.

There is no record that alcohol was officially allowed to be consumed by St. John's students on (or off!) campus over the following 100 and more years until the early 1970s. Fr. Aidan McCall, O.S.B., of happy memory, Vice President of Student Affairs, set down the first guidelines that permitted drinking when the legal age in Minnesota was changed from 21 to 18 and then 19, and the ban was experimentally adjusted to accommodate the now adult "requirement."

This, of course, was by no means the introduction to student drinking here, excessive or otherwise. With the safety advantage and selective clarity that time often affords, less recent alumni of most any class readily confess cherished memories of having participated in events that were not wanting for alcohol in the privacy of student rooms or other campus coves. However, those secret attractions didn't always escape the seasoned eye of Fr. Boniface Axtman, O.S.B., or the clever tongue of Fr. Daniel Durken, O.S.B., and other frayed Deans of Men!

Occasional socializing over a few drinks for those who are free to choose has its own rewards. Such behavior is not the subject of continuing concern on college campuses across the country. The stubborn topic is abusive drinking among many people in academic communities, younger and older, students and faculty, staff and administration, religious and lay.

It would be of little comfort to know that patterns of alcohol consumption or reasons for drinking or extent of abuse may be no more serious at St. John's than elsewhere. The matter of widespread documented destructive behavior associated with alcohol is a problem as alarming as the solution continues to be baffling.

We are by no means immune to the devastating impact of this drug of choice, even though we work hard at making our campus better. A disturbing number of people are regularly drinking too much with astounding consequences on any measure. To deny the problem is to embarrass even the fabled ostrich.

All the statistics are horrible and not improving for the most part. The National Institute on Alcohol Abuse and Alcoholism's recent data still indicate that over 18 million American adults and an additional nearly 5 million teenagers have severe alcohol-abuse problems. Some 45,000 babies are born in our country yearly with serious birth defects because of alcohol. About 500,000 Americans are injured annually in alcohol-related motor vehicle accidents with an additional 25,000 killed.

The cost by some estimates approaches 100 billion dollars. That's likely to become meaningful, however, only when our neighbor is killed, or mother, or classmate; or when a friend is a headlined victim of sexual assault, rape or spouse abuse that nearly always involves alcohol.

And it looks like much of this is our fault, even allowing a generous disposition to genetics and disease, in how we accede to the advertising associations of drinking with feeling good or showing importance or being a winner.

What's it like for college students? If the overall national statistics are harsh, what about the 12 million American college students as a group who drink even more? College students generally have a higher drinking prevalence than people their same age who do not attend college. According to the National Clearing House for Alcohol and Drug Information, some 40% of college students will engage in heavy drinking (five or more drinks in a row) at least every two weeks, over 70% will drink regularly and only about 12% will be able to resist the enormous pressure and abstain all together. Half a million college students will drink every day. It should be noted that men drink more often and in greater quantities than women but there is evidence that women become more impaired than men when drinking the same amount of alcohol.

A recent study by the University Minnesota indicates that binge drinking by underage students has risen alarmingly in recent years, a statistic that some tie to the change in the legal drinking age.

The alcohol of choice among students, of course, is beer, about four billion cans in America, enough stacked end to end to reach the moon and beyond, perhaps a goal of the "serious" drinker. The typical American college student consumes over 34 gallons of alcoholic beverages annually for a staggering total of 430 million heavily advertised gallons by manufacturers who deny that their promotions attract new consumers! That's an olympic-sized swimming pool of booze for each of the 3,500 college campuses in the States every year.

Who drinks the most? The more vulnerable are probably younger students on rural campuses who are lonely and bored, away from home and parental control, and who want to belong, need to conform, and worry about being excluded. With some exceptions, students who do poorer academically drink more than those who are in high academic standing. Is it saying the same that those who drink more get worse grades? Most students, however, do not make this connection. It is estimated that about 7% of any freshman class throughout the country will discontinue college because of alcohol-related issues and these people will earn throughout their lifetime significantly less than their college counterparts.

And what do college students say about all this? They agree for the most part but would contend that the "problem" is even worse in as much as their perception of the drinking norm is higher. They report that about a quarter of their friends get drunk at least once a week. Curiously, 60% of college students feel that their friends drink too much. "Holding one's liquor" is prized among peers, and especially if they are athletes, a judgment call that is likely to be grossly overestimated. And the more a college student drinks in one sitting and over time, or anyone else for that matter, the greater that person is likely to distort his or her ability to overcome the consequences, including driving.

College textbooks are terribly expensive. Most everybody complains about that rip-off, but the typical student will spend more money for alcoholic beverages than for all his or her textbooks and, on a representative campus, the student body's private expenditure for alcohol will far exceed the total operating costs of the library.

As one who has influenced directly the shaping of attitudes and behavior on the subject at St. John's over the years, I am persuaded that on-going education about drinking fortified by explicit expectations and attractive alternatives provides worthwhile learning objectives and appropriate incentives for life-long change.

Our alcohol policies and related programs affirm specific standards of personal health and community living. Although such persistent efforts may be criticized by some as a hopeless countercultural blockade, they are based on the belief that life is valuable, people are important and education, even without credit, makes a difference!

Under the prophetic leadership of Fr. J. P. Earls, O.S.B., Vice President of Student Affairs, we began re-examining our campus-wide alcohol programs and policies in 1976 when it became evident that events were compromising people, destroying facilities, distorting academic priorities, and jeopardizing hospitality.

By 1980, St. John's and St. Benedict's were working together on the problem. In accord with our Benedictine tradition of encouraging personal maturity through responsible decisions that demonstrate a respect for self, others and property, the two colleges joined hands in supporting the right of individuals to make choices about alcohol use within the evolving guidelines established for decent academic community living. We think that alcohol can be a refreshing part of our educational environment (prohibition is neither practical nor ideal) and that policies ought to reflect a respect for law, academic and residential priorities, and tolerance for learning.

We also recognize that we drink for many reasons that include boredom, peer pressure, relational discomfort, academic disappointment, career ambivalence, personal conflicts, family struggles, drinking history, few alternatives, availability of the substances and social encouragement. Isn't it interesting, however, that the reasons for drinking change very little over a very long time. Any reason, however trivial, appears to be a wholly adequate one if there is a need to drink. But the libations intended to bring people together often become the wedge that drives them apart.

Our attention to the problem of good people drinking excessively attempts to address a number of concerns concurrently: the destructive effects of alcohol on individuals, the disabling consequences of abusive drinking on educational objectives and the disproportionate impact of drinking on both younger and older adult behavior.

I am encouraged by and proud of our student initiatives. Our student community is demonstrating an increasing sensitivity to the matter of drinking and is helping to refine policies that exact accountability. Already in the mid-80s, the St. John's Student Senate and the St. Benedict's Student Administrative Board were sponsoring National Collegiate Alcohol Awareness Week (October), and, in later years, Drinking and Driving Awareness Week (December), National Collegiate Drug Awareness Week (March), and Safe Break Week (April). The University Peer Resource Program is actively engaged in floor pitches to promote responsible partying.

Other efforts that recognize the influence of students on themselves in modeling behavior saw the development of the Alcohol Abuse Prevention Program for St. John's Varsity Athletes, Student Advocates against Sexual Assault, and the extraordinary student attention to responsible planning of co-campus student festivals and dances.

All freshmen by floor are required to participate in the "Alcohol and Other Drug Education Program" during the January Term. We welcome the Drug Free Schools Act guidelines in distributing literature to each student and channeling video programming into all student rooms.

For those in need, individuals may be required to participate in an assessment and recommended treatment program as a condition of continuing enrollment. Students who are cited for DWI (DUI) disqualify themselves from varsity sports and may not hold a position of student leadership until they meet the conditions of requalification.

Faculty, administration, staff and guests are also being encouraged to exercise special care in the use of alcohol that reflects adherence to state law, consideration of example and compliance with University regulations. Policies affect such events as the Corporate Employee Christmas Gathering, Homecoming, Swayed Pines Festival and other celebrations as well as summer events.

Some years from now when this article is again revisited, in all likelihood the global statistics will not change constructively very much and we may become discouraged. Many people will still suffer a lot. But this is a matter in which change must be measured one person at a time.

We will be fortunate to stand still if we move fast. There are things each of us can do that would be progress:

1. Continue to emphasize in families and communities the importance of infinite compassion for people, defined margins for learning, and no tolerance for compromise.

2. Insist on an enforcement of alcohol-related public safety laws with severely-inconveniencing sanctions that cannot be commuted or plea-bargained.

3. Support continuous education efforts that provide accurate information and that target peers for influencing positive change.

4. Create attractive incentives for responsible social alternatives to drinking.

5. Encourage tithing: Challenge producers, distributors and retailers of spirits and brews to contribute 10% of the money allocated for advertising to promote education and responsible choice programs.

There isn't much new to be said. But our sweat will have been worth while in making campuses better by not tolerating alcohol-related behavior that compromises college students in those ways they are most vulnerable—suicide, drunk driving, sexual violence, gender and minority discrimination, and academic failure.

The goal of all our hard work continues to be a safe and friendly learning environment, with the resources to be persuasive, that supports respect, rewards moderation, forgives error, and forbids excess.

Our tradition is one of recognizing that people do not live on (Johnnie) bread alone. Just as alcohol is part of our past, we want it to be a wholesome element of our future in the oasis behind the pine curtain.

—*Saint John's,* May 1992

Substance Abuse: Reflection Questions

1. How does the production and trafficking of illegal drugs violate the moral law?

2. Do you think of drug use as a "sin" or just a "vice"?

3. How do you respond to those who suggest there is nothing wrong with street-drug use because "I'm only harming myself"?

4. Do you agree that those on campus who drink most are bored, lonely, or need to conform?

16
And, in the End . . .

Revelation 21–22:1-5

Then I saw a new heaven and a new earth; for the first heaven and the first earth had passed away, and the sea was no more. ²And I saw the holy city, the new Jerusalem, coming down out of heaven from God, prepared as a bride adorned for her husband. ³And I heard a loud voice from the throne saying,

"See, the home of God is among mortals.
He will dwell with them as their God;
they will be his peoples,
and God himself will be with them;
⁴he will wipe every tear from their eyes.
Death will be no more;
mourning and crying and pain will be no more,
for the first things have passed away."

⁵And the one who was seated on the throne said, "See, I am making all things new." Also he said, "Write this, for these words are trustworthy and true." ⁶Then he said to me, "It is done! I am the Alpha and the Omega, the beginning and the end. To the thirsty I will give water as a gift from the spring of the water of life. ⁷Those who conquer will inherit these things, and I will be their God and they will be my children. ⁸But as for the cowardly, the faithless, the polluted, the murderers, the fornicators, the sorcerers, the idolaters, and all liars, their place will be in the lake that burns with fire and sulfur, which is the second death."

⁹Then one of the seven angels who had the seven bowls full of the seven last plagues came and said to me, "Come, I will show you the bride, the wife of the Lamb." ¹⁰And in the spirit he carried me away to a great, high mountain and showed me the holy city Jerusalem coming down out of heaven from God.

¹¹It has the glory of God and a radiance like a very rare jewel, like jasper, clear as crystal. ¹²It has a great, high wall with twelve gates, and at the gates twelve angels, and on the gates are inscribed the names of the twelve tribes of the

Israelites; [13]on the east three gates, on the north three gates, on the south three gates, and on the west three gates. [14]And the wall of the city has twelve foundations, and on them are the twelve names of the twelve apostles of the Lamb.

[15]The angel who talked to me had a measuring rod of gold to measure the city and its gates and walls. [16]The city lies foursquare, its length the same as its width; and he measured the city with his rod, fifteen hundred miles; its length and width and height are equal. [17]He also measured its wall one hundred forty-four cubits by human measurement, which the angel was using. [18]The wall is built of jasper, while the city is pure gold, clear as glass. [19]The foundations of the wall of the city are adorned with every jewel; the first was jasper, the second sapphire, the third agate, the fourth emerald, [20]the fifth onyx, the sixth carnelian, the seventh chrysolite, the eighth beryl, the ninth topaz, the tenth chrysoprase, the eleventh jacinth, the twelfth amethyst. [21]And the twelve gates are twelve pearls, each of the gates is a single pearl, and the street of the city is pure gold, transparent as glass.

[22]I saw no temple in the city, for its temple is the Lord God the Almighty and the Lamb. [23]And the city has no need of sun or moon to shine on it, for the glory of God is its light, and its lamp is the Lamb. [24]The nations will walk by its light, and the kings of the earth will bring their glory into it. [25]Its gates will never be shut by day—and there will be no night there. [26]People will bring into it the glory and the honor of the nations. [27]But nothing unclean will enter it, nor anyone who practices abomination or falsehood, but only those who are written in the Lamb's book of life.

22 Then the angel showed me the river of the water of life, bright as crystal, flowing from the throne of God and of the Lamb [2]through the middle of the street of the city. On either side of the river, is the tree of life with its twelve kinds of fruit, producing its fruit each month; and the leaves of the tree are for the healing of the nations. [3]Nothing accursed will be found there any more. But the throne of God and of the Lamb will be in it, and his servants will worship him; [4]they will see his face, and his name will be on their foreheads. [5]And there will be no more night; they need no light of lamp or sun, for the Lord God will be their light, and they will reign forever and ever.

Until We See God Face to Face   *William C. Graham*

"Let me show you fellows something," Tom Dougherty would routinely say as he drove his funeral home's limousine filled with pall bearers from a Duluth church to Calvary Cemetery. "Here's a piece of work by one of the world's best salesmen."

Into the cemetery gates, around the circle where the diocesan priests are buried, and straight back, he'd point to a tombstone:

Mother-well

The world's best salesman had persuaded a grieving family to purchase a tombstone on which their name was hyphenated. Obviously the stone-carver had used letters which were far too large for the narrow monument. He did not fix, but rather sold, his mistake. That mistake has become something of a landmark for funeral directors, pall bearers and priests, and for others who visit the cemetery when not lost in the mists of grief.

The Motherwell family lives in collective memory as those who financed another's mistake. Usually we live with the consequences of our own activity. The Motherwells live with the consequences of the careless stone-carver and unscrupulous sales associate.

Perhaps they will meet Another who will challenge them.

"You've never seen a hearse pulling a U-Haul, have you, Father?", Tom Dougherty would often ask sometime on the limo ride back to church from cemetery.

He puts an unusual spin on a common Christian truth. Like Job, all people might proclaim, "Naked I came forth from my mother's womb, / and naked shall I go back again. / The Lord gave, and the Lord has taken away" (1:21).

We who make life's journey will be called to stand before the Just Judge of all, the creator of the universe, the Compassionate One who is Lover of human innocence.

The constant call of the Christian is to hear the Gospel and reform one's life.

Then shall we stand in God's good presence, joining Job and all the choirs of saints and angels, announcing, "Blessed be the name of the Lord" (1:21).

HEAVEN

690 Jerusalem, My Happy Home

1. Je - ru - sa - lem, my hap - py home, When shall I with you be? When shall my sor - rows have an end? Your joys when shall I see?

2. Your saints are crowned with glo - ry great; They see God face to face; They tri - umph still, they still re - joice: In that most ho - ly place.

3. There Da - vid stands with harp in hand As mas - ter of the choir: Ten thou - sand times that we were blest That might this mu - sic hear.

4. Our La - dy sings Mag - nif - i - cat With tune sur - pass - ing sweet; And all the vir - gins join the song While sit - ting at her feet.

5. There Magdalene has left her tears,
   And cheerfully does sing
   With blessed saints, whose harmony
   In ev'ry street does ring.

6. Jerusalem, Jerusalem,
   God grant that I may see
   Your endless joy, and of the same
   Partaker ever be!

Text: Joseph Bromehead, 1747-1826, alt.
Tune: LAND OF REST, CM; American; Harm. by Richard Proulx, b.1937, © 1975, GIA Publications, Inc.

And, in the End . . . : Reflection Questions

1. What is the incomparable destiny which Paul VI anticipates as waiting for Christians who honor their vocations? How does that challenge you?

2. What does it mean to suggest that one does not see a hearse pulling a U-Haul®?

3. What does it mean to suggest that the constant call of the Christian is to hear the Gospel and reform one's life? How does this idea challenge you?

4. Explain the profound theological principles behind this cartoon:

An Index to the *Catechism* of the Catholic Church

Some readers may wish to consult the *Catechism of the Catholic Church* for further reading. Following are some suggested paragraphs.

origin of evil:
   derived from sin: 403, 1607
   human limitations: 844
   permitted by God: 412
   scandal as inducement to evil: 2284
physical evil: 310
prevention of evil: 1431
question about evil to be answered only in faith: 385

Faith: 26, 142, 146, 150, 155, 176
"analogy of faith": 114
and eternal life: 163–65
and science: 159
and understanding: 156–59
as answer to evil: 309
as assent to revealed truths: 150
as foretaste of eternal life: 163, 184
as God's grace: 153, 179, 224
as human act: 154–55, 180
as source of moral life: 2087
as source of prayer: 2656
as theological virtue: 1813–16
certainty of faith: 157
content:
   Christian faith:
      in God: 178, 223
      in God the Creator: 14, 229
      in the Holy Spirit: 14, 152, 202
      in Jesus Christ: 14, 108, 147, 151, 202, 463, 573
      in the one God: 150, 200, 202, 222–27, 228, 233, 2086
      in the signs of revelation: 156
      in the Trinity: 234
   consequence of faith: 222–27
   cooperation of intellect, will and grace: 155
   crises of faith:
      conflict with reason: 159
      doubt regarding faith: 2088
      separation from God by one's own free choice: 1033
      support from the witnesses of faith: 165
      trials: 164
   duties of faith:
      duty to a life of faith: 13
      duty to preserve the faith: 162

Index